DUNKIRK AND BATTLE OF BRITAIN TOP GUN

DUNKIRK AND BATTLE OF BRITAIN TOP GUN

WW2 Ace Pilot Officer William McKnight

The Most Outstanding Canadian Fighter Pilot in the first half of the Second World War

16½ confirmed kills in eight months
Leading ace of Dunkirk
Leading Canadian in the Battle of Britain
First Canadian in the Second World War to win a Bar
Leading Canadian fighter pilot in the first half of the Second World War

SHELLY McELROY

AIR WORLD

AIR WORLD

DUNKIRK AND BATTLE OF BRITAIN TOP GUN
WW2 Ace Pilot Officer William McKnight

First published in Great Britain in 2026 by
Air World
An imprint of
Pen & Sword Books Ltd
Yorkshire – Philadelphia

ISBN 978 1 03614 926 0

A CIP catalogue record for this book is available from the British Library.

Typeset by SJmagic DESIGN SERVICES, India.

Printed and bound in the UK by CPI Group (UK) Ltd.

The Publisher's authorised representative in the EU for product safety is Authorised Rep Compliance Ltd., Ground Floor, 71 Lower Baggot Street, Dublin D02 P593, Ireland. www.arccompliance.com

For a complete list of Pen & Sword titles please contact

PEN & SWORD BOOKS LIMITED
George House, Units 12 & 13, Beevor Street, Off Pontefract Road,
Barnsley, South Yorkshire, S71 1HN, England
E-mail: enquiries@pen-and-sword.co.uk
Website: www.pen-and-sword.co.uk

or

PEN AND SWORD BOOKS
1950 Lawrence Rd, Havertown, PA 19083, USA
E-mail: uspen-and-sword@casematepublishers.com
Website: www.penandswordbooks.com

FSC www.fsc.org
MIX
Paper | Supporting responsible forestry
FSC® C013604

Contents

Contents

Foreword

Sometimes – and I speak from long personal experience – it is possible, I believe, for the living to forge what I call a 'posthumous friendship' with the deceased, someone, for example, much admired. That, I would suggest, is the case here. William Lidstone McKnight was a Second World War Canadian fighter ace from Calgary in Canada – coincidentally the home town of one Shelly McElroy. Cutting a story short – no spoilers – Shelly learned of McKnight's story and was both moved and inspired by it. Consequently, Shelly determined to research and share this courageous young man's story, yet another cut down before even the prime of his life, in so doing maintaining the currency of it and sharing 'Bill's' story much more widely.

As Shelly explains, Canadians very much understate their achievements, arguing that, conversely, Americans elevate their war heroes to sometimes mythical status, and Britain being no far off. The latter I cannot entirely agree with. Britain is the home of the understatement, and that, I suspect, may go a long way to explain Canada's culture in this regard, given our two nations' long association through the Empire and Commonwealth. Indeed, as the clouds of war gathered during the 1930s, that close relationship may well also explain why aviation-minded and adventurous young men like Bill McKnight travelled from their homes far away to Britain, volunteering to fight in a distant war – but one which threatened the future of all the western democracies. In truth, for a very long time, that reaffirmed future seemed assured – but today the world is again a troubled and uncertain place; for that reason this book should resonate with us all – and especially with Canadians, for here is an all-Canadian hero deserved of being remembered and whose story must be told.

Most books in this genre are written by military aviation historians, which, by her own admission, Shelly was not – at least when embarking upon this self-set endeavour. Now, clearly, Shelly knows much more about the subject – and has done a commendable job in providing a very readable and accurate narrative. Most importantly, Shelly provides much background context to anchor the main character and events in space and time. For example, Bill McKnight flew during the early war period in 242 Squadron, commanded during the Battle of Britain by the legless Squadron Leader Douglas Bader, a well-documented story already – so what I personally found very interesting was the material presented by Shelly around the preceding period, when 242 suffered heavy losses during the Fall of France. That story is not an oft-trodden path, and will, I am sure, be of interest to many.

In sum, Shelly has done a remarkable job in reconstructing Bill McKnight's all too brief and mercurial life and times, in the process doing a great service to his memory, his family, and Canada – and in so doing has enriched the bibliography and our knowledge of the violent past.

I commend this book to you, and congratulate Shelly McElroy on a job well done.

Dilip Sarkar MBE FRHistS FRAeS BA(Hons)
Honorary Vice-President,
Battle of Britain Memorial Trust CIO
February 2026

12 January 1941

Three patrols known as 'Mosquitos' were organised that day for No. 242 Squadron. While Douglas Bader and Stan Turner flew out for the first of the day, Bill McKnight was getting ready to fly out on his own patrol. He tossed his logbook on the table; it was later updated that for that day, recording a Mosquito patrol. '"E" Boat and troops strafed with PO Brown' was written in a different hand.

Bill gathered his belongings. For the last time, he banged the lid shut over his heavy Royal Air Force trunk, the annoying shelves intended to hold shoes and toiletries threatening, as always, to tumble out before the top swung closed. He shrugged into his sheepskin-lined bomber jacket, turning the collar up against the cold. He and Marvin Brown could see their breath clouding in the air as they walked out into the courtyard. Waving goodbye to Noel Barlow, they strode across the frozen tundra of the grass airfield to where the four Hurricanes had been assembled. Pilot Officers Hugh Tamblyn and Bruce Rogers were coming along.

Bill was wondering vaguely what supper would be. Perhaps there was the hopeful prospect of a decent bowl of soup and fresh bread to look forward to instead of the house speciality – the unlimited, lifetime supply of cooked-to-death vegetables smothered in ketchup. He pulled his goggles down over his eyes. His feet, attached to the short, aching legs, walked along the strong wing of LE A. The sturdy wings of the Hurricane that had supported and lifted him for so long did not vibrate rhythmically with his footfalls. They were too heavy to move under the weight of a man, and quite a slight man at that. They throbbed to the Merlin engine thrumming them in sustained, non-musical growls.

With the Rolls-Royce Merlin engine roaring, the Hurricane hurled itself down the runway. Bill gunned its engine, aiming into the headwind. The solid wings and powerful engine lifted it into the sky as he drew back on his stick. The ground fell inevitably away.

The Reaper had long waited quietly, sensed, but silent. Unseen by anyone, it had turned its exacting, irresistible, selecting finger at last.

Prologue

My connection to William Lidstone 'Willie' (though he was more often called Bill) McKnight is both unlikely and intriguing. I grew up in Calgary, Alberta, just as he did. Each evening, I watch the sun set behind the rugged peaks of the Rocky Mountains – the same view Bill once knew. I'm familiar with the shape of Nose Hill; so was he, although his Calgary in the 1930s had far fewer buildings than mine in the 1980s and '90s. My dad attended the same elementary and high schools as Bill, and I lived only a few kilometres from McKnight Boulevard.

I only learned about him a few years ago.

If Bill had been British or American, I'm convinced his name would be celebrated in households across Canada, and perhaps beyond. For American readers, it might help to understand how Canadians see themselves in relation to the U.S., our closest trading partner. Americans magnify their stories, battles, and heroes, elevating them from impressive to nearly mythic proportions – whether it's George Washington or the B-17 bombers. In the U.S., historic achievements are met with fervent national pride. Admittedly, this can sometimes seem excessive to outsiders, but at least Americans honour their heroes.

In Canada, we approach history differently. When something noteworthy – a law, an invention, an exceptional individual – emerges, we dissect it, compare it unfavourably to a British or, especially, an American version, and often diminish its significance. We downplay our own achievements.

That's why I believe that William 'Willie' McKnight, had he been British or American, would be far more widely recognised in Canada. Despite his accomplishments, he remains relatively unknown in Alberta and Calgary, where he grew up. It took years before a major road leading to the airport in Calgary was named in his honour – a story in itself.

If Bill were American, Hollywood would surely have turned his life into a blockbuster: a rebellious main character, a bittersweet and doomed romance, a complex hero with a heart of gold (well, he had his moments), a fighter pilot who became the top ace at Dunkirk, led the Canadian scores during the Battle of Britain, and shot down a confirmed down sixteen and a half enemy aircraft – half of which were the deadly Bf 109s – in under eight months. On top of all that, he offered a nuanced perspective on the extraordinary times he lived in, recorded in letters to his friends and family.

I've compared Bill to other aces – New Zealand's Alan Deere, fellow Canadian greats Stan Turner, Johnny Fauquier and 'Buzz' Beurling, and Britain's Douglas Bader. No matter how much I analyse, I can't dismiss Bill McKnight with my typical Canadian indifference.

More than a just combat pilot, Bill was a person, worth getting to know. I hope you'll find his story as compelling as I did – not only as Willie, Canada's most outstanding fighter pilot of the first half of the Second World War, but also as Bill, a young man from Calgary facing the challenges of early adulthood. He had much to prove to himself, did his best to find his place in the world, and he left an indelible mark, both on those who knew him and people like me who never met him.

Meet Bill

I am interested in agriculture, industry, and social histories that focus on the under-reported stories of women and children in their communities. I'm fascinated by cattle, cream separators, vintage tractors, textiles, and even sadirons. What is missing from this list of assorted areas of interest is the military. So how did this connection ever happen, given that the only thing I knew about Willie McKnight was that he was Calgary's Second World War flying ace, that he flew in 242 Canadian Squadron of the Royal Air Force, and that McKnight Boulevard (located only a few kilometres away from my childhood home) was named for him? There was also a rumour circulating that he wasn't really called Willie. So, I referred to him as William.

As Bill himself was to remark later, we owe it all to Cami Kepki. Because luckily, I like football too (the kind of football with a oval ball, not a round one). In 2020, GlobalTV in Calgary did a story on my research linking the history of the Calgary Stampeders to the military. This happened in the fall of 2020 as the Covid 19 pandemic was making its implications strongly known, so I couldn't even invite Cami into my house or offer her a cup of tea. She had to stand outside the door to film me while I sat a few feet away. In the interview, I spoke about a pilot called Don MacQueen, a young Calgary Bronks football player who had been shot down in France in 1940. I told the audience that Don had been in the same Royal Air Force squadron as the most famous member of that squadron … a guy called William McKnight.

Little did I know that William McKnight himself was watching.

Of course, it wasn't THAT William McKnight, but rather his nephew. Bill reached out to GlobalTV, who passed his details along to me. When I followed up, I realized immediately that I was talking to a person who had a lot on his mind, and in his heart. He told me that he was the son of Ted McKnight, Bill McKnight's youngest brother, and he had things that he wanted me to see. We met up at Calgary's Central Library so that he could show me his treasures and tell me about his family's simultaneously world-famous and invisible story.

I realized that I was looking at a precious archive of documents, photographs and letters, and hearing a vibrant, well-rounded history that only family lore can produce. While I am going to walk you through the story known nationally and internationally – Bill as the leading ace of Dunkirk, arguably the greatest Canadian fighter pilot in the first half of the Second World War and a tough fighter pilot who has a major road in Calgary named for him – I'm also here to share with you the family memories and perspective of his brief life.

Bill Was from Edmonton

The famed Canadian warrior William Lidstone Knight was descended from the kings of Scots, and he was born on the day that the First World War Armistice was signed. At least, that was the version of events he told when he was trying to impress his not very impressionable high school friends.

The more prosaic reality was that our story begins, as not too many good stories do when you think about it, in Edmonton, Alberta, Canada.

Because that is where this famous Calgarian was born. Bill's parents, Rosella ('Rose') Elizabeth Lidstone and William Crozier Campbell McKnight (who may have been called 'Mac' but who will be known in this text as William to distinguish him from the bewildering number of Bill McKnights who populate this history), were married on Christmas Day in 1917. William was born in Glasgow in 1893, emigrating to Alberta in 1911 at the age of seventeen.

Rose's father, John Lidstone, was born in Dartmouth, England. His family had emigrated to Canada in 1873. Rose was born in Montreal and came to Alberta in 1906 with her family. John Lidstone initially took a homestead in the Leduc area of Alberta, but the family ultimately relocated to Edmonton.[1] Rose and William were the best man and bridal attendant in Rose's sister's wedding a few months before they were married themselves, indicating a budding courtship with close mutual connections.

Bill McKnight was born on 18 November 1918. He told people that he was born one week before, linking his birthday with the momentous signing of the Armistice. It was classic Bill – misleading other people with a tale about himself that cast him in the starring role and aligning himself with noteworthy dates and important people. A personal myth if you will. Heavy on the myth. I'll tell you one thing: for any little boy born in the 1918 – 1919 – 1920 date range, it doesn't particularly matter what day of the year is it, does it? Your heart stands still for him, just like it does for all the little boys born around 1895 a generation before.

There were to be three McKnight boys altogether. Raymond 'Ray' Clifton was born on 11 January 1921, and John 'Ted' Arthur arrived in 1930. In 1921, long before Ted joined the family, the McKnights had moved 300 kilometres south of Edmonton to Calgary.

Photographs, letters and postcards from the McKnight Family Archive recorded outings such as swimming, golf and trips to the Rocky Mountains – Banff National Park is approximately an hour's drive from Calgary – and everyday scenes from family life, such as Ted practicing the piano … and looking miserable about it!

Calgary in the 1930s

When Bill was born, the place that we now call Calgary was a scant forty-five years old, but the alterations it had seen over the span of a generation or two had been profound. The province of Alberta was transforming itself from a hunter-gatherer society into an agricultural superpower at a rapid rate, and there had been enormous changes along the way. Bill's world was shaped by the First World War, by agriculture, by the Bow and Elbow Rivers, by the herds of bison that he had never seen and that had vanished only decades before he was born, and by the high stately bluffs that rose above the floodplain where the rivers converged.

In 1875, the Northwest Mounted Police had first glimpsed the confluence of the Bow and Elbow Rivers when they had ridden over the hill at a spot that would one day become Crescent Heights, Bill's neighbourhood. Then, the herds of bison, the signature species of the Great Plains, had sauntered down the strange, straightforward drop of present-day Edmonton Trail to their hereditary crossing place at the confluence of those rivers as they had done for millennia. When the Northwest Mounted Police arrived in 1875, those herds, which had numbered in the millions, had less than a half decade left.

The first decade of the twentieth century had seen Calgary, and indeed all southern Alberta, experience a boom. Calgary increased its population from roughly 4,000 in 1901[1] to more than 40,000 in 1912, an accelerated pace of growth that influenced real estate, manufacturing and businesses in the thriving, optimistic city. New neighbourhoods appeared on city planning maps, but they don't exist today because by 1913 Alberta was experiencing a bust, and all the hectic growth essentially went off a cliff. There wouldn't be another boom in Alberta for sixty years, and the projected communities were never built.

For Calgary, the period between the wars was shaped and influenced by agriculture, the heartbeat of the provincial economy. Farming impacted everything, and there were stern lessons to be learned as settlers tried to use agricultural practices from Great Britain and the eastern half of the continent on the Great Plains.

The boom may have ended, but by the 1920s Calgary was becoming a proper, grown-up, modern city. It had daily newspapers, three railway lines (Canadian Pacific Railway, Canada National Railway Company and Grand Trunk Pacific Railway) and expanding neighbourhoods, schools and places of worship. There was great disappointment when Calgary, which had been passed over in the selection of the provincial capital of Alberta, was also rejected as the site for the first provincial university, which was also built in Edmonton. But Calgary had its own light transit rail system. It had parks, movie theatres and sporting teams and facilities.

In 1929, Bill's neighbourhood, Rosedale, was the fastest-growing residential district in Calgary. The budding community coexisted right across the road from pastures of cattle and farmers using horses to pull hay rakes. Local children walking to school heard the carolling of meadowlarks and other prairie songbirds. As for the enormous Rocky Mountains, they were almost a character in themselves for a Calgary childhood. They were shining with snow in the mornings, and provided a spectacular sunset backdrop on the way home at night.[2]

And, more and more often, flight and aviation were beginning to shape the landscape.

Alberta had made a respectable contribution of aces in the First World War. Calgary supplied Fred McCall, via Vernon, British Columbia. Jock Palmer was from Lethbridge. Edmonton had provided Wilfred 'Wop' May.

Bill attended Stanley Jones Elementary School and later Crescent Heights High School. The nearest municipal airport in his community was commonly referred to as 'Renfrew Airport', or even 'Stanley Jones Airport'. It was perched on the cliff above what is the present-day Deerfoot Trail, a major thoroughfare. The airfield was approximately a 2km walk or perhaps a short bike ride away from Bill's home, and it was directly north of his elementary school. At the time, there was a charming bygone tradition of exchanging coupons from cigarette wrappers for lifts in aircraft when you had collected enough of a particular brand, and both Bill and his brother Ray enjoyed doing this.[3] What an image to imagine Calgary's First World War ace Fred McCall striding off the airfield right past the little lad perched on a nearby fence who was destined to be Calgary's Second World War ace. We don't know that it happened, of course, but it makes for a delightful and not too improbable vignette.

Rutledge Air Service Ltd opened in 1929, one of several such companies that operated from the airport. It boasted the first complete set of runway beacons in Canada, but – no runway! Very few airports had paved runways at the time; aircraft landed and took off from a large open grass airfield. In 1930, a beacon was mounted on the top of the Hudson's Bay Company building in downtown Calgary. It had a three million-candlepower beam that guided aeroplanes through the darkness.[4]

Aviation was transforming Canada, and indeed the world. The Alberta aces who had returned from the First World War with extensive flight experience had ideas and innovations for how aircraft could be used during times of peace. Remote Canadian communities could be more easily reached with medical supplies, mail and groceries. Aerial photography of growing communities and neighbourhoods became popular. Horrifically dangerous but crowd-pleasing aerobatics became common, with barnstorming and wing-walking stunts included at local events. Calgarians gathered by the hundreds to attend airshows. On one unforgettable occasion, an engine failure forced Fred McCall to plant an aeroplane on top of a merry-go-round at the Calgary Stampede instead of landing on the racetrack where an automobile race was in progress. The resulting photographs were memorable, to say the least.

So, Calgary in the 1920s offered considerable local inspiration and opportunities for an impressionable budding ace, and first-hand experiences with aeroplanes and airfields right in his own neighbourhood.

The 1930s were a different story. The environmental, fiscal and humanitarian devastation of the Great Depression were catastrophic in Alberta communities. Key businesses and industries in Calgary were partnered with agriculture or were closely linked to it. Grain elevators, the railways, the stockyards and the packing plant were major employers. Farm equipment dealers, the Robin Hood Flour Mill and manufacturing all offered agricultural products and services.

The financial downturn of the 1930s had an impact worldwide, but arguably, nowhere saw it worse than the Great Plains. Western Canada had already experienced years of drought, and the farming practices that had caused widespread damage to soil in the 1920s got even worse. 'Black Blizzards' were dust storms caused by the wind vaulting topsoil into the air and flinging it in choking black clouds across the prairie. Those storms were unstoppable. While there had been drought and damage early in the 1920s that caused widespread abandonment of homesteads, the 1930s added even more significant national, and indeed, global economic despair into the mix.

While the Calgary area was spared the worst of the dust storms, families in southern Alberta and across the rest of western Canada were struggling to survive. Homelessness, unemployment and poverty were widespread.

This economic toll certainly had a widespread influence on Canadians, including some of Bill's future squadron mates. But Bill's family does not appear to have been among those who were struggling. Bill's father worked for MacDonalds Consolidated, which became the present-day retail grocery chains Safeway and Sobeys, and he evidently did well for himself, purchasing large and comfortable homes in upscale neighbourhoods in Calgary for his family. While grocers were indirectly employed by agriculture, even during the worst years of the Great Depression, Bill's family wasn't experiencing the desperate poverty that was the scourge of the prairies during those years. However, hungry people occasionally came to the doors in Rosedale, looking for something to eat. They were given coffee and sandwiches by local moms. Neighbourhood children spoke with the unemployed and unhoused people on their way to school.[5] No one was afraid of them. They were respectful people who were down on their luck under conditions and circumstances completely beyond their control.

The McKnight family attended the North Hill United Church where Bill's mother Rose worked with the Ladies Aid. The society offered social and charitable opportunities for local women, holding afternoon teas and planning refreshments to offer at the Calgary Stampede. The beautiful Canadian Rockies were close at hand, and a journey from Calgary to the world-famous Banff or Lake Louise was an accessible day trip away. The McKnight family enjoyed visiting Calgary's beautiful mountain backyard for skiing, swimming and camping.

The life of a child growing up in Calgary included plenty of winter pastimes, including skating parties and tobogganing. Any Canadian kid can tell you what a close brush with death is like. It is flying down a hill that looked like a modest slope from the bottom and turned out to be a cliff on the way down. And Canadian parents can relate to opening the door to a wailing child on the front step after a fun afternoon on the snowy slopes gone awry. Calgary kids used skis, sleds or pieces of cardboard on the sledding hills.[6] One of Bill's exploits was to – accidentally of course – ride his toboggan full tilt into a parked car, smashing his face quite badly and receiving a deep gash above his eye. The next day, to the amazement of neighbours, the little boy was back outside with his sled, a big bandage and a railway track of stitches decorating his forehead.[7]

As a teenager, Bill was known as 'a dark and quick-moving little chap', a well-rounded athlete who played basketball, hockey and rugby.[8] He was also enrolled as a private in a Lewis gun section of the Calgary Highlanders, an infantry regiment. He seems to have been a very high-energy person, described by his father as 'confident' and 'fearless'.[9] He was a fixture of his community, and his pals included Bill and Mike Peglar, John McKinley, Louise and Olive Riley, Andy Little, John McKinlay and Harry Booth.

For a sweetheart, it was the prettiest girl in school, Miss Marian Glover, the girl practically next door, who caught his eye. Marian had dazzling blue eyes and a mouth that went down at the corners when she smiled, a charming effect rather like a smirk. The duo met when they were fourteen years old, and they went skating on their first date. Marian thought Bill had a wonderful grin, with short, curly hair and a great personality.[10] They dated in an on again, off again style for approximately four years during high school.

In addition to being the class beauty, Marian was an accomplished pianist[11] and she had a soft spot for animals. Her kitty was Boots, who had little white socks on his feet. She joined the Band of Mercy, a precursor to the Humane Society, at age eleven.[12]

Games, dances and suppers were part of the fun community events that well-to-do Calgary teenagers enjoyed and looked forward to. School was the social hub. Which was a good thing, because when it came to school, the priority was not necessarily the academics as far as Bill was concerned! His yearbook entry in the 1937 edition of the Crescent Heights *Bugle* displayed his decidedly lackadaisical attitude towards schoolwork. His favourite pastime was chronicled as 'explaining to the teachers that he never heard them say anything about homework'. Indeed, Mr Macleod, the luckless instructor of the class of '37, must have had his hands rather full. Classmate John McKinley mentioned that his own favourite expression was, 'What did you get for this answer, McKnight?'[13] Harry Booth's pet aversions and pastimes were, respectively, 'Being called names by McKnight' and 'Calling McKnight names'.[14]

Harry's prospects didn't include writing biographies according to the *Bugle* but it did foretell that Bill would become a chemical engineer.[15] Mike Peglar thought his own future lay with 'Hollywood and M. West'! and shamelessly admitted that his hobby was 'talking back to his teacher, Miss Wylie'.[16] As for the fascinating Miss Glover, her own interests ran to skating and especially to dancing, which she particularly loved. She was a member of the school's dramatic club and oversaw the secretarial duties. In 1937, the dramatic club's featured production was *Daddy Long Legs*.[17] Marian's potential career path was prophesied to be 'winner of a beauty contest', although of his former girlfriend Bill would later say that she had had business ambitions.

The young people were a generation coming of age in Calgary, not altogether sheltered from the misery and scourge of the Great Depression that encircled them, and their lives were moulded by the Great War, which was currently in a pause, the half-time of a deadly global conflict that was headed straight for them and would mark them all forever.

Bill's Moms

Bill's childhood may have been economically comfortable, but he had his own adversity to face.

His first brush with the Reaper came unexpectedly when he was very young, and it cut from his life the person who was utterly essential … his mother.

Bill was scarcely twelve years old when Rose died giving birth to little Ted. This must have been most unexpected and heartbreaking for everyone involved. Rose's obituary bears the shocking development out; amidst all the trauma, the newborn had not even been given a name yet and is simply referred to simply as 'baby'.

Rose, the source and symbol of love, belonging and nourishment for her little boys, was gone. Life was now a place where death could happen to anyone, including a happy, healthy young woman. It created a profound and lasting impact. Bill's own life would never really feel safe or happy again. He was devastated by the loss, and to add to the disorientation and stress he was experiencing, his father remarried only a few months later.

William, at thirty-seven, was now a widower with three young sons who needed a mother. He met twenty-five-year-old Doris Ingram when she was working as a comptometer, the 1930s equivalent of a billing clerk, at MacDonald's Consolidated. The pair were married in 1931, a scant year after Rose's death. William and Doris had a little daughter together when adorable Hazel Sandra joined the family in 1932. Bill was being asked to absorb considerable change at a breathtaking pace, just as the turbulence associated with adolescence was beginning. 'Grandma Doris' was spoken of with great love in later years by McKnight family members. But Bill himself apparently had very different opinions about his new stepmother. He started spending more time with his friends and their families.

Mike and Bill Peglar lived across the alley and Marian's place was just around the corner. Bill began turning up in the Peglar kitchen in the evenings for a nightly visit while the Peglar brothers did the washing up.[1] Mike later reported that his family 'kind of' kept in touch with Bill, but the letters Bill sent to Mike in later years revealed that the connection was very significant to him, and it may have been one of the few roots that he had.

The loss of his mother may explain the behaviours that people noticed about Bill during this time. We can appreciate that losing one's mother at a young and impressionable age would be a very tough thing for any child to experience. There is a natural inclination to impose ideas about how adults grieve onto children, and that can lead to a great deal of misunderstanding about the way that children and adolescents mourn.[2] Mike Peglar would later say that Bill missed his mother 'to a very deep degree'[3] and he appeared determined to make sure his father and his new stepmother knew that she wasn't welcome.

Some developmental norms of grief for adolescents in Bill's age range include pulling away from their families and relying on peers for support, struggling with schoolwork, hypervigilance, and feeling ambiguous about how they belong in their own families.[4] Other behaviours that could be noticed in a grieving adolescent include anger, which may be conveyed in a passive or sullen manner, or by lashing out at other people. Boys are more likely to engage in dangerous driving, fights, drug-taking – it would have been drinking in the 1930s – and testing authority.[5] And what better place to test a power structure than with an unwanted stepmother?

Understandably, there was yearning from this boy for the mother he loved so much, as well as loyalty towards her and deep ambivalence towards anyone trying to replace her. Bill's sorrow could have been expressed in rage or disregard for what his father and stepmother wanted for him, even if they were sincerely doing their best. Ray did not respond the same way his big brother reportedly did, and as for little Ted, he was extremely attached to Doris, who was the only mother he would ever know.

Of course, healthy and natural mourning can happen too. When bereaved children are well supported by family, they can display resilient and empathetic behaviour, such as taking responsibility for siblings.[6] It sounds like this happened as well, with little Ted being adored and spoiled by his big brothers. Ted would provide a very important eyewitness account about his big brother in the future.

I personally believe that Bill showed examples of both healthy and unhealthy grief. He clearly loved his family and repeatedly expressed concern and care for his siblings. He could be responsible and generous, saving up to buy things that Ted wanted. But he was a kid, and he was hurting. Even if he was trying to hide his grief, everyone around him, including other children, could see that he was struggling. When interviewed much later, Mike Peglar noted that Bill was 'having trouble finding himself' and that there was 'a troubled situation at home'.[7]

Rebel

Bill had a reputation for being a rebellious person with an unruly spirit and very little time to spare for authority figures. He often self-reported conflict with people who were supposed to be in charge. His family and friends also had stories to contribute about his risk-taking behaviours, and they recalled many examples of Bill's total disregard for dangerous situations. Either he didn't understand how unsafe his actions were, or he didn't care. It was a pattern of behaviour.

Family stories about Uncle Bill that his nephew grew up hearing included that his uncle was a speed demon; like all the McKnights, he drove fast. Bill and a friend picked up a hitchhiker in a rural area; by the time they got back to Calgary, the terrified passenger could barely stand up and couldn't wait to get out of the car.[1] The car they were driving apparently wasn't Bill's. Ray was the one who owned a car, although he couldn't afford to drive it too often. One day, Ray decided he wanted to go for a spin. He found his beloved car sitting in the alley. It was missing two wheels entirely and the other two were pushed back on the rims.[2] The culprit, his cherished big brother, had been hoping that Ray somehow wouldn't notice the write-off-level damage. Either way, Bill's parents cannot be faulted for being unimpressed.[3] Other antics included shooting a car across the top of the Glenmore reservoir at maximum speed.[4] Risky and risk-thrill-seeking behaviours were described again and again, and that gives us another look into Bill's mind. 'William was the kind of guy who was always looking for fun and excitement,' Ray recalled.[5]

Fun was one way of looking at it.

Bill's need-for-speed attitude was dangerous and disruptive in a quiet neighbourhood setting, but those nerves were going to serve him very well in another context.

Mike and Marian recalled that Bill increasingly turned up on their doorsteps and in their kitchens. Marian said that he called her own mother Mom.[6] He wasn't happy or settled at home, and Marian, to whom Bill was deeply attracted and attached, found his immature behaviour to be a major turn-off, despite their 'chemistry' (her words). Marian remembered an odd occasion of Bill telling her that his birthday was on 11 November; she was invited to a family supper on 18 November, only to realize with embarrassment that this was Bill's birthday party, and she had not brought him a gift.[7] Another of Bill's delusions of grandeur was the claim to have been descended from the ancient kings of Scotland. Marian noticed that there was a string of stories – lies – just like it. Making up fiction that cast himself in a more grand and interesting light seemed almost compulsive. Bill's tall tales may have given him an inflated sense of self-importance or significance, but ironically it had the impact of making the young sweetheart he adored feel as though she couldn't trust him to be honest with her. It wasn't what she wanted for her life.

Other memorable moments. Football seems to have been Bill's favourite sport, and he played halfback. Marian remembered that Bill had once called the play for his team by quoting a line of poetry.[8] Then there was a dramatic incident at school that was short on details but that had centred around a bottle of ink. Given the dangerous mischief that teenagers can sometimes get into, an event with a bottle of ink does not sound like it should have been of any particular importance, no matter what had happened. But decades later, Bill's classmates remembered it. And for the 1930s, it had been a big deal. Bill had been involved – or flat out committed the crime. Whatever it was.[9]

Bill graduated from Crescent Heights High School in 1937. He had decided to attend medical school at the University of Alberta in Edmonton. This had mixed results. Bill became a commissioned lieutenant in the university's Canadian Officers Training Corps, which sounds like a promising start, but perhaps unsurprisingly, he continued his childish antics.

Both Ray and Ted McKnight remembered that their oldest brother had famously started a disruptive conga line in his class as a prank.[10] Other reports stated that the dance began in a pub. Either way the party spilled out into a street, disrupting traffic. Bill's instructors – and his parents – were furious. Naturally, excessive qualities of alcohol were involved. While both Ray and Ted retold the stories as hilarious, coming-of-age pranks, Bill's father was reportedly livid with his son's actions. The University of Alberta was similarly not amused. What seems breathtakingly obvious is that Bill wasn't ready to be there. According to Mike Peglar, Bill was expelled from the university because of his behaviour.[11]

When I was describing Bill's antics to a Calgary psychologist looking for information about how children process and express grief, she surprised me by commenting, 'It sounds like he has ADHD.'

Attention Deficit Hyperactivity Disorder (ADHD) is a new name for an old affliction. The condition was noted by physicians as early as the late eighteenth century. By 1902, the condition that we now know as ADHD was described by the British pediatrician Sir George Frederic Still as 'an abnormal defect of moral control in children'. Still noticed that there were children who could not control their behavior as typical children could, but he also observed that their condition did not reduce their intelligence.[12] Today, we know that people with ADHD appear to have lower levels of a neurotransmitter called dopamine. Thrill seeking and daredevil activities may be their attempt to raise those levels naturally.[13]

Of course, we must be very careful about venturing back into the past and imposing our present-day understandings and sensibilities onto it. It is like going to a foreign country and trying to overlay your beliefs onto a completely different culture. However, the teenagers around Bill were from his own time and they noticed that there was something different about him and his behaviour too.

We have no way of knowing whether Bill had ADHD, but I have cautiously explored this here because it was recognised as a possibility by an expert. It was intended in the spirit of giving a list of Henry VIII's symptoms to a contemporary physician and asking for their thoughts. I have received pushback about including this material in this book, particularly from members of older generations. Fellow millennials were typically interested in and open to the information. The fact of the matter is, we don't know, and we never will.

What we can see is that whether it was influenced by his grief, feeling displaced at home by a stepmother whom he did not like, a condition such as ADHD, or a combination of all the above, Bill appeared very young. He struggled to communicate his true feelings which, as it turned out, were deep, but also deeply hidden. Mike was getting his career under way. Other childhood friends were also getting on with their lives, finding jobs and planning weddings.

Marian still cared for Bill, but she was pulling away from him. This greatly affected him, for Bill would later say that he decided to leave Alberta because of his feelings for her. Perhaps he believed, or imagined, that if he could impress her, she would reconsider. The two young people were not on the same page at all.[14]

How and where the idea to join the air force occurred to Bill, we don't know. Was it an impulse decision, or had he been thinking about it for a while? By 1938, it was becoming increasingly clear that another conflict with Germany may well be on the horizon. For the moment Canada was looking for ways to support Britain while avoiding becoming combatants themselves. Aviation was a focus. Plans were under way for Canadian manufacturers to build bombers and other aeroplanes for the Royal Air Force.[15]

There was also an acknowledgment that pilots and other personnel were going to be recruited from the Canadian population. The Royal Air Force was enlisting young Canadian men who were interested in joining up. The recruits were to be taken on conditionally and paid accordingly.[16]

The Royal Air Force had been advertising for prospective pilots in western Canada. For a region still clawing itself out of the abject poverty of the Great Depression, it is not hard to understand how the prospect of adventure, travel and above all a steady pay cheque would have greatly appealed to the young people. Bill was not the only person from Alberta who was attracted by the prospect. The opportunity certainly appealed to Bill's fellow Albertan, Noel Barlow. Noel was from a farming family at Carseland, located about 70km east of Calgary. Noel, who at twenty-seven was somewhat older than Bill, paid for his own one-way ticket to Britain. He was already a licensed pilot and thought he would be an automatic fit for the Royal Air Force.[17]

There were no guarantees that the young applicant would be accepted, so paying for the train ticket to travel to Ottawa – as Bill was about to do – for the precursory round of screening was a gamble. The young men would be assessed physically and academically, and their character and level of education would also be considerations. For those accepted, the next step towards a Short Service Commission (SSC) would be to attend the Central Flying School in England. The courses were four months long and offered advanced training in both flying and technical matters. Following their training, the young men would be employed in the Royal Air Force as commissioned members, serving for five years.[18]

Bill, attending university in Edmonton, saw newspapers running headlines declaring 'Reich Expels German Students from Universities' and referencing the immense crowds of Romans who had turned out to welcome Hitler when he visited Italy in the spring of 1938. Those stories marched along right next to reports about the Royal Air Force's activities in Canada and the opportunities it was offering to Canadians. With the benefit of hindsight, it's all very ominous. It undoubtedly seemed ominous at the time, too.

We have referenced the economic despair that Canadians were facing on the western prairies in the 1930s. Booking a one-way ticket, sometimes literally on a cattle boat, to go to Britain was not simply answering the call of adventure for young people who had never owned a new set of clothes in their lives. Their own country offered them no hope, limited opportunities and no economic future. There are estimates that 1,800 CAN/RAFs – Canadians in the Royal Air Force – were already in Britain when the Second World War broke out, and the fiscal position of their own country goes a long way towards explaining why.

While Bill didn't share the economic desperation that other recruits were facing, for a young person who appeared directionless, the Royal Air Force's offer was undoubtedly intriguing. His life was increasingly aimless and the things he was trying weren't working out. Although he was not motivated by the financial hardships that had driven other people from Alberta, he hoped to impress Marian. Perhaps he could prove something to himself as well.

He wasn't expecting to be gone forever, and he would later reference the intention to continue his medical studies. Have fun, travel, meet new friends, try something else. As a young person in his early twenties, he was exploring, trying things, searching for his place in the world. Some of that would include ruling out things that weren't the right fit after all, something that many of us can relate to, recalling our own tentative first steps into adulthood. We gradually found our path and ourselves through trial and error, working out what we liked, what we were good at, and where we belonged. This seems to be what Bill was trying to do. He could spend time in England, become a pilot, and then serve in the Royal Air Force. Would he be a good fit as an instructor? Work in the navy? Return to Canada to train other Canadians?

Unlike most of us, however, a massive historical event was straddling his path and was about to intervene in his life in a powerful, critical and unforeseen manner. That five-year agreement with the Royal Air Force was coming at a very critical juncture for anyone joining up in 1939.

Bill was on his way to Ottawa for the first round of screening, paying for his own train ticket.

He was about to find something that he was very, very good at.

The Fledgling

Until now, January 1939 had been mild in Calgary; daily temperatures had hovered around zero. 21 January dawned at a reasonably pleasant – by Canadian standards – -7.

Bill said goodbye to Calgary and to his family on the broad Canadian Pacific Railway platform beside the stately sandstone Palliser Hotel. Surely it was too cold for little Hazel and nine-year-old Ted, who were already accustomed to the comings and goings of their biggest brother, to go to the train station. He had been an intermittent part of their lives for a year or two now as he travelled back and forth to university, trying to figure out his future. Goodbyes were likely said in the warmth of the cozy childhood home on Alexander Crescent before the departure for the station. But surely Bill was accompanied by his father, and perhaps Ray.

The coming separation would not necessarily be a long one, but the distance between Calgary and England is after all terribly far. Likely no one dreamed or imagined that the goodbye was forever as the farewells were spoken on the frigid Canadian Pacific Railway platform.

The sun sets early in Calgary in late January, around 5 p.m., often in a pretty blue and pink prairie palette over the shoulders of the Rocky Mountains. An hour later, utter darkness. If the wind shifted, the smell and sounds of the cattle at the stockyards, only a few blocks away from the grandest hotel in town, circled the train platform.

The train was coming; its lights and noise and rhythm swept up to the platform. He stepped aboard.

Behind him in the darkness, Calgary grew smaller and smaller. Pinpoints of light, miles away, flared and flashed brilliantly as they do on the level land, with even the most minuscule points of light visible miles away. Stops at familiar eastern locales – Langdon, Gleichen – steadily faded behind him as the train travelled farther east. Had he already nodded off when they reached the Saskatchewan border, or was he too wired and excited?

That night, the temperature would plunge to a frigid -18.

The *Calgary Herald* society pages had reported on the big occasion: 'Mr William L. McKnight, son of Mr and Mrs W. C. McKnight, is leaving this evening for England, where he will join the Royal Air Force. He will go to Uxbridge.'[1]

In later years, Marian would recall the night before Bill left Calgary. He came to say goodbye to her family, and as he was leaving he had turned to her and told her that when he returned they would 'start up again'. This cryptic message didn't fully make sense to her at the time, but she didn't forget about it, either. What she had not said is that, under the circumstances, she knew what she wanted, and it wasn't him. But it turned out that she did not have the full picture. Decades later, she would learn what Bill had been wanting to say.[2]

Travelling across the enormous span of his own massive country, Bill wrote two postcards to his family, both mailed on 25 January. One showed the Mink Tunnel at Lake Superior, Ontario, and contained a brief note saying that he had just passed through it but couldn't write much, thanks to the motion of the train – although he was appreciating the wonderful sights. 'Love Bill'.

The second postcard had a photograph depicting the rugged shoreline of Lake Superior. Bill had a more important news bulletin on this one:

> Arrived in Ottawa today. Had a good trip. Passed all my tests O.K. but had a bit of trouble with my ears. However, specialist passed them. One chap failed. Will write again from boat. Am staying at Y.M.C.A.
>
> Love, Bill.[3]

History could have been halted in its tracks if the screeners in Ottawa had decided that William Lidstone McKnight's ears would not be able to tolerate the dramatic altitude changes to be experienced by pilots!

Bill embarked for England not aboard a cattle ship but on the Canadian Pacific Railway liner *Montclare.* He was not the only former Calgarian on board. Richard Bedford Bennett, the former Prime Minister of Canada (serving in 1930–35), was on his way to a recently acquired retirement property in Surrey. Both former Calgarians were headed into a state of affairs that would be impossible for them to predict or imagine, with Bill looking for a purpose and adventure and Bennett dreaming of a relaxing retirement. It is improbable that the two met while on the *Montclare*, though surely Bill learned that the former Prime Minister was aboard. The deadly and dramatic global conflict was in the paths of both men when they landed in England and went their separate ways, Bennett to his new estate and Bill to Warwickshire to join his two-month training program at No. 9 Elementary and Reserve Flying Training School, the next step in his journey.

Also aboard the *Montclare* were two other young Canadians, Arthur Deacon and Robert Hill, and their paths would cross with Bill's later in the year. They were all destined to become members of the Royal Air Force's all-Canadian squadron. But that was all in the future as well.[4]

Bill had left behind the intense, high-altitude energy of Calgary. The wide-open spaces, endless blue skies and the climate of nearly perpetual sunshine, with the Rockies stretching along the western horizon, had been exchanged for the soft watercolour palette of the British Midlands in winter. The pointillist effect of the landscape was glimpsed through rain-spattered train windows, which fogged up immediately if you leaned too close. Already, the grass in England was faintly threaded with green, and the sky was a misty gray affair, with a near permanent skin of cloud between the sky and the sun. The effect was a great contrast to Alberta and an exciting exchange of backdrops for a new chapter in his life.

There was a marked difference in attitudes towards flight and aviation between the two places as well. For Canadians trying to survive the fiscal devastation of the depression, their own Royal Canadian Air Force had offered limited and unappealing opportunities throughout the 1930s. The Royal Air Force had been throwing out a lifeline, a rescue from homelessness, hunger and exhausting poverty.

Meanwhile in Britain, aviation was in a period of expansion. The Air Ministry was planning major projects, building airfields throughout Great Britain in 1938, and the intention was to train the pilots and the other ground crew needed to keep aircraft and airfields running. The uneasy situation on the Continent was creating a dynamic of preparation and attention for whatever the future might bring.

The recruits visited the No. 9 Elementary and Reserve Flying Training School at Ansty in Warwickshire for evaluation and assessment. This was Bill's first stop on his journey. Air schools were privately operated by civilians, employing instructors who were RAF Reserve officers. The instructors had completed their four- or five-year Short Service Commissions as pilots and their career paths had led them to engagements as flight instructors, which was a possibility for Bill when and if he completed his own Short Service Commission.

As for the airfield itself, when Bill arrived early in 1939, all the airfields were grass. Can you imagine trying to take off from a muddy grass airfield in a heavy bomber? The trainer aircraft ringing the airfield included Avro Cadets, Avro Ansons, Airspeed Oxfords, and North American Aviation Harvards.

Bill arrived at his temporary new home on 6 February. There was no time for sightseeing or settling in. He was in the air the very next day. Flying Officer Hudson was Bill's new instructor, and it seems that he promptly became Bill's nemesis, as frequently befell anyone in a role of authority in Bill's life. Bill and Hudson went for a forty-minute trip from the No. 9 Ansty Aerodrome on 7 February. They were flying in an Avro Cadet; Bill recorded the big occasion in his brand-new logbook as 'Effect of Controls' and 'Air Experience'.

Bill was essentially attending the kindergarten of the Royal Air Force, and the little Cadet biplane was basically the tricycle version of an aeroplane, but it is not really fair to assign training wheels to the Cadet, because it was not an easy aircraft to manage. A taildragger, it was more difficult to land and to manage on the ground than an airplane with a nosewheel. Bill's would have had a five-cylinder air-cooled Genet engine. The student sat in the front seat and the flight instructor sat right behind him. In the open-air cockpit with the engine roaring and the wind whipping past, communication was all but impossible. The technology at the time was Gosport tubes, allowing the instructor to talk to the student, but that was all. The instructor had their own rudder pedals, throttle and stick, but they would ideally take over only to prevent a crash. Cadets did not have brakes.

There was no typing of pilots at this early stage, no evaluation of whether the person would be a better fit to fly fighters or bombers. The assessment was a sudden-death situation to determine whether the recruit would become a pilot or not. Pass or fail. For the washouts, their professional choices would narrow to supporting roles such as navigators or gunners.

The July 1937 issue of *Flight Magazine*[5] had provided details of what life was like for the newly arrived No. 9 Elementary and Reserve Flying Training School recruits:

> In batches of about thirty, A.S.T. take young men, mostly raw to flying, who have applied for entry into the R.A.F. In their eight weeks' sojourn at Ansty they have to embrace a good working knowledge of airmanship, navigation, engines, aircraft construction and rigging, and armament.
>
> In the same time about fifty hours' flying are completed, of which twenty-five are solo. The usual period of dual instruction before the first solo is about ten hours, but fifteen hours is the maximum allowed under normal circumstances.

There was also a physical component to the preparation, including weekly 5-mile cross-country races. Bill claimed to have lost 18lb in his first few months of training.[6] The healthy new habits were offset with sampling the local beer, which he allegedly limited to a pint a week. If Bill were around today, I suspect he would have thoroughly enjoyed the microbreweries that are trendy in the 2020s.

London was an exciting new experience. Dancing, both locally and in the big city, did not come naturally, as the styles were unfamiliar to a Canadian, but he was willing to try.[7]

Bill's Royal Air Force Pilot's Flying Log Book[8] will be a major source of the information shared throughout this book. A logbook was a very personal document for a young pilot, a record of their professional milestones such as first solo flight, awards and participation in significant events. It also provides a rich record of the day-to-day activities that are so important for historians. A logbook was expected to be kept up to date, but it was acceptable for a pilot to make up their entries a few days later. The information was signed off on by a superior officer on a monthly basis, ensuring that the material would be more or less accurate.

We will also trace Bill's escapades through letters sent to his family and his friends Bill and Mike Peglar back in Calgary, and you will see for yourself that not infrequently Bill's version of the events differed greatly from the verified and more prosaic realities. Impressing his buddy Mike and the dutiful family missives represented 'on brand' aspects of Bill's experiences, recording his own interpretations and impressions of what was happening in his exciting new life.

And then there was what was actually happening.

Both make for fascinating reading. Bill could be a legend in his own mind, and his version of events often painted him as a character in a melodramatic comic book or action movie, with occasional comedic elements – even if what he was really doing was flying Cadets with Flying Officer Hudson cramping his style and eating awful British food.

'Tell Ted I'm Sorry About the Train'

Bill knew that he had passed his exams, both flying and written, and he had progressed to the No. 1 Royal Air Force Depot in Uxbridge by the time he wrote a letter to his parents on 18 April 1939. He described a typical day in his life:

> We get up at six in the morning and work until four – then we have tea and have two and a half hours before dinner. We have to dress – mess kit – for dinner and that takes up a good while, so when dinner finishes about nine I feel like going right to bed.[1]

Bill's missive included travel plans for his two weeks' leave in July to visit Aunty Jean, his father's sister, in Scotland. He had also decided to make the most of the fine weather that had finally arrived in England, including making recreational plans for swimming, squash, tennis, and golf 'when I can afford to buy some clubs'.[2]

The letter from Bill to his family is preserved from April 1939. At this point, he was merely in training, and the Commonwealth was not at war yet. This is the letter historians didn't previously know about from the McKnight Family Archive. It reveals that while most of his class was preparing to fly bombers, Bill was training on fighters.

The letter expresses love and concern for family members, including little Hazel, who has been ill. Bill was generous to his family members. 'Tell Ted I'm sorry about the train,' he writes, saying that he is saving up to buy a train set longed for by Ted, but that he must pay for his uniform first. A sense of responsibility in providing things that his little brother enjoyed, such as toys, or a coveted sticker book, displayed Bill's kindness to the people he loved, and we will see this again. Older children can have a sense of obligation to their siblings, particularly when a parent has been physically or emotionally absent, and Bill's actions seem to reveal this. And how easy to imagine the security that little Ted must have felt with his idolised big brother showing care not only for his needs but also for the things that are important to young children (their toys). Bill also sent a flying helmet to Ray to wear while motorcycling, because he had acquired a newer and better one.

Of course, he uses a formal tone in writing to his parents. It is only one side of Bill. But it does show a caring, attentive and generous family member. Just over a year later, he would be flying a Hurricane in the defense of doomed France. But for now, he was a young man who had spread his wings and flown across the world, writing to the family who, unknown to all of them, he would never see again.

Bill's letter to his family left out a dramatic training incident that may have happened just a few days before, on 14 April. It is in a letter dated 3 May 1939 to Mike Peglar that Bill revealed what had happened, from his point of view.

Until then, Bill's training had been restricted to stick and rudder flying. His first solo flight was recorded on 24 February 1939, a ten-minute flight in an Avro Cadet. The training regime outlined in Bill's logbook records a measured, step-by-step program that even to an aviation outsider certainly appears to be designed to make the pilots succeed in a careful series of experiences and exercises that build on one another. Stalling, climbing and gliding, taking off into the wind, approaches and landings built into climbing turns, steep turns without aerobatics and landings with and without engines. As Bill's chief instructor, Flying Officer Hudson was along for the ride.

Bill's letter to Mike was written from No. 6 Flying School in Little Rissington; he had arrived there on 29 April 1939. He was through to the next round. Bill told Mike that he had been switched to flying bombers. He must have been referring to the Avro Anson. The Anson was originally a maritime reconnaissance aircraft that had been adapted to many roles, including training duties, but Bill evidently was not impressed with bomber aircraft, which were incapable of the rollercoaster-style aerobatics that he enjoyed.

The boring old Anson could only fly straight and level. And as for the six other passengers on board, Bill was not amused at being 'a taxi driver'[3], which was rather surprising. Previously he seemed to have been quite extrovert and enjoyed partying and being around other people. But not if he had to fly a bomber, apparently. Bill said he had applied for a transfer back to his fighters but was irritated in the meantime as he expected it to take six months.[4] His first solo flight in the Anson was made on 11 May 1939.[5]

Bill had bigger problems.

He told Mike that he had been in a confrontation with his instructor, whom he does not name but was likely Flying Officer Hudson, that had led to a major blowout. Bill claimed that they were flying formations, and that the instructor had confronted him about flying too close to his tail. Bill described that he had responded soothingly, 'If he was afraid to fly in front why didn't he let somebody else do it and as far as I was concerned he could go to hell anyway – he's about the biggest louse I've ever met.'[6]

Unsurprisingly, this went down like a lead balloon, with Bill's actions being reported to the commanding officer and Bill receiving two weeks of the Royal Air Force's version of a time out for insubordination. He was confined to camp for fourteen days and commanded to report to the orderly officer every two hours until 10.30 p.m. To add insult to injury, he had to wear full mess dress to dinner every night. One can only imagine Mike shaking his head over the incident, the 'Classic Bill' behaviour that must have surely been all too familiar as he remembered his friend's challenges with his family and the circumstances that had caused him to leave medical school only months before.

However, this incident simply could not have happened the way that Bill described it. Not only does Bill's logbook not record any incidents of formation flying during April of 1939, but it would have been a completely inappropriate training exercise for such a new group of pilots to participate in.

While we don't know exactly what Bill was referring to, the Canadian aviation historian – and pilot – Richard de Boer has proposed a theory. We can make an educated guess about what happened because on 14 April 1939, Bill had recorded in his logbook his first occasion of instrument flying. He and Flying Officer Hudson went for a nearly fifty-minute-long flight. The significance of that for this very grounded historian was entirely lost; however it is evidently a major event for a pilot.

Bill's experiences before that date had been of the stick and rudder variety, a 'drop a primate into an aeroplane' sort of flying. The purpose of instrument flying is to teach you to distrust the most basic instruments you have: your senses. You are to become a bird, or perhaps more accurately a bat. Your flight instruments tell you that you are right side up when you feel like you are upside down, for instance. The experience for almost everyone is stressful and disorienting, and it is nearly impossible to prepare for what it is going to feel like. Flying Officer Hudson, who had been Bill's principal flying instructor, was present that day and this is likely when the incident took place.

Perhaps something happened that scared everyone; Bill had only fifty-four hours and fifteen minutes of recorded flight time by this point and if he was going to mess up, it would likely happen when he was doing something new and dangerous. It seems possible that this happened, because afterwards Bill did not record any other flying activity for three weeks.

Naturally, Bill did not share this story in the letter he sent to his family. 'Highly strung fiery lads get the fighters, cooler and more phlegmatic heads are assigned to the bombers' was the accepted wisdom at the time.[7] Somehow, the monikers 'calm' and 'cool' don't sit quite right when describing Bill McKnight.

Conceivably his instructors were having trouble getting their own heads around where Bill's strengths and gifts would lie. Bill may have been flying bombers, but he was a fighter pilot by nature and by preference. Fighter pilots were expected to be aggressive and to have a '$%^& you' attitude because it served them well in the risk-taking and dangerous situations they would be expected to face. After a stressful day and a demanding new experience, mistakes and volcanic tempers were perhaps to be expected but it showed that Bill had not progressed emotionally from his time at medical school. He blamed his instructor, lied to Mike about what had happened, and did not take one shred of responsibility for anything.

However, he may have taken the occurrence more seriously than he was willing to admit, because he also recorded more soberly that a fellow pilot had failed his exams. Bill had passed his own exams with an unimpressive 70 per cent, and he observed that, 'I've been really sweating like hell to get a good mark,' and offered a surprisingly sober assessment of his own academic strengths and weaknesses.[8]

Bill's correspondence to Mike during the summer of 1939 is simultaneously invaluable and worthless as a source document because, true to form, he perpetually inflated his adventures, exaggerated and flat out lied about what he was doing. He gives us a window into his day-to-day activities, talked about what he enjoyed and showed snapshots of his personality, which were typically of a sunshine/shadow dichotomy. However enjoyable his stories are, and as valuable as they can be for giving us glimpses into his experiences and impressions as a pilot in training, the problem is that many of them are simply not true.

Another excellent example of this in the 3 May letter is the graphic description Bill shared with Mike of night flying, which seemed to scare him:

> We've started night flying also and it's really fun. You don't know whether you are five or five thousand feet above the ground, and the first few landings scare hell out of you. We don't use beacon lights or anything for landing, just flare lights, and after they die out you might just as well be landing with your eyes shut. If you want to get a very faint idea of what it's like, try driving a car along a dark road you don't know on a dark night with your lights

> out – that's only a fair idea. These planes land at 90–95 miles an hour, so if you slip you very rarely get a second chance.[9]

This paints a wonderful picture to a civilian such as Mike – or myself – of what night flying is like when you are the one in charge of the aircraft. It is unsettling and intimidating, and if it has managed to daunt Bill McKnight, one can well appreciate that this is something that requires good, steady nerves and a high level of skill.

The problem is, Bill does not record any night flying in his logbook until 19 June 1939.

As an etiquette instructor Bill may leave something to be desired, but he also passed along a message for Mike to give to a mutual acquaintance, adding, 'Oh, by the way, tell Barnes I really don't give a damn whether he answers my letter or not, but it's only customary politeness to at least drop a note in return for a letter.'

Despite claims to the contrary, he sounded angry and hurt to be ignored.

The effect of the letters seems to indicate that Bill was repeating a pattern that he had been struggling with for years: conflict with authority, a short fuse, and very little patience for himself and those around him. The McKnight men were not big people, but their tempers were so volcanic that others generally backed down in the face of their rage. It was like dealing with a wolverine. Even a grizzly bear might decide that taking them on was just not worth it.

Surely a warning bell must have been ringing away at the back of Bill's mind, reminding him of the failure at the University of Alberta. Despite the bravado, the impression left is that he did not want that to happen again. Angry and scared, and not wanting a repeat of that experience, he may be telling his friend in a devil may care attitude of his larger-than-life experiences. Behind it, there was a determination to succeed, some self-assessment, and a willingness to work harder. He was planning a route to reach his goals. We can perhaps conclude that he had taken the occurrence somewhat seriously, even if he blamed other people for what happened.

He was seeing real world consequences happening to other people and was learning from them, just a little. Not that we will see much evidence of this for a few months.

Despite the blowout, there was good news to report. Bill had received his pilot's certificate of competency for flying all types of private landplanes on 16 March 1939. And Bill's chief flying instructor rated his proficiency as a pilot as 'above average', a rarity from the praise-grudging Royal Air Force. It was the unofficial code for 'a natural pilot'.[10]

Summer of '39

The summer of 1939 stretched invitingly ahead. There were more exams to come and more to learn about flying Ansons, but there was the prospect of a summer holiday in Scotland with Bill's father's family and considerable good times too. His new instructors included Flying Sergeants Grossey and Lewis, Flying Officer Oldbury and Flying Lieutenant Fothergill.

Meanwhile, the Canadian Pacific Railway liner *Empress of Britain* had arrived in England. It was bearing King George VI and Queen Elizabeth, who had spent the better part of a month in Bill's home and native land. On 26 May 1939, Calgarians, including the McKnight family, had waited anxiously to get a glimpse of them when the royal couple arrived in Calgary by train on an extensive, month-long rail trip across Canada. In the spring of 1939, war with Germany was starting to appear increasingly inevitable. The visit was a chance for the King and Queen to visit an important Commonwealth country and it seemed that they were both looking for and offering reassurance and support.

The King and Queen began their day in Calgary at City Hall, where they signed a registry book. Then they were driven to the Mewata football stadium, where they met with 2,000 First Nations peoples from the Siksika, Kainai, Pikani, Tsuu Tina, and Stoney Lakota tribes, who presented them with a portrait of Queen Victoria.

Returning to England on 21 June, the couple were welcomed by their daughters and a salute of naval guns. Bill reported to Mike Peglar in a letter dated 25 June 1939 that his training squadron had had the great honour ('so they say' he added rather acerbically) of being selected as an escort for the couple when they arrived home. He sounded considerably nonplussed as he reported to Mike that he had flown for four hours and had been more tired than overawed by the supposed honour. Bill did not record this event in his logbook. As we well know, Bill exaggerated his adventures and even lied about them when he was writing to Mike. The medium may have been letters rather than

Snapchat or TikTok, but even in 1939 young people wanted their lives to look more impressive to their friends than they actually were.

If Bill did participate in the event in some way, he claimed that he was not impressed by the occasion. He had stronger views about the local beer and cider. Bill did not appear to have been a food critic, but when it came to alcoholic beverages, he had his opinions. He approved strongly of the English beer. 'It's just like drinking the nectar of the gods,'[1] and it was cheap. Bill had done the first-hand research to know how many people could get drunk for $0.75 – it was a gang of four or five, if you want to know his precise calculations – approximately $20 CAD (£11) in 2025.

He had more to say about night flying, which he was currently practicing. He went for his first night flight on 19 June with Flight Lieutenant Fothergill. Bill found night flying to be a thrilling and disturbing experience, and to be fair night landings are often described as horrifying and disorienting by new pilots. He also mentioned that he did not like flying the #2 position in a formation as you were either flying into #1 or #3.[2]

On top of everything else, he was back in time out. He had been confined to camp for two weeks for going AWOL on a weekend but had been 'persuaded' to go to see the musician Jack Hylton performing (it seems rather unlikely anyone was twisting his arm). Unfortunately for Bill, karmic lessons seemed to be quick and immediate. The commanding officer and his wife were attending the same concert, and Bill ran into them. The next day, Bill was informed in no uncertain terms that he would lose his rank if he was guilty of any further insubordination. He reflected that he would have to change his ways, 'at least for a while'.[3]

Truthfully, the commanding officer must have had his hands full, because according to Bill, the CO's own commanding officer was coming to investigate the ongoing antics at No. 6 FTS. But why don't we let Bill describe the situation in his own colourful language? 'The C.O. gave us hell [and] said we were rapidly getting a nice reputation and the A.O.C. is coming down to-morrow to find out what's been going on down here lately.'[4]

Bill claimed that more than half of his class had outright failed in their mid-term exams; a dismal 20 per cent score had been the average. Bill also announced that there had been three terrible flying accidents, one of which had destroyed an aircraft and sent a young pilot to the hospital with extensive injuries. 'His instructor only got a broken arm.'[5]

Bill recounted the merits of a Bristol Blenheim, which he seemed to admire and credited with far more capacity than it had. He joked that he had purchased several uniforms, promising that Mike can 'have them cheap' if he forgets to pull out during a diving practice exercise.[6] I don't know if we would have encouraged Bill to try improv, but he might have been rather good in a stand-up set. He did have a rather dry sense of humour and slipped sly comical observations, often at his own expense, into his letters.

All joking aside, the fact that so many of the young pilots were evidently struggling with both the practical and written portion of their training indicated either a breakdown with the leadership or that their squadron specifically had systemic issues.

While Bill had a well-deserved reputation as a rebel and had few cares to spare for people in authority, he had told Mike that he intended to study hard. And he must have, because he had passed all his exams but one and had a respectable 82 per cent average. Academically, he was doing well. He also demonstrated self-reflection and self-assessment about the parts of flying that he was good at and the parts that were hard for him.

He did not seem to regard crashes as things that could happen only to other people. While he made jokes, he seemed to have a 'this could happen to me' attitude, an understanding that can sometimes be difficult for young people whose brains are not fully developed. Immaturity had long been a defining trait for Bill, something that he was known for. Now, just a little, he was showing that he did understand cause and effect, and that he set and achieved his goals. There was a wariness about things that were truly dangerous, such as night flying, which unsettled him noticeably.

In addition to drinking and dancing, the young men had of course their fledgling experiences with love, romance and sex to navigate. Mike had recently been through a stormy patch in his love life, splitting up and getting back together with his girlfriend, Olive Riley. Bill responded empathically and shared his experiences with his own break-up. He was still thinking about and trying to forget 'a certain person' – code for Marian. There were other young women around and he found them distracting, but not compelling. Still, he was glad to hear that his friends had patched things up.[7]

Ever so faintly, there were signs of hope that our young Calgarian was growing up. Ish.

'You can spot a Canadian right off'

You can spot a Canadian right off, and if you can't see them, you can hear them – shouting and swearing, drinking more than they can hold, and generally with the worst-looking whore this side of either of the two places.

So how did our allies feel about the Canadians who were turning up throughout Britain as the Commonwealth prepared for the war that was looking ever more unavoidable? The above is a blistering and most unflattering quotation from an eyewitness about Canada's finest that I am choosing to include here. Who would say such a thing about our heroes in uniform? I will reveal this later, but first, let's explore this period through Bill's eyes. It might shed some light on the Canadians who would find themselves on the receiving end of this bad publicity.

Canadians admittedly had some adapting to do. First, there were cultural differences around food. And the food, to be fair, was terrible. Canadians were criticized for the disgusting practice of putting ketchup on everything (porridge, pancakes ...). Stereotypically, Canadians are fans of ketchup; Canada is the home of the ketchup potato chip after all. However, the counter-argument from the Canadians was that they had to use ketchup to make the awful food edible.[1] In Hell, the English are the cooks!

Bill's 10 July 1939 letter to Bill Peglar was a newsy affair that covered personal and professional ground. It was Bill at his worst. He was dismissive of the Hurricane, the aircraft with which he would become synonymous. He claimed they were outdated, which was not true. He then informed Bill Peglar that he was flying Blenheims, Hamptons and even a Spitfire. His logbook prosaically reveals that he was flying nothing but Ansons, and that same logbook indicated that he did not fly any other type of aircraft until November. His pattern of bragging and exaggerating about himself and his adventures was on full display.[2]

Bill noted that he had logged 150 flying hours and described a hilarious night out participating in blackout drills. He claimed that he and a friend had flown their bomber to shoot up his friend's girlfriend's house as a prank. The police were still on the trail of the culprits, but Bill thought that they would get away with it, serenely confident that law enforcement couldn't see in the dark.[3] Blackout exercises and practice runs were indeed carried out in June, July, and August of 1939, but Bill's logbook for June and July of 1939 did not mention any participation in the exercises. What he recorded on 10 July were two flights and three landings, indicating that they were practicing circuits.

Was he full of it in other ways? Bill noted the changes around him that were leading towards the outbreak of war; both men and women were appearing in uniform. His own uniform had an appealing side effect – there was a magnetic result on women. An instructor had disclosed the sobering information that Britain expected to lose a thousand pilots a week for the first month of the war.[4]

Bill's main concern upon receiving this disturbing news was ... well: 'It's funny, you know, that when a country gets a sort of war scare creeping over it, the women all loosen up and give – and I mean really give. There's absolutely scads of beauties in town.'[5]

Bill claimed to be dating a wealthy and beautiful girl called Jo, but he was using her car while she was away to pick up other girls! Jo was supposedly dating other people as well.[6]

Did Jo = flying Spitfires?

As the summer stretched on, he was studying for exams, balancing school and sports days. He visited London. He sampled a peppery German beer, which he liked. He was looking forward to seeing the musician Ray Fox perform at an upcoming ball where everyone was projected to get plastered, including the commanding officer.

In the final paragraph of the letter, Bill did something that an insightful friend of mine calls the doorknob effect. A person you've had a conversation with puts their hand on the doorknob, ready to leave, and they say the thing that has really been on their minds the whole time. The last few sentences of this letter were Bill at his very worst, in an absolutely terrible mood. It seemed that he had found out that Marian Glover had started dating someone else. He shredded Marian's reputation and criticized her for setting physical boundaries with him. It seemed that he regretted respecting them.

'I came over [here] principally because of the way I felt about [Marian],' he admitted. He took no responsibility for the way their relationship had ended. In fact, he blamed Marian for being too 'prim' to take their relationship to the next level, resentful that she – and perhaps others – had thought of him as a bad influence. He was the victim, he was 'very disappointed', he was 'finished'.

But, despite it all, she was the girl for him.

'I don't think I shall ever go for anybody else like I did for her – I hope not.'[7]

It sounded remarkably like a temper tantrum. The ferocity and intensity of the legendary McKnight anger flashed across the page; the emotional weather was decidedly stormy. Bill was doing his best to make sense of the world, and everything hurt. He was not being fully honest with himself about what was happening, and why. He even threatened Marian, implying that if he could live life over, he would have ignored her physical boundaries, and at least in that moment, it seemed that he meant what he said. There was an oblique reference to suicidal thoughts. It appeared momentary as he was still making future plans, something that someone with a serious intention to kill themselves would not have done.

Still, he confided: '… it's sort of made me feel like quitting for a minute.'[8]

Unknown to Bill, the feelings Marian had for him were still there. She, unlike the young women who he claimed swarmed and swooned at the sight of his uniform, did not care about the uniform. She had really liked him. What he was unable to see was that what Marian, and perhaps some other people back home in Calgary, did not like was his behavior. He had been acting out, full of grief for the loss of his mother, and resentful of his stepmother. He was a high-spirited person with a lot of energy; his anguish had been expressed in rebellion and rage. But Marian it seemed had made up her mind; she did not want to be lied to and misled. So, she did not want him. Rejection is so painful.

Late July saw Bill in a better mood. There was a lighter tone to the letters home as the summer wore on. The sporting competitions had come and gone – he had come second in the broad jump. The concerts he had attended included performances by musicians Joe Loss and Geraldo.[9] The summer carried, at least for him, the signature of beach vibes. Exams were beginning. His logbook reported a variety of activities such as taking off, landing with one engine and more night flying. The logbook contained this feedback from an instructor: 'Tends to be careless, must be supervised.'

Overall, he seemed relaxed and happy. He thought that he might be going to Singapore at the end of his course. 'I hope so.'[10] Luckily for him, he did not.

'… the dame I was telling you about was a bit of allright and I had my evenings well taken up,'[11] he told the Peglar brothers. Was he finally having sex? A mysterious Alice was mentioned. It could certainly account for the good mood.

When not – according to him – flying Spitfires and terrorizing the local innocent civilians, the partying continued. One night, Bill and a group of friends returned drunk to their base. They were ordered to go to bed after irritating a 'very' senior officer with their intoxicated antics. Instead they continued the party. Someone threw beer on the walls and smashed glasses in the fireplace. At this point, their flight lieutenant lost all patience with them. Bill received a two-week open arrest for being the perpetrator of a riot and spent another two weeks confined to base for his behaviour. 'Christ that's all I ever get from this place.'[12] He was exasperated with the people setting limits, but never with himself for what he had done to earn the penalties. It was always someone else's fault.

I've never had the impression that the people around Bill found him to be a mean or cruel person. He was never described as creepy. He did not hurt animals or have a reputation for stealing. For the most part, he was harmless, aside from his terrifying driving. What was clear was how immature he was. At times he was thoughtful, and he did have the capacity to assess himself and set objectives (knowing when he needed to step up and study hard for exams, for instance). However, his antics often sounded like the capers of an awkward, disruptive kid on the verge of adolescence. Risk taking and authority challenges were intended to impress other adolescent boys. No one else was enjoying or appreciating it. He was a typical young guy in some ways, but there was also a different tone when alcohol was involved.

He had a new life, a new career and his own time and freedom to manage. The judgmental interfering family was far away. Travel had offered a new culture and customs to explore. It was all an elixir for growing up. Pain, mistakes and having things not work out the way that he had hoped was part of that, too.

Knowing as we do that this was the last lighthearted summer that Bill would ever have, it is kind of hard to begrudge him.

Prime Minister Mackenzie King and Canada's Political Situation

> *I appeal to my fellow Canadians to unite in a national effort to save from destruction all that makes life worth living, and to preserve for future generations those liberties and institutions which others have bequeathed to us.*
>
> Mackenzie King, Prime Minister of Canada

While Bill was living it up during the last carefree summer that he would ever experience, the leaders of nations were preparing for the gathering storm. While the occasional strong thunderclap may have been heard sporadically by Bill, the intense dark clouds menacing the horizon were no longer avoidable for the Prime Minister of Canada.

Mackenzie King was the Canadian Prime Minister during the lead-up to the Second World War that was about to have so many implications for little chess pieces like Bill McKnight. King was going to be guiding his nation through the political elements of the coming death grapple and preserving 'the liberties and institutions that make life worth living' for Canadians. He, like so many others who remembered the awful realities of the First World War, did not have the stomach or sensibilities for a second one.

Like Winston Churchill, King was a career politician, but he had a different temperament and outlook to his British counterpart. King had held to a strategy of placation and concession with Hitler throughout the 1930s. While Hitler had lavished almost unlimited spending upon the German military, with a concentration of that investment being made on aircraft, by the time Bill arrived in Britain, expenditures on the Royal Air Force were high.[1] As for Canada, as we have seen it had endured an environmental, fiscal and humanitarian crisis during the 1930s, and probably luckily for King, his predecessor R.B. Bennett had to deal with the political fallout from the worst half of it.

King had skill and experience as a mediator. His background included high-profile work that he had done for the Rockefellers. He was familiar with high-stakes negotiations and finding common ground between opponents. That approach was the very worst thing that anyone could have done with Hitler, although to be fair, others had tried that tactic, too.

As a sovereign nation, Canada's parliament debated the decision to join the war. It could have taken advantage of the fact that Canada was separated from Europe by a vast and convenient expanse of ocean. It could have sheltered alongside the might and power of the United States with its indifferent neutrality.

Instead, Canada declared war, separately from Britain, on 10 September 1939.

Sick as Hell

Bill seemed too young for most of the first half of this story. He was too old for the rest of it. There is a literal dividing line, and the switch occurred just over a month later.

Writing from Little Rissington, Bill composed a letter to Mike Peglar that contained two letters in one, written on two different dates. The first half, penned on 16 September 1939, followed his two-week military time out. Canada had declared war on Germany six days previously, after Germany invaded Poland on 1 September. The implications had evidently not had time to sink in. Bill had learned nothing from the consequences of his actions. He had been partying with his cousins in Scotland, taking advantage of the nightlife in Glasgow and 'Edinbourough'! There was such a high percentage of Scottish women to Scottish men that he was moving right along, living his best life.

The letter was completed on 24 September 1939. After the first graphic paragraphs along his familiar themes of wine, women and song, it could almost have been written by a different person.

He had achieved a major milestone, become a pilot and received his commission. But rather than making decisions that should be accompanying the next steps of his career, war had confronted him. It was really happening at last. He was a pawn, inanimate and disposable, frozen in place as other people made decisions about where he would go and what he would do. The resulting chaos and uncertainty were rumbling across every aspect of his young life. In the space of two weeks, war had transformed everything.

No sooner had Britain declared war on Germany than Wellington bombers had flown out to the Kiel Canal and bombed German warships. Some of the crew from No. 149 Squadron who had taken part in the mission were stationed at Little Rissington, and as a newly appointed bomber pilot, that had implications for an impressionable young guy who had just attained his wings. In the disorganization of the very early days of the war, the Royal Air Force hadn't decided what to do with McKnight just yet, but he thought that he might be sent to France. Already there were rumours that Canadian squadrons would be arriving to join their allies in Britain.

The weather had taken a turn for the worse in mid-September, a harbinger of what was to come that winter. Bill wrote to Mike that he was patrolling the coast and supervising guards, all while operating on three or four hours of sleep a night. Single-handedly winning the war it seemed.[1] Whatever the rumours were, and whatever exciting adventures he was reporting to Mike, his logbook reported nothing but training exercises on Ansons for all of September and October of 1939. He was rated as an average pilot that autumn.[2]

Being sent to France to confront the Luftwaffe was a different prospect from provoking the authority figures who had the power to mess up his summer vacation. There was no mention of shirking, although he knew that men had been lost in the Kiel raids. For the moment, his prospects seemed to be leading in the direction of flying fast medium bombers. He seemed to think that the survival rates were rather good (they were not).[3] Despite its reputation for being 'dangerous as hell', Bill advised Mike Peglar to join the Royal Air Force.[4]

Prominent First World War aces had begun turning up in the flying schools, taking refresher courses to update their skills. They were a somewhat mixed blessing, because while they had expertise and celebrity, they were under no illusions whatsoever about what was about to happen. The grim songs from the first war supposedly contained cheerful lyrics such as 'Good luck to the next man who dies' and 'A poor wounded airman lay dying'.[5]

As if a war was not enough to occupy his mind, the weather turned bad, making the flying difficult. War or no war, there were always other concerns. Bill could not help thinking of Calgary, of home and familiar faces. The 'swell chaps' he had spent the summer with were no substitute for old friends. He advised Mike on how to be safe if he joined the air force and offered praise and encouragement for Mike's career path. He also sent good wishes to mutual friends.[6]

Facing a war should perhaps have obliterated everything else, but life does not work like that. Even as a traumatic global event began to shake the world around him, Bill was longing for Marian. Sex and girlfriends and the young woman who he had wanted to be a permanent part of his future occupied his thoughts, too. He now openly regretted the way he had treated Marian. Far from changing his mind, the longer he was away and the more of the world he saw, the more he missed her. At only twenty years old, he realized that he might never see her again.[7]

For months, he had been wanting to admit that he couldn't get over her.[8] He wanted to say that he knew he had made mistakes, but he thought that with another chance, he could change her mind. He had even amazed himself with his progress at times.[9]

There was a certain amount of kindness and maturity to his self-assessment. His reflection might very well have impressed a young woman who wanted a grown-up man to love. But even the supposedly fearless Bill McKnight had his limitations. He was not too afraid to go to France, but he was 'too stubborn'[10] to tell Miss Glover what he thought. The letters had been crumpled up in the bin, shoved under the little blue book of Officers' Mess Rules that he had never opened in his life, or composed only in his mind, because they were never sent.

So, he wrote to Mike instead.

The feelings were there, and the war was making them visible. Anyone who has lived through an emergency can agree that a sense of what matters becomes unavoidable, that the implications become real very quickly. The version of his life where he spent time in the RAF, got his commission and returned home to woo Marian and start up their romance again was being erased. After a seemingly light-hearted summer where he had done his best to be happy, with considerable numbing thanks to alcohol, the future now frightened everybody, not just a young person trying to sort out his life.

The direct threat to their home must have taken a toll on the British pilots, giving the coming conflict a stressful personal element that the recruits from the Commonwealth could not totally appreciate. For the Canadians, their home and native land was protected both by proximity to their imposing southern neighbor and by a helpful vastness of ocean. Yes, they were in the fight, but their homes and loved ones were safe.

But that safety had a trade-off. Home and family were protected precisely because they were so far away. The unique circumstances that Canadian families confronted as the war began were the prospects of a long separation with no foreseeable ending. As a Canadian in the RAF in his early twenties, Bill was dreadfully young. He would face the war disconnected, potentially for years, from the people who loved him, without hugs from Ted and Hazel, and the food he liked best on the weekends to look forward to, even if it was a rationed version.

As Germany invaded and dismantled Poland, Canada and Britain had declared war separately but neither came to Poland's rescue. An eight-month 'phoney war' lay ahead, but for the moment, no one knew that there would be an interlude.

Is there anything less poetic than an upset stomach?

Bill reported that the recruits from the colonies promptly began reporting tummy aches – they were 'sick as hell'. The Medical Officer was dutifully trying to have the food seen to.[11] As we've already touched on, the food was bad, but it had been bad the whole time.

I don't think everyone was sick because of the food.

Meet No. 242 Squadron: The Official Troublemaker Squadron

As Bill was in the midst of writing his two-part letter to Mike Peglar, on 13 September 1939, the British High Commissioner to Canada, Sir Gerald Campbell, was doing some problem solving that was going to have an impact on Bill's immediate future. A telegram was sent that day to Sir Gerald's superiors inquiring, among other things, whether Canada would be willing to have units of Canadian air force personnel assembled 'as soon as sufficient trained personnel are available overseas for this purpose'.[1]

There were a lot of Bill McKnights in Britain in 1939. Known as CAN/RAFs, they were Canadian-born members already serving in the Royal Air Force. Some had followed a path like Bill's, taking up the RAF on their Short Service Commission offers, while other Canadians had been in Britain – and the Royal Air Force – since the end of the First World War.[2]

While there was more than enough Canadian manpower to form a squadron composed almost entirely of pilots and ground crew from the Dominion, the Canadian government had no capacity to outfit a theoretical all-Canadian squadron with aircraft or indeed with any equipment at all. The newly created squadron would be relying on Britain for equipment, a development that was to have some frustrating implications.[3]

On 26 September, Sir Gerald was informed by the Dominions Office that Canada was being invited to form a Royal Canadian Air Force squadron overseas as soon as possible. The squadron would be formed of Canadians who were already trained and in Britain.[4]

The 26th was a busy day; Canada's Prime Minister, Mackenzie King, also committed Canada as a training ground for pilots and other airmen from around the Commonwealth. Citizens from Australia, New Zealand, Britain, other Commonwealth countries and homegrown Canadians would be taught to operate guns and radios, and to work as engineers, air gunners and navigators.

Training bomber and fighter pilots was by far the most time-consuming and labour-intensive part of the preparation, and Canada was offering to do that too. And Canada would assume the lion's share, three-quarters of the cost, a total that would climb to upwards of $1.6 billion CAD.[5]

But this would all take time.

For their part, the British wanted the British Commonwealth Air Training Plan to get off the ground. If Canada was volunteering to provide training for pilots and ground crew from all over the Commonwealth, constructing airfields and providing that training largely at its own expense, then politically creating a Canadian squadron in the Royal Air Force made sense.

It also made sense to add Dominion squadrons to strengthen the Royal Air Force. But while the creation of a Canadian Royal Air Force squadron was of political importance, there were practical elements for consideration as well. Mackenzie King was clearly looking for meaningful ways to support Britain, but Canada was not ready for war. Military spending in Canada had been increasing since 1935, but when war broke out, Canada's navy consisted of seven outdated destroyers and a few other random vessels.[6]

In the meantime, the formation of a Royal Air Force squadron composed of Canadian personnel meant that Canada could contribute immediately to the war effort. The Canadian leaders also wanted a visible presence overseas, so the value of such a squadron for propaganda was recognised at once. The members of the new squadron were to become what we now call influencers. They impressed on enemies and allies alike that Britain was not engaging in a war with Germany as a vanity project. It was supported by key Commonwealth countries around the world.[7]

The views in the Royal Air Force itself were somewhat different. In the 1920s and '30s, the RAF drew pilots from the sons of aristocratic families who had attended elite schools such as Eton. The service was looked upon as a private adventure club with exclusive membership, an established hierarchy and deep political undercurrents. The CAN/RAFs who were joining the RAF at the critical juncture just before the start of the Second World War were outsiders. They were going to be perceived as interlopers who would never be as good as the old British establishment to whom the air force really belonged. The RAF was not a meritocracy, and there was a top-down prejudice that was shared by the commanding officers. The politicians may have been satisfied with using CAN/RAFs to create a Royal Air Force squadron, but that view was not universally shared by the senior brass at the RAF, and they would not have been happy with the appointment of an outsider as a squadron leader.

However, there was a war on, and diplomatic matters outweighed cultural norms. The Canadian government and the Air Ministry agreed to the formation of an all-Canadian Royal Air Force squadron. It was to be known as No. 242 Squadron, and it was based out of Church Fenton in Yorkshire. Fowler Morgan Gobeil was selected from the Royal Canadian Air Force to be the squadron leader, and he arrived at Church Fenton on 1 November 1939.

A native of Ottawa, Gobeil had been promoted to squadron leader in April and had spent the summer of 1939 in Britain on an exchange posting.[8] Gobeil was a competent man with a respectable and varied record of experience with the Royal Canadian Air Force. If nothing particularly spectacular marked his career, neither did he have a reputation for incompetency. He had at least flown fighter aircraft before, which was not something many members of the Royal Canadian Air Force could say in the 1930s.[9] It was his first command, but he was a solid choice as a candidate, at least from a Canadian perspective. But Gobeil was also an outsider and colonial, and he was partly French Canadian. He was a trespasser in the Royal Air Force in every possible way.

Assembled

As squadron leader, Gobeil's first task was to recruit both pilots and ground crew for his new squadron. By October 1939, he had four experienced pilots[1] and he needed to find aeroplanes for them to train in. At the beginning of November 1939, he had no aircraft. The Canadian authorities had high expectations for the unit he was building, so there was considerable pressure as he began his new role.

The creation of a squadron composed of Canadians was good news for Noel Barlow. Bill's fellow Albertan was already a licenced pilot; Barlow had received his certification from the Calgary Flying Club. Barlow, born in Wales and raised in southern Alberta, had arrived in Britain in 1937 hoping to become a pilot with the Royal Air Force.[2] As previously noted, there may have been as many as 1,800 CAN/RAFs in Britain before the outbreak of war.[3] That indicated that Canadians had wanted to join the RAF directly, bypassing their own country's air force. The Royal Canadian Air Force in the 1930s offered limited chances for both adventure and advancement, and the high numbers of Canadians serving in the RAF also spoke to the desperation of Canadians to find employment.

Barlow learned that he had missed the birthdate cut-off by three months. He was too old to become a Royal Air Force pilot. As a person of Welsh descent, Barlow had an indifferent attitude towards English authority at the best of times and the arbitrary cut-off date seemed ridiculous to him. He was stranded 6,000 miles from home.[4]

As frustrated as he was with the RAF for passing him over for the job he wanted, Barlow later reflected that not becoming a pilot at that deadly interval in history probably saved his life. We don't know how Bill McKnight learned about the newly formed all-Canadian squadron, but Barlow saw an advertising notice. Barlow applied and was accepted. He had joined the RAF after all – as ground crew.[5] Barlow was exactly the sort of Canadian whom the newly formed squadron was looking to put to work, and it proved to be a great fit for him.

The other pilots who began to arrive were new recruits selected from various flying schools. None of the young men had any combat experience whatsoever.[6] The average age of a pilot in No. 242 Squadron was twenty-three, rather old for a pilot, and making Bill one of the youngest members. Bill joined up on 6 November 1939, just a few days before his twenty-first birthday. On that date a veritable tidal wave of Canadian recruits arrived in Church Fenton.

Yet another Albertan, Don MacQueen, joined the squadron on the same day as Bill.[7] If Bill didn't personally know Don, he might have known of him. As a football fan, Bill may have watched Don in action as he played semi-professional Canadian football for the Calgary Bronks. Don had joined the team in 1938. The Bronks were competitive; year after year they came close to vying for a championship, but they could never claw their way past the West Final to get to the Grey Cup, the national championship. In 1939, the Bronks had finally battled past the team from the neighbouring province in Saskatchewan. It was the squad from Winnipeg, in the province of Manitoba, that put the nail in the coffin of the Bronks' championship dreams. Both Don and Bill had to follow this news through letters and newspapers. Don was not a part of that play-off tussle on the football field, because like Bill he had joined the Royal Air Force in the winter of 1939.

No. 242 Squadron's flight commanders were Flight Lieutenant John Sullivan, previously a Royal Canadian Mounted Police officer, and Flight Lieutenant Don Miller. In combat, flight commanders were the principal attackers in air-to-air combat. The other aeroplanes in their flight were tasked with supporting and protecting them from counterattack. Since no one was going to be in combat for the immediate future, No. 242 Squadron's flight commanders were being tasked with the instructional duties necessary to turn the squadron's inexperienced recruits into fighter pilots, and it also meant trips to pick up the training machines that Squadron Leader Gobeil was tracking down.[8]

Pilot Officer Peter MacDonald joined the squadron as the adjutant on the same day as Bill. MacDonald was an example of someone who had been born in Canada and who had stayed in Britain after the First World War ended. He hailed originally from Halifax, Nova Scotia, and he had served in the 85th Battalion of the Canadian Expeditionary Force. MacDonald had become a member of the Royal Air Force Volunteer Reserve in 1937. His varied career path also included serving as a Conservative Member of Parliament since 1924, representing the Isle of Wight. He would continue to sit as an MP while simultaneously handling No. 242 Squadron's administrative tasks as the adjutant.[9]

The pieces were falling into place.

The squadron would ultimately be composed of young men from across Canada and from a wide range of backgrounds. They included Flying Officers Lorne Chalmers, John Graafstra and Richard Coe. Pilot Officers were Robert Davidson, Robert Grassick, Arthur Deacon, Dale Jones, James Mitchell – Bill noted that 'Mitchey' had come over with him – Hugh Nicols, Joseph Smiley, Garfield Madore, Hugh Niccolls, James Howitt, William Waterton, and Russell Weins.[10] Also incoming were Pilot Officers Marvin Brown and John Latta, both of whom would have a major tie with Bill in the future. On 20 November Stanley Percival (to be known as 'The Bull') Turner signed up.[11]

The situation had the potential to be great for Bill. He was energized and motivated by other people. His new squadron was a haphazard cross-section of Canadian life. Previous occupations of the other pilots included a former miner, a fisherman, a hardware store manager, a grain elevator operator and a lifeguard – and more.[12] Surely the Canadian content created a home-like atmosphere, with the irritating British formalities and useless protocols to some extent sidelined. Here were familiar accents, people who liked hockey and who knew the rules of REAL football. There were friends in common back home, providing much-needed social support and opportunities for that greatest of all Canadian pastimes: rather judgmental gossip.

Bill, assigned to the squadron's A Flight, was finally flying something other than the dreaded Anson. In November, he and his new flight lieutenant went for an hour-long flight in a Miles Magister. He finally flew a Blenheim, too.

The Blenheim was not a trainer aircraft. It was all metal with fabric ailerons, two air-cooled Mercury engines and a top speed of more than 250mph. It was a bomber, with an internal bomb bay capable of carrying up to 1,000lb of explosives, but there were also fighter versions. Bill also flew a Harvard, an American-designed-and-built trainer, later that month. It was big, heavy and had an air-cooled radial engine that pumped out 450 horsepower. It had a reputation for being a difficult aircraft to fly. In December, he also flew a Tiger Moth. He was getting experience on a variety of aircraft now.

The squadron was visited by politicians and journalists. It was exciting, and perhaps it added to the feeling of connection with home. There were high expectations for them and for their squadron leader. On 9 December, Canada's High Commissioner to Britain, Vincent Massey, Canada's Minister of Mines, Thomas A. Crear, Wing Commander F.V. Heakes of the Royal Canadian Air Force and Air Commodore Lloyd Breadner visited. The resulting interviews and photo ops were covered by both the British and Canadian press.[13] Those stories received a lot of attention, particularly in western Canada. When questioned about the aircraft they preferred, all the pilots said they wanted to fly Spitfires. There were Spitfires ringing the airfield at Church Fenton, but the Canadians were not flying them.[14]

That entire day was a busy one. After the appointment with the media and political figures, there was a wedding to attend. Flying Officer Richard Coe and Hazel Browne were from Kelowna, British Columbia. Even though the future had a very uncertain cast to it at present, they had decided to go ahead with their marriage. Squadron Leader Gobeil gave the bride away in the afternoon ceremony that followed the interviews and photographs.[15]

The political introductions proved to have lasting benefits. Canadian High Commissioner Vincent Massey hosted the squadron over the Christmas holidays. Bill may have been economically well off back in Calgary, but this was a whole other level. The young men went to shows in London, and an orchestra played as they ate delicious meals prepared by a French chef. There were mouthwatering turkeys, oysters and pies.[16]

No ketchup required.

Fighters and Fatalities

No. 242 Squadron experienced its first fatality in January, and it was a particularly sad crash. In December the squadron had learned that it was to be assigned Hawker Hurricanes and it was equipped with twelve old Mk Is. The Hurricanes arrived in late January; the mechanisms of death and war were calling to themselves, gathering the parts together. The harsh, snowed-in winter was nothing but a pause. Spring was guaranteed to bring nastiness.

Hurricanes weren't Spitfires, to be sure, but they were a significant step up from a Blenheim or a Battle.[1] Gobeil was unapologetic as he advocated for his squadron, and in his view, the Royal Air Force command did not appreciate this. He had not been asking for Hurricanes, he was lobbying for Spitfires. The RAF was used to people who knew their place and who obediently followed orders, instead of asking pointed questions and not taking no for an answer.

Well, if you want a pony, start out asking for a Spitfire.

While the Hurricanes had been promised in December, the terrible weather had made ferrying conditions dangerous and had caused delays, and the weather cost one young pilot his life.[2] Richard Coe, whose wedding Bill and the rest of the squadron had celebrated mere weeks previously, was killed when he tried to force-land the Hurricane that he was ferrying under horrible conditions. Coe was the first member of No. 242 Squadron to die.[3]

Bill and the rest of No. 242 Squadron put in their time during the winter of 1939–40 following a business-like training program that included solo flights, practicing circuits and landings, use of the radio, tactics, signals, armament, battle orders, 'flying' in the link trainer, revolver practice, aircraft recognition, rigging, organization, care and maintenance of engines and studying navigational aids.[4] Their downtime included occasional trips to London and sports such as squash.[5]

Bill wrote in a 25 February 1940 letter to Mike Peglar describing the training regime. 'We are off to France soon now,' he confided, and said that his squadron was spending hours in the air, practicing their formations and attacks.[6]

And night flying:

> … when night comes we generally fly all night practicing night interceptions – we started our flying formation at night about a week or so ago and it's the most hair-raising thing I've ever done. Before the war you could use the navigation lights of the leader as a mark to formate on but as we're not allowed to use navigation lights we have to use the exhaust flames as a guide. Most of us have grown half a head of grey hair since we started and hope we never have to do it again once we've got it buttoned up.[7]

Bill was now the old hand; he found the new Canadian arrivals to be a source of great amusement with their reactions to their new surroundings. The dimensions of the British aerodromes and landing strips seemed miniature to them after the vast territories covered by the airfields back home. One unnerved pilot flying a Tiger Moth overshot his landing entirely, to the delight of the onlookers.[8]

Only a few months later, Bill observed with disgust the behavior of his fellow Canadians, and he had very damning and judgmental comments for their actions. He saw that they were unpopular with English people and found himself siding with the locals, who saw Canadians swearing, drinking too much and associating with women of ill repute in their pubs and cafes.[9]

'You can spot a Canadian right off, and if you can't see them, you can hear them – shouting and swearing, drinking more than they can hold and generally with the worst-looking whore this side of either of the two places.'[10]

This quotation roasting Canadians was Bill's own! His disapproval was steeped in irony because he clearly had no appreciation for the fact that the behaviour he criticized was virtually identical to his own antics six months before.

Bill found himself having a heart-to-heart conversation with his flight lieutenant, Don Miller. 'He did most of the talking,' he noted, adding, 'We've been getting on marvellously since.'[11] What was intriguing about this revelation was that Bill must have done most of the listening. And as his capers and conduct had proven thus far, he really did need to listen. He was communicating. Growing up.

No. 242 Squadron had been divided into flights, A Flight and B Flight, each commandeered by one of the squadron's flight commanders. Bill was in A Flight. Don Miller was from Saskatoon, Saskatchewan. He had joined the Royal Air Force in 1936, escaping from the poverty and unemployment that had been stalking the plains in Saskatchewan. That had been a gamble, because on the day that Miller learned he had been accepted into the Royal Air Force, he had less than £4 in his pocket.[12] He had lived through a stressful financial situation that Bill could not imagine. Miller must have managed to get through to Bill, and that is a compliment to Miller. Also, I cannot help but wonder about the toll it would take on Bill when, less than four months later, Miller would have a nervous breakdown amid conditions of unbelievable strain and be invalided out.

Bill, it turned out, had a pronounced distaste for being in charge. In February, he was promoted. He described the job this way: 'I'm being made a section-leader, which means I lead one formation of three machines in a flight (there are six in a flight).'[13]

While he loved flying, he did not like overseeing other people and preferred flying in the #1 spot, where he had 'the best position and half the responsibility'.[14]

Learning to fly was a dangerous business. There had been a string of horrible accidents. Death was already selecting among from the recruits, who had yet to see a single battle. Some of the crashes happened for no observable reason, although the most common causes were pilot error and weather conditions. Even flying with an instructor was dangerous, because pupils who panicked tended to forget that there was someone else in their aircraft. The rearview mirror was positioned so that the instructor could monitor the young face for signs of alarm, but they may have had only seconds to correct serious mistakes.

There was a particularly perilous time for pilots who – like Bill – had logged between 100 and 200 flying hours. It was a period when they had just enough knowledge – and self-assurance – to overestimate their own abilities. As we know well, Bill had a strong streak of over-confidence. He had already witnessed training accidents. Now, they were becoming routine. He wrote to Mike that one of his friends had been killed when a Spitfire collided with his aircraft. Another pair of young pilots had been playing around in a Magister and shot up a train as a joke. The prank went sideways when they subsequently crashed their aeroplane. While both the pilots had survived, they had serious injuries and their careers were finished. In yet another horrifying accident, an entire aircraft had disintegrated around its pilot, fuselage and all. There was nothing left but the seat and the terrified young man sitting on it.[15]

Then, a young Canadian corporal was inadvertently shot in the head. An armourer working in a Hurricane's cockpit had unintentionally fired the aircraft's guns. Bill rather callously reported that his own uniform had been ruined with blood and brains. Immediately, a locking ring around the firing button was fitted as a safety device to prevent similar accidents, but they made the guns harder for the pilots to use. Bill was irritated with the 'dumb airman' who had caused the accident and was making his life more complicated.[16] He blamed individual pilots for the accidents. He knew that fooling around and taking risks was dangerous and stupid but admitted, 'We all do it.'[17]

The Royal Air Force stance towards the accidents was typically not to comment on them, behaving almost as though a crash was as normal as a successful landing. A rowdy dance or party with lots of drinking was the routine mental health support. What everyone was thinking privately as the pieces of the pilot and the aircraft were gathered up was another matter.

In early February, another chess piece arrived at RAF Duxford in the form of Guy Mayfield, who was to be the station chaplain. The glancing reference that Bill had made the previous summer to the huge die-off of pilots that was expected had been taken far more seriously by the RAF than it had by him at the time. Mayfield's role as a spiritual advisor was the only mental health support, aside from alcohol, that anyone in 1940 had to offer.

Most of the pilots were heavy drinkers, which did not inspire confidence considering that they were operating deadly weapons. Take your pick: voluminous quantities of alcohol or God. Perhaps some ungainly combination of both. Mayfield kept a journal that provided a record of day-to-day life over the violent approaching summer. That journal surely must have served as a mental health support to Mayfield himself at times. He and the other Royal Air Force chaplains walked through the Valley of the Shadow beside young, healthy men who knew that they had weeks, or in some cases, only days, to live. The journal would become a witness to lives lived under the unapologetic and pressing influence of the Reaper. Bill's family had attended church in Calgary, but truthfully, we don't know what his religious stance was. Nevertheless, Mayfield came to know him rather well as we will see.

Pilot Officers John Benzie and Noel Stansfield reported to No. 242 Squadron on 2 February. A photograph taken in early February captured the squadron arranged around Gobeil. The group of uniformed Canadians regarding the camera appeared at least semi-professional for their photoshoot but rather nonplussed. The young men were facing their future, tied to the survival of Britain and to each other. They were to witness each other as novice pilots, through ferocious, thrilling battles, through desperate life and death situations. Ahead of them were girlfriends and marriages, high honours and awards, losses, close calls, and their own deaths.

For now, they were idling on the runway, waiting for their turn to climb into the sky and either prove themselves or be picked off.

Family and Friends

Bill's family, meanwhile, at last had reason to be proud of him. He was certainly bragging rights for his grandparents! In February 1940, the *Edmonton Journal* reported that Bill's maternal grandparents, the Lidstones, were celebrating their golden wedding anniversary. The couple had been in Alberta since 1906, and the story recounted their pride in their grandson who was serving in the Royal Air Force. Bill, 'Mr. William McKnight' himself, had, in the proudly worded narrative, 'left his university work here a short time ago to go to England, where he joined the R.A.F. as an instructor of Canadian men'. The tone had a very different ring to it than the gossip and concern Bill must surely have inspired a year previously, when he had left university following a string of immature and juvenile incidents. Now he was seen by his family as important and successful, and there would be far more significant tidings for his family to share in the future.

Bill was navigating the unique situation of being a member of a community that was thousands of miles away. In addition to photo opportunities and newspaper interviews, members of No. 242 Squadron made radio appearances on the BBC. Bill's parents were 'thrilled to death' to hear his voice over the airwaves in February 1940.[1]

Letters included back and forth inquiries about the wellbeing of mutual friends and family members, with Bill asking Mike Peglar whether a buddy from school had joined the service yet. Bill, meanwhile, was dutifully looking into the posting of Mike's brother-in-law. With Mike's sister Helen expecting a baby, everyone was anxious to know whether the child's father was posted somewhere safe in France. (In April of 1940, the answer was yes. Three weeks later, there were no safe places in France.) Bill was not above playful teasing. He said he thought that Helen's baby would be cute – if it looked like her and not its father!

Bill was growing up, and the unthinkable had happened. For the first time, he appreciated that his stepmother loved him. Doris McKnight had greeted

Bill's friends warmly when they visited, delighted to see them. He knew that the way he had treated her when she joined his family had been unfair. 'I don't think I ever gave her quite a square deal when she first came into the clan but she sure earned one if anybody did.'[2]

He added supportively, 'I guess, from what I can gather, that she has had quite a job around the family this winter and can quite imagine how she would look forward to a little entertainment once in a while.'[3]

And while Bill, the rest of his squadron and indeed all the British fighting forces were preparing for the dangerous months ahead, back at home in Calgary the last ski meet of the season was being held at the Sunshine Ski Resort in Banff, Alberta. Enticing conditions were being reported in the Rockies, with plenty of the fine powder so beloved by skiers. Temperatures were hovering just below freezing, and the requirements were perfect for a competition. Among those participating were Marian Glover and a certain Carl Jones.[4] Carl had caught Marian's eye after he rented the basement suite in her family's home.[5]

Life for Carl, Marian and the rest of Bill's friends in Canada was proceeding rather normally despite the disturbing conflict in Europe.

The gap between the life experiences of Bill and the people he had known, and in the case of Marian, loved, was widening.

Where to?

The winter of 1939–40 was one of the worst in years. Operations ferrying Hurricanes to France (as early as January) should have been under way earlier, but the terrible weather held it all up. It was an awful time for the highest snowfall in forty years.[1] Adapting to the situation, the squadron pilots concentrated on ground training and joined the airmen to shovel snow off the runways. The Canadians had the advantage of familiarity when it came to dealing with snow removal, of course.

Bill thought that there may have been another reason for the hold-up. The squadron was being told that they would likely be sent to France, but in the meantime there was another serious situation developing in Norway and he thought it was possible that his squadron might be sent there, too.

Norway had declared itself neutral. There were evidently conversations about sending Royal Air Force squadrons to defend it, and Norway did receive assistance from Allied troops, but Germany officially seized control of the territory on 9 April 1940. This meant that between their control of Denmark and Norway, the Germans now had unlimited access to the Baltic Sea. With troops now desperately needed to defend France, the Allies left Norway entirely early by June 1940.

No. 242 Squadron may have been formed partly as a public relations exercise. But even by the spring of 1940, the RAF was reneging on the commitment they made in October 1939 to keep No. 242 Squadron of purely Canadian content, for good reason. They were now in a life and death showdown with a ferocious adversary and they would post their Canadians wherever they chose.

The first operational sortie was a brief excursion on 25 March that year when Bill and five other pilots from No. 242 Squadron provided protection for coastal shipping fleets.[2]

Meet the Hurricane

Bill's first recorded flight in a Hurricane, which was to become his signature aircraft, was logged on 10 February 1940.

Fighter pilots had a stereotype, body, mind and spirit. Physically, Bill fit the requirements. He was not a big person, which was fortunate since Hurricanes were not intended for anyone tall. But the RAF also valued athleticism and stamina in their pilots. Bill's background in sporting events would serve him well in the endurance tests that were the back-to-back patrols. Experience driving or operating equipment, whether it was a motorcycle, farm machinery or a car, was also desirable in a pilot. It seemed that Bill's old habit of terrorizing his sedate Calgary neighbourhood with his aggressive driving had all been a test flight.

In temperament, fighter pilots also had a stereotype. They reacted quickly, they talked quickly, and they lost their patience quickly. Although some could be tough and belligerent, the stereotypes were just that as there were also serious and studious young men amongst them. No matter their temperaments, they would be expected to get up and fly for their lives every day. The people and country Bill was protecting were his by ancestry and adoption, but it was not his home. Victory was far from assured. The façade was jarring because the men were so young. Bill in his crisp, professional uniform still looked like a teenager, and the sketchy moustache he ill-advisedly would decide to grow at some point later that year did not help.

Bill had always been a high-spirited person and his lack of impulse control and thrill-seeking had scared the daylights out of the people around him in Calgary. As a fighter pilot, those quick, nearly automatic responses in dangerous situations were an asset. People who could handle the physical and mental pressures of this particularly risky and traumatic job could not be expected to enjoy birdwatching and growing succulents in their spare time.

Unlike their pilots, Hurricanes were tall. They stood significantly taller than Spitfires. They were a tough and sturdy aeroplane with the capable air of a truck or a sport utility vehicle. Walking along those strong, straight wings for the first time must have been a thrilling moment for Bill. Here at last was a real, proper aeroplane, a grown-up fighter that flew at speeds exceeding 300mph and had eight bristling guns mounted in its wings.

Hurricanes represented a quantum leap in aviation from the biplane fighters of the First World War. Biplanes had been the front-line RAF fighters into the mid-1930s. The Hurricane was the first monoplane fighter, and the first with a retractable undercarriage. It was also the first combat aircraft – of many – to be powered by the Merlin engine.

Swinging his short leg over the edge of the fuselage and planting his foot on the seat to climb into the cockpit, Bill lowered himself into a space that was roomier than that of a Spitfire, and far more so than the horrible, coffin-like design of the competition: the Messerschmitt Bf 109. There was room for a coffee cup holder, though there wasn't one. It kind of seemed like there could have been. No heat, though. One's own parachute, in a seatpack-style apparatus hanging from your back end, served as a seat cushion. Whatever you do, don't drop anything. There is absolutely no room to bend down around the exceedingly businesslike controls. And there were no floorboards. If something fell, it would have to roll around under your feet in the fuselage until you could catch it again, or, more likely, until the flight was over. Thread your feet along the two narrow channels that lead to your rudder bar. Not exactly a LazyBoy.

Bill's sharp eyes wandered across the dials. The Hurricane was not a night fighter; it was the pestilence that flew by day. Equipped with a green glass screen for the gunsight, the coloured glass acted as sunglasses for the harsh 20,000ft plus sunlight. There was a rearview mirror mounted on the outside of the cockpit, right above your forehead; catch a glimpse of your own simultaneously excited, scared face. The mirror was there to aid in the spotting of Messerschmitts sliding up treacherously behind you, something Bill was destined to excel at. The stick was a comfortable spade grip, fitting snuggly into one's right hand. It slid smoothly forward, back and side to side, controlling the pitch and roll. The trigger was right there in the stick too, invitingly designed for your thumb to work the safety off, then press the button in. The left hand closed around the throttle.

The Merlin engines coughed to life with a scream and began to snort. Chocks away. Time to go. Exhaling in a professional, dragon-like way, the Hurricanes coasted on their way to taxi, warming the oil up to 80 degrees Fahrenheit before the run up. 900 RPM, propellers whirling. Then, charge down the runway, hurling into the sky seconds later. Retract the landing gear.

Spitfires significantly outperformed Hurricanes, as we will see, so why wasn't No. 242 Squadron issued the planes the pilots wanted to fly? In a letter to Mike Peglar, Bill had stated that the Hurricane was outdated, but it was more accurate to say that it had been outcompeted by both the Spitfire and the Bf 109.

So, let's meet the Hurricane. Introduced by Hawker in 1935, it was a member of a family of light bombers and fighters such as the Fury, Hart and Demon. It achieved spectacular speeds of 335mph. In aerobatics, it rolled faster and required less muscle on the ailerons than a Spitfire.[1] It was also extremely strong and could turn and climb better than a Spitfire. Best of all, it was a marvellous gun platform, with straight, thick wings that reduced recoil.[2] In a breakdown between the Spitfire, the Hurricane and the Bf 109, a pilot who has flown them all reports that Hurricanes have the best field of view, stability, and firepower.[3] For Bill, who would prove to be an excellent marksman, the Hurricane would make a good teammate.

While the Hurricane handled rather nicely on the ground, for a warbird it was not an easy aeroplane to trim off, and pilots needed to keep their wits about them and their hands on the controls while flying it.[4] Fighters were fast, agile and accelerated quickly. The design trade-off was constant, nervy instability because it made them more maneuverable. That meant pilots needed to have their hands on the stick and their feet on the rudder bar all the time. No cruise control.

The peace, the big picture quality, the 'away from it all' experience of looking on the earth from thousands of feet above it was considerably diminished by the lack of creature comforts, although pilots who had flown biplanes might well have argued that the enclosed cockpit was a real plus! But when it was hot outside, it was an inferno in the cockpit. Sliding the hood open, taking care not to lose an arm in the slipstream, helped to cool off at least a little and it also protected against carbon monoxide poisoning. The lack of ventilation meant that the pilots climbed out of their aeroplanes with their flight suits soaked with sweat.[5] If there was no ventilation, neither was there any heating. When it was cold outside, the cockpits were freezing. Needless to say, there were no bathrooms.

Layered on to that, close formation flying as practised by the RAF early in the war was difficult and potentially dangerous, requiring a lot of concentration. Since the pilots were watching each other, it reduced their ability to scan for the enemy.[6] Do that three or four times a day for weeks at a time, all while potentially being shot at and sitting 6ft away from roaring exhaust pipes attached to a deafening 1,000-plus horsepower engine. It was a very full-on experience, and it added to fatigue.[7] It also goes without saying that when landing, putting down the landing gear was important, but sometimes pilots did forget to do that. Once 'safely' on the ground again, the Hurricane had little or no braking until it slowed right down.[8]

Like other aeroplanes constructed during the 1920s and '30s, the Mk I, introduced in 1936, was partially constructed of wood and fabric. The fuselage had a tube steel construction, and the wings were of all-metal structure, skinned in fabric. The upgrades being made included changing out the standard issue two-blade wooden Watts propellers to three-bladed, metal, constant-speed ones.[9] Metal wings were also manufactured and replaced on all production lines and existing Hurricanes. Armoured plates for their seats and self-sealing fuel tanks were also being added to protect the pilots.[10]

The Hurricane had been a tough and cutting-edge fighter in its day, arguably the most extraordinary development in flight since the end of the First World War. But that had been in 1936. It was the last in a long line of conventional aviation technology, using wood, fabric and tube steel construction. A strange but perhaps helpful metaphor is to liken the Hurricane to the IBM word processor. Everything that could possibly be done to optimize a typewriter had happened. They were the best typewriter in history. But if the Hurricane was a typewriter, the Spitfire and the Bf 109 were computers. Spitfires were built completely of metal – although they did have fabric-covered control surfaces in their rudders and elevators – and they had curved elliptical wings rather than blocks of wood.

The reasons given for the use of the Hurricane over the Spitfire were that the RAF wanted to standardize the fighter types they were using in the field. Spitfires also had a reputation for having more delicate landing gear than Hurricanes, meaning that they might not withstand the dodgy landing and take-off conditions in France, where access to good runways was not assured.[11] Pilots who have flown both Hurricanes and Spitfires tell me that this is not a major concern.[12] As for standardization, the RAF could have certainly standardized using Spitfires.

These were legitimate reasons that obscured the pragmatic truth: the RAF feared that they were going to lose everything that was going to France, and they had no intention of leaving Spitfires behind when that happened.

The Competition

Meanwhile, Germany had been preparing for war since 1933, when Hitler had first ordered new fighters and bombers. By the end of the 1930s, the Luftwaffe had a stable of impressive aircraft, the most feared of which was the Bf 109.[1] It was all metal, with a closed canopy and retractable landing gear. Like the Spitfire, it was a monocoque design. By the end of the war, it would score more kills than any other aircraft. The top three fighter aces of the Second World War were all German, and Erich Hartmann, Gerhard Barkhorn and Günther Rall all flew the Bf 109. While small, it was designed for performance. Its splayed landing gear made it a nightmare to handle on the ground. It was a different story once it was in its true element, the air.

Primitive-looking, deadly and heavily armed, mounted with two 20mm cannon and two machine guns, the Bf 109 was fashioned in a lean, mean, dart-like shape. They were professional killing machines, and so were the pilots who were flying them. Unlike most of the young RAF pilots and 100 per cent of the pilots in No. 242 Squadron, the Luftwaffe pilots were battle-tested, and they had been victorious.

You are going to want to remember these unstoppable Bf 109s, because Bill McKnight is going to stop a lot of them.

Willie McKnight: The Action Starts

There wouldn't be any letters from Bill for several months, so we will follow his adventures through his combat reports and logbook entries. The weeks ahead would be transformative ones, revolutionizing Bill McKnight from a kid from Calgary who was having a sobering and grown-up adventure into Willie, the action hero, whose exploits would be perfectly at home in a blockbuster film or a comic strip. As his infamy grew, he would be given a new name to match the growing legend. But his own voice will not be heard again until July, and in the meantime, everything would change.

The hectic, in-at-the-deep-end texture began almost immediately, with the first few days of May teetering on the edge of an ominous precipice. The smell of death was in the air, and the tension must have been unbearable. Bill's logbook at the beginning of May recorded repetitive engine tests and local flying. On 10 May, he was flying a night patrol as the quick collapse of Norway was swiftly followed up that same day by the synchronized German invasions of Belgium, Luxembourg, the Netherlands and France. The Maginot Line stretched along the border with Germany, bristling with guns and armaments. It was a 750km barrier constructed after the First World War with a view from the French that they never intended to go through anything like that again. It was created to be impenetrable. So, the Germans didn't penetrate it. If this was presented as an animation, it would show the German army circling around the top of the Maginot Line and seeping like a bloodstain into France.

The intense German assault had begun. Despite how stressed and scared the young 'colonials' – and likely everyone else – had been at the start of the war, since September there had been only a few brief skirmishes, earning the previous six months the moniker 'the Phoney War'. That Phoney War had really been over since the occupation of Denmark and the invasion of Norway in April, but now that it was directly affecting Bill's own life, it had well and truly ended for him, too. The gathering storm had been looming for years; on 10 May it officially broke.

Six RAF fighter squadrons were already in France. The service responded to the 'Blitzkrieg' – the quick, intense, surprise attack – by summoning reinforcements; pilots from No. 242 Squadron would be among those despatched.

The Luftwaffe was targeting the French airfields, and that strategy would prove to be hugely effective. The Hurricane squadrons did a great job shooting down the slow, heavy bombers. But of course, it wasn't as simple as that, because those bombers were escorted by either the ferocious Bf 109 or the versatile Messerschmitt Bf 110 Zerstörer, which was termed a heavy fighter aircraft but was also used as a fighter-bomber. The Bf 110s were needed to open a route through the defensive fighter screens and to protect the German medium and dive bombers. Bf 110s were just as fast as the Hurricanes, but they lost points against them because the Hurricanes could easily outmaneuver them. The Hurricanes also accelerated more quickly. The Bf 110s were really no match for a Hurricane. It was a different story when the Bf 109s showed up.

The RAF in France would suffer severe casualties over the next few weeks as it became clear that this was a new style of warfare for a new generation. The First World War had introduced a new battlefield – the sky. This war would expand the importance of that combat zone; it was now essential.

And amid all the drama, a very significant political change was occurring on 10 May. Winston Churchill was taking over as Prime Minister from Neville Chamberlain.

Bill's logbook recorded a night flying patrol on 11 May. There is no entry for 12 May. Whatever the group from No. 242 Squadron did on the evening of 12 May, whether they spent it together or apart, eating in the mess, playing darts, attempting to read, listening anxiously to the radio, listening to music, waiting, waiting for instructions, everything in their lives was about to change. That configuration of young men, the original No. 242 Squadron, would never be together again.

On the morning of 13 May, No. 242 Squadron were instructed to supply enough pilots to bolster the RAF units already in France. Every member volunteered, so a selection was made.[1] Bill, along with Flight Lieutenant Sullivan, Bob Grassick and Stan Turner, was sent to Manston. They were being attached to No. 607 Squadron, and they left that evening. The next day they flew to France, reinforcing units that were already there.

Despite over a year of training and 253 hours and thirty minutes of recorded flight time, Bill had no combat experience. That changed immediately as he flew in two patrols on his first day in France. Flying patrols above Louvain, Bill recorded a dogfight on the morning of 14 May. Twenty-four Hurricanes met a force of fifteen Hs 126s – a twin-seat reconnaissance and observation aircraft – and, more importantly, their lethal protective escort of forty-five Bf 109 fighters. The result was a literal bloodbath, with ten enemy aircraft being claimed as destroyed. But so were four Hurricanes, and one of them had been flown by Flight Lieutenant John Sullivan. He was the first flier from No. 242 Squadron to die in action, and it was reported that he may have been shot while parachuting out of his Hurricane.[2] He is buried at the Perwez Cemetery in Belgium. He was only twenty-one years old.

For Bill, there was no time at all to integrate what he had just witnessed and participated in, because the dogfight at Louvain was no sooner over than he was then flying a second patrol at Zeebrugge over Belgium. On the 15th, he recorded an offensive raid over Lille-Cambrai and then a patrol over the same on the 16th. On 16 May, Bill and Stan Turner and Bob Grassick were transferred to No. 615 Squadron, flying out of Belgium. They flew two patrols with their new squadron that day. Bill flew another patrol on the 18th and two on the 19th.[3]

19 May would prove to be a long but exciting day, with a big ending.

19 May 1940: First Kill

At 19.40 in the evening of 19 May, Bill was flying another patrol with four other Hurricanes from B Flight of 615 Squadron over Cambrai when he got his first kill. They met up with a group of fifteen Bf 109 fighters that dropped down from 10,000ft to attack the Hurricanes. The enemy fighters were protecting a group of He 111s, the German medium bombers. The first seven enemy aircraft appeared from abruptly behind; Bill spotted them first and radioed an alert to the rest of the flight immediately. Then eight more Bf 109s joined the formation. It was a circle of the ultimate assassins, the best of both German aircraft and pilots. They had the advantage of height and a shot from behind was as close to automatic as you could get.

Bill climbed sharply to the left and settled in behind one of the Bf 109s and followed it through the sky. He closed to 250 yards and fired at it in four quick, staccato bursts. Smoke rolled from the wounded aeroplane. Bill followed and continued to shoot at it until it struck the ground, the most feared aeroplane in the Luftwaffe a ruined, smoldering carcass.[1]

Within the space of a week, Bill had been separated from his main squadron, sent to France and then to Belgium, flown in patrols, and shared in his first dogfight. Now he was a blooded man, and he had shot down one of the Luftwaffe's single-seat fighters. He had quickly spotted the danger, warned everyone else in the squadron, and then kept his cool as he climbed behind one of the terrible Bf 109s, setting himself up for the clear shot, and then shot it down without mercy. He had responded to an extremely hazardous situation like an experienced fighter pilot with no nerves – or humanity – to speak of. The 'dark-haired and quick moving little chap'[2] that the people back home in Calgary had known was becoming Willie McKnight, action star.

Later, he would express how he really felt before a battle began. Terrified. It was when the fighting started that he was able to focus. In fact, there was nothing to do but focus. But beforehand, it was awful.[3]

He returned to England later that night. He had been away for six hectic, chaotic days. The loss of Flight Lieutenant Sullivan must have been a sobering blow that perhaps none of the young men had time to process while it was happening; they had been in a literal life and death situation themselves. And Bill may well have survived the Battle of France because of a mix-up; on 19 May, when he returned to England, he was given seven days' leave.

The operations in France were a traumatic and dramatic start for the young Canadians. We don't know what Bill did on his first leave; his fondness for beer, music and beautiful young women were his go-tos. He was not to our knowledge a particularly religious person. We know that he processed his experiences in a rather therapeutic way in letters to Bill and Mike Peglar, but he didn't write to them during this time. Another No. 242 Squadron pilot, Bill's buddy Pilot Officer Bob Grassick, had also recorded victories. Thrill, pride, a sense of purpose and accomplishment, guilt, trauma from the loss of a friend and an officer and near misses with mortality themselves – yet, we have no record of what Bill did during his week of leave.

In fact, that seven days' leave had been immediately revoked. While we can appreciate that it was considerably more difficult to contact people in the 1940s than it is today, as early as 1918 there were procedures in *The King's Regulations and Orders for the Royal Air Force* that outlined exactly what the pilot's responsibilities were in a situation like this one and he should have made sure he was contactable. Whatever Bill was doing on his time off, he had messed up again, this time in a serious situation where his help was badly needed.

And this may well have saved his life because behind him, on the Continent, France was being overrun.

The Rest of the Battle

The original No. 242 Squadron had been separated when Bill, Pilot Officers Bob Grassick and Stan Turner and Flight Lieutenant Sullivan were parted from the rest of the group and sent to France on 13 May. Six more of No. 242 Squadron's pilots had followed three days later, joining No. 85 Squadron at Lille-Seclin. The rest of the squadron were under Squadron Leader Gobeil's command and relocated from RAF Church Fenton to RAF Biggin Hill on 21 May. The young men were being dispatched around France and England like chess pieces. The rest of the squadron had the remaining intense fighting during the rest of May to face, and unlike Bill on his unintentional reprieve, they would get no respite.

We'll experience the fighting through the eyes of a fellow member of No. 242 Squadron, Don MacQueen. The fighting over the north-east corner of France intensified as the Germans cascaded over undefended Belgium. Squadron Leader Gobeil, Flight Lieutenant Miller, Brown, Chambers, Wiens, Deacon, Stansfield and Donald MacQueen were in the heart of those extreme and futile battles as the Luftwaffe punished the French airfields.

On one occasion Don was forced to land his aeroplane when its engine misfired. The conditions were hideously unsafe. Don hid under his plane and miraculously avoided any injury until his attackers flew away and he could take off again. On another occasion when his plane went down in rural France, Don reported that his high school French became critical as he attempted to explain to the suspicious farmers that he was not a German.[1] Understandably, the rural French population was on edge and would jump to conclusions. A foreign pilot would be assumed to be German, and they were guilty until proven innocent; Allied pilots bailing out of their aeroplanes could be shot out of the sky, not only by their enemies but by the local population. Don also had his wins; on 22 May, he shared a kill with Pilot Officer Stansfield as they patrolled the shores north of Doullens, France, bringing down an Hs 126.

The conditions for the pilots were brutal. Don described that sleep was snatched in power naps lasting an hour or two. There was no time for a shower or any sort of personal care, he never changed out of his clothes, and there was little time to eat. 'Boy, it was rough,' he wrote to his father.[2]

Squadron Leader Gobeil reported that his pilots were patrolling for upwards of eighteen hours at a time and that one of his most reliable junior pilots had landed his aircraft with the landing gear up because he was so exhausted.[3] In later years, Gobeil would tell his daughter that he believed that No. 242 Squadron was being given missions that the British didn't want to do themselves. While he could not outright refuse to follow an order, there were ways to sidestep commands that he thought were suicide missions. There wasn't enough fuel, perhaps, or there weren't enough operational aircraft available.[4] The squadron would suffer terrible losses anyway.

As the month concluded, No. 242 Squadron had been credited with shooting down six enemy aircraft between them. On 25 May, in an inconclusive action, Gobeil himself was credited with shooting down an Bf 110 Zerstörer. But they had suffered their own substantial losses. Sullivan was dead, Chambers had been captured, and Brown and Weins were both injured.[5]

When Bill reappeared on 26 May, the hardest fighting was yet to come. No. 242 Squadron were now going to be defending the retreat out of France in the skies over Dunkirk, and Bill was about to have a string of his best days in history.

Dunkirk: Operation Dynamo

After the declaration of war on 3 September 1939, Britain had honoured its long-standing commitments to its ally by sending over 350,000 troops to France. The Royal Air Force had contributed two elements to the British Expeditionary Force, including the Advanced Air Striking Force, which was tasked with bombing operations. Meanwhile, the No. 22 Army Cooperation Group was to work closely with ground troops; it included four Hurricane squadrons. The months since deployment had been spent enduring the admittedly brutal weather of the proceeding winter, but there were minimal engagements with the enemy.

A scant ten days after the invasion of France had been launched, the German forces had reached the Somme Estuary at the Channel coast, where a large, protected bay drains into the English Channel. It created a critical situation for the Allies. The British Expeditionary Force, the French First Army, and the Belgian Army were now isolated from the French troops positioned further south. The Germans continued their rapid advance northward along the coast, placing port cities at risk and threatening to encircle the British and French units. This essentially sealed the escape routes for hundreds of thousands of Allied troops in northern France, so they began travelling slowly toward Dunkirk. A week later, it would be the lone point of evacuation.

Dunkirk was a prettily situated port town on the northern coast of France, approximately 200km south of the border with Belgium. Impressionist paintings from the late nineteenth century illustrated a harbour full of tall and graceful ships and a long shore with a powdery white sand beach, a wonderful destination spot for a summer vacation. Visiting artists had created appealing coast scenes, showing tourists sauntering along the long sea wall.

The images that stretched beneath Bill and the rest of No. 242 Squadron would have been unimaginable to the residents and tourists of Dunkirk who lived in the Impressionist era, and there would have been inhabitants living in Dunkirk in 1940 who were old enough to recall it. Nothing less like a postcard, or a painting, could be imagined. The people who had enjoyed the lengthy, broad beach and strolls along the pretty quay were about to live through a torturous era, and Dunkirk was merely one of the French beaches that were to be polluted by oil, wreckage and blood in the years to come.

By the time Bill was sent to Dunkirk in mid May, the RAF had withdrawn most of its squadrons from France. The Fairey Battles and Blenheims of the Advanced Air Striking Force had not exactly proven a challenge for the Luftwaffe, and they had sustained heavy losses. Air Chief Marshal Hugh Dowding did not want to send the fighter squadrons that French Premier Édouard Daladier was pleading for to the Continent; he knew that the Battle of France was over but for the technicalities.[1] The priorities of the RAF were now balanced precariously between supporting the rescue effort for the men of the British Army who were funneling through the French countryside to the evacuation site at Dunkirk harbour and conserving resources for the defence of its own nation.

The Hurricanes traced through the silver sky with the sea wrinkling below. The sun and clouds alike could obscure the presence of predators, the enemy that the RAF were now tasked with keeping away from the helpless men waiting on the Dunkirk beach, and from the ships that were needed to save them all. Bill and the rest of No. 242 Squadron played a significant role in the heroic rescue effort that unfolded over the next six days.

The Germans were headed for Dunkirk, too.

27 and 28 May 1940

So, what was going on for Bill? As this tense situation unfolded beneath him, he began to shine and then to sparkle. He had a string of big days.

Flying out of RAF Manston in Kent, the sea of blue stretched to the horizon, displaying the curvature of the earth, not so different really from the sea of green on the great plains where Bill had been raised. There was no need to ask the way to Dunkirk. The Luftwaffe were bombing the town heavily, and that included the docks.[1] On the edge of the horizon, a poisoned plume stretched into the sky, a finger pointing the way to the pilots of both air forces, and to the flotilla of little boats that would soon be sailing to the rescue through places in the sea where it was black with oil. The Royal Navy cruisers and destroyers and the massive Merchant Navy ships were waiting in the harbour to load their cargo.

At midday on 28 May, No. 242 Squadron flew a patrol over Ostend along the Belgium coast. A squadron of approximately twelve Bf 109s were sighted flying between 6,000 and 9,000ft. The enemy's squadron leader climbed for better position and assaulted the Hurricanes from behind. Bill picked a fight with an enemy aircraft that was trying to turn away from him and opened one burst of fire from 250 yards away. The aircraft's engines failed immediately, and it dropped, writhing, out of control into the sea.[2]

There was no time for a victory high because immediately the original group of enemy fighters were reinforced by another host, this time numbering roughly sixty aeroplanes, striking from above and flanking No. 242 Squadron. In the resulting dogfight, three enemy aircraft and two RAF aircraft and personnel were lost. Bill's combat report described that during the ensuing melee his own Hurricane was hit by enemy fire, disabling its coolant system. This meant that he had less than five minutes left before his engine overheated and seized. Dropping to a lower cloud base, he found out for himself what it was like to have a maniac trailing his wounded aircraft. He was caught up 'in a determined and sustained chase' with an enemy fighter right on his tail as he flew for his life back to the base at Manston.[3]

However, the damage to Bill's Hurricane may really been caused by a friendly fire incident with another No. 242 Squadron pilot, Bill's soon-to-be fellow ace Stan Turner. If it was, Bill protected his friend. Stan later said that Bill confronted him heatedly about the accident when they got back to Manston and then laughed it off. Bill's official account does not mention Stan.[4]

29 May 1940

The men waiting on the beach were in a precarious position as the enemy bombers began to sweep along the coastline, bombing and shooting as they went. Dunkirk was already alight thanks to the 27 May bombardment, and that included oil tanks. As the water supply had been disabled, the fires could not be extinguished.[1] One witness described watching the planes dropping 'stick after stick' of bombs as the Luftwaffe passed overhead.[2] The men who must surely have felt waves of relief when they at last reached the shore were now faced with the horrible dilemma of diving for cover as the bombs fell, taking shelter from the air attacks, or losing their place in line. They were waiting for hours in the cold rain, their feet wet, sand in their socks, with no bathrooms. Waiting for their turn to board the ships, for safety, to go home.

At daylight on 29 May, the Luftwaffe attacks intensified. A *Schnellboot*, the German fast attack craft termed an 'E boat' by the British – 'E' was for enemy – hit two destroyers loaded with evacuees. Eleven British and two French ships were attacked. Five were destroyed.[3]

The Luftwaffe were concentrating on bombing the ships, not the men on the beach, but it was not a merciful choice. It was a devastating tactic. That afternoon, large formations of German aircraft began to appear overhead when there were gaps in the Hurricane and Spitfire patrols.[4]

The decision for the RAF was how to manage that situation. Should they deploy conservative smaller patrols, flying almost continuously? Or should they have massive, multi-squadron detachments, a huge show of strength, but flying more infrequently? To start with, they relied on the first strategy, then switched to the second. Apparently, that was unnerving for the men on the beach, because there were complaints that the RAF had abandoned them. Perhaps it was better for morale if there were always at least a few friendly aircraft overhead. Screaming Rolls-Royce Merlin engines were the most reassuring sound the personnel of the army could hear; it meant solidarity and protection, that they were not abandoned or forgotten.

Late on the afternoon of 29 May, around 5.20 p.m., patrolling the skies north-west of Dunkirk, a group of twenty-five Bf 109 fighters were intercepted. It was a very, very bad time for an enemy aircraft to meet up with Bill McKnight. Bill's group soared higher to prepare for the assault, while even farther above them, another group of Bf 109 fighters was approaching swiftly. Bill and another Hurricane were tag-teaming an attack on one enemy aircraft, but before Bill could open fire a Bf 109 appeared on the tail of the other Hurricane. Bill responded immediately, turning to the right and opening fire at point-blank range. The enemy aeroplane promptly rolled onto its side and dove unceremoniously into the sea.[5]

Bill wasn't finished. As he was turning away from his kill, he spotted another Bf 109 pursuing a Hurricane and dived after it; after a short burst from Bill's guns, the fighter was precipitously dropping for the shore. Bill followed it but was unable to catch up to conclusively finish the job; he was credited with a 'probable' rather than a 'kill'. As he was rejoining the dogfight, Bill noticed a light bomber above him. He climbed his Hurricane behind the Do 17 and with the first burst of bullets, its engines were disabled. With the second burst, the bomber crashed. Its smoking carcass crumpled lifelessly on the beach as Bill soared above his prey. Like a young eagle.

Or a vulture.

'My ammunition being expended I returned to base,' Bill's combat report concluded the dramatic events rather matter of factly.[6]

Almost as though shooting down Bf 109s wasn't that hard after all, all in a day's work.

Although he didn't report it himself, after shooting down a pair of fighters and a bomber, Bill still wasn't finished that day. He may also have attacked ground targets, strafing a railway being used to transport German artillery as he flew away from the dogfight. If he did this, he demonstrated solid problem-solving skills, disrupting the enemy supply line. He would also have caused a high number of German casualties. It must have impressed someone who was watching, because the incident is mentioned in the citation he was awarded, but Bill didn't reference it in his logbook or combat report.[7] He finally had something real to brag about, but he didn't mention it.

I have never experienced an attack by an enemy on my country, so I cannot imagine what the soldiers on the beach were experiencing, or what Bill McKnight and the rest of the RAF meant to them. Staring into the sky, wondering if you were deserted by your own air force as you waited for a rescue that you weren't altogether confident was coming, watching the terrible, terrifying dogfights stacked over your head, perhaps there was a grim satisfaction to watching a Hurricane kicking the s*** out of two fighters.

With little else to cheer for, perhaps there would be a wild lift in the heart, because someone needs to do something. Someone needs to stop this, even though it seems like no one can. Except for the kid from Calgary.

Willie McKnight: three enemy aircraft down. 4,000 to go.

30 May 1940

By the next day, 30 May, the Royal Engineers had constructed makeshift jetties so that more men could be evacuated. However, only 31,000 soldiers were rescued that day compared to 60,000 on previous days.[1] To the evacuees waiting on the beach, in the water, and clinging to the makeshift piers, there was a clear and observable correlation: when there were no British fighters overhead, the Luftwaffe would appear and bomb the ships.

Both the Merchant and Royal Navies had a brutal day; nine large ships and other smaller ones were destroyed. Although the focus for the Luftwaffe was on sinking the ships, their bombers also dropped explosives on the beach and shot at men swimming for their lives in the freezing cold sea.[2] For those waiting for their turn to board a ship that would carry them to home and safety, the sight of enemy bombers slicing through the clouds and flinging down their deadly cargo was deeply distressing. Witnessing massive ships sinking with the people aboard simultaneously being incinerated and drowned was enough to make a person question whether you wanted to be on board or not.

On 30 May Bill and the rest of No. 242 Squadron carried out two patrols, one over Dunkirk and the other over Furnes.[3] Along with No. 229 Squadron, they were providing high cover to squadrons that were engaging bombers headed for the rescue ships, but no enemy aircraft were spotted.

But how could we ever forget the most important and predictable feature of any battle or any scene of destruction: a group of politicians having their photographs taken. No. 242 Squadron were visited by the Canadian dignitaries Group Captain Walsh and Governor General Vincent Massey on this day, right in the middle of Operation Dynamo.[4] Facing havoc and annihilation, there was a pause for a promotional photo opportunity. The Canadian government wanted to be sure that their squadron was, visibly, in on the action. One can almost imagine the public figures announcing to the assembled squadron, 'Now see here, everyone! You must all pitch in and do your best work! McKnight can't be expected to do everything by himself!' And then, as the assembled company begins to disperse, Governor General Massey reaches for Bill's arm as he passes by and draws him aside. 'McKnight, you're going to have to do everything by yourself.'

31 May 1940

Bill certainly wasn't doing everything by himself. On 31 May, the two most intense days of aerial fighting were ahead, and two members of No. 242 Squadron were going to become aces. However, the vile weather impacted both air forces. Most of the day was spent waiting around. It was mid afternoon before eight Hurricanes from No. 242 Squadron were back in action. They were now flying regularly with Nos 64, 229 and 610 Squadrons, forming their own team in Big Wing-style formations. In the target-rich environment of the Dunkirk evacuations, twenty-seven Hurricane pilots achieved ace status over the next few days. The top scorers were to be Bill, of course, and his friend Stan Turner from Toronto. Bill would be credited with nine confirmed kills since the start of May (three of his claims could not be confirmed) and Stan with seven.[1]

Their first patrol that day was unremarkable, but when they finished, they circled back in an unsuccessful scouting mission. They were looking for an observation balloon that had been surveying for the German guns that had been bombarding Dunkirk.[2] It was on the way back that they met up with a formation of roughly twenty-five to thirty Bf 110 heavy fighters and Do 17 light bombers, flying at between 9,000 and 10,000ft. An intense fight developed. Bill reported it this way:

> While patrolling around Dunkirk, was quite a way behind the formation, I climbed higher then dived in to attack. At the same time a formation of 25–30 Me 110s dived down. I fired at the leader of the first group of them and hit him causing him to swerve and break up the formation. I continued to fire on No.2 in the formation, but half way through my burst number 1 and 2 collided and went down in flames.[3]

By now, Bill was out of ammunition and had to fly back to base at Manston.[4] It was a triumph for No. 242 Squadron; Pilot Officers Plinston, MacQueen and

Stansfield all had their own victories to report.[5] The formation that they had attacked and halted had been heading straight for Dunkirk. Instead, it had been forced to retreat. Best of all, there were no casualties to report.

After rearming and refuelling, No. 242 Squadron headed straight back out on another reconnaissance mission looking for yet another surveillance balloon two hours later. On this occasion, they found themselves in an extremely dangerous situation, sandwiched between two enemy formations. The Hurricanes were attacked from behind, above and starboard, very nearly fenced in. They were caught unless they could fight their way out.

A Bf 109 confronted Bill from the rear. The enemy fighter lined up for a perfect shot. Bill switched into evasive tactics, the erratic behaviour of a prey species, darting and rolling, when another enemy fighter suddenly turned right in front of him. Bill instantly fired at it and thought it was disabled, but he was unable to confirm this. Grassick also submitted a combat report for a damaged Bf 109; it could have been a shared kill, but neither was able to confirm that the aircraft was destroyed.[6] No. 242 Squadron had managed to claw themselves out of the trap. Four German fighters were believed to have been shot down, but only three could be confirmed, and Pilot Officer Stewart, who had joined No. 242 Squadron only the day before, had been killed.[7]

The inexperienced young aviators who had flown out to protect France only three weeks before were rapidly turning into tough, savvy combat veterans – or dying – under the harshest and most unforgiving conditions imaginable.

1 June 1940

As the sun lifted itself over Dunkirk on 1 June, the day of the heaviest aerial fighting stretched before the RAF; battles raged all day long. Bill had another outstanding day, although describing it later, he declared it was more of a mistake. 'I got separated from the squadron and was sort of pissing about on my own – you know, boots shaking, knees knocking, etc.,' he would later relate.[1]

Fearless, not so much.

Around 4.35 p.m., cruising at around 2,500ft off the coast 6 miles south-west of Dunkirk, he and Pilot Officer Stansfield flew into a cloud of fifteen Ju 87s. Bill himself called Ju 87s 'Junkers'. They were also referred to as Stukas, a dive-bomber aircraft used to destroy ground targets. They were also proving to be brilliant anti-shipping aircraft, with automatic dive brakes under both wings, engineered to be sure that the aircraft could pull out of a steep attack. Stukas were also equipped with air raid-esque sirens mounted to the main gear legs that let out a distinctive eerie scream as they dived, a sound that became familiar – and hated – for people watching them from the ground. When left unopposed, it demolished its targets with great efficiency.

This formation of Stukas was attacking rescue ships. Bill chased after one and found himself drifting, worryingly isolated, amid the rest of the enemy formation. The bomber was plunging into its strike on a ship when Bill shot at it, and it toppled straight into the sea. Bill immediately climbed and fired at another bomber from underneath it. Smoke rolled out of the aeroplane, and it too lunged abruptly into the Channel. He then attacked another Ju 87; it was smoking as he lost sight of it climbing back into the clouds. Another dive-bomber whirled in front of him, and he fired at it; he believed that his attack was successful, but he was running low on ammunition. He used the rest of it to chase off a few other aircraft.[2] Stansfield had a probable hit as well.

This all begs the question, what were the German bombers doing on their own without the protection of fighter escorts? The truth was later revealed – the bombers had not been alone at all. In fact, the Germans had a tactic of positioning fighter aircraft above their bombers, waiting to swoop down out of the sun and attack once the RAF fighters had moved in. As if Bill and Stanfield's own battle had not been thrilling enough, little did they know a second dogfight involving the rest of their squadron had been raging above their heads and a curtain of thick cloud cover at 5,000ft.

'The funny part is that while I was doing this the rest of the boys got jumped by 109s as usual right above me on top of the clouds, so while I was having all the fun, they were keeping everything away from me,' Bill later related. 'I got lost in some clouds and had no idea where the others had gone. I dropped down and found four Junkers before me doing their stuff right over a convoy. It was a jam. I knew I got two of them, but wasn't certain about the others for a bit until the navy confirmed my report.'[3]

The overhead clash had inadvertently protected Bill and Pilot Officer Stansfield from the horde of enemy fighters that had been escorting the bombers. While he had an impressive showing, if even one of the Bf 109s had turned up it would have changed the tone of the fight considerably, and Bill knew it. Then again, he had an impressive record at dealing with Bf 109s. Still, he regarded his own coming decoration as the product of an accident.

The people on the ships that the bombers had been targeting must have experienced utter relief to witness the Hurricanes show up and begin impressively to pick the Stukas off, one by one. From terror one minute to watching an exciting dogfight the next. It had not seemed like much of a fight, really. And now there were four Ju 87s drowning. Instead of you.

It was a day of wall-to-wall madness. As the sun began at last to melt into the sea, the RAF had lost thirty-one aircraft. However, the Luftwaffe had also taken their share of destruction because they had lost nineteen bombers and ten fighters. A further thirteen Luftwaffe aircraft had been damaged. Bill was responsible for an impressive proportion of those enemy losses, with two confirmed hits and two probables. He later said that the Royal Navy had confirmed his probables.[4] However, he never updated his logbook or combat report to reflect that change, so they remain unconfirmed.

Bill had reported another terrific day. He was the highest-scoring ace at Dunkirk. Alan Deere, the great New Zealand ace, claimed five hits during May 1940. During Dunkirk, Bill had ten claimed and eight confirmed victories. That would make William McKnight of Calgary, Alberta, Canada, the leading ace of Dunkirk.

There was a day or two left to go, of course. Bill's logbook recorded an offensive patrol of Dunkirk on 2 June; by 4 June he was patrolling in Canterbury and the evacuation of Dunkirk had ended.

On the political front, Churchill had taken over from Neville Chamberlain as Prime Minister on 10 May. When briefed by Air Marshal Hugh Dowding on 3 June, Churchill was informed that if the Luftwaffe were to attack Britain with its full strength, it was estimated that the RAF had the aerial resources to hold out for forty-eight hours.[5]

Many of the air battles of Operation Dynamo had taken place inland or out at sea. The RAF squadrons had been doing their best to intercept enemy aircraft before they ever got near Dunkirk. The weather had also been terrible. The clouds had created a screen of sorts over the sky; when the enemy bombers sliced through them, the navy and infantry personnel witnessed attacks on targets that seemed unimpeded, unaware that there was often a gritty battle going on above their heads. The conservative patrolling strategy and the careful managing of precious aerial resources also explains why the navy and the infantry had felt neglected by the RAF at Dunkirk. They believed that they had been deserted, although nothing could have been further from the truth.[6] There was an unbelievably cautious and strategic handling of resources that was playing out behind the scenes. It would be in the months to come that the value of the RAF would be understood, and the debt that they were owed by everyone.

Between 31 May and 1 June, No. 242 Squadron claimed the destruction of thirteen enemy aircraft.[7] That forty-eight-hour period had been a desperate, frantic race against time and a superior foe and No. 242 Squadron had been in the thick of it. They had done what they had been asked to do, and the situation had created aces. Bill claimed the lion's share. He was credited with a Bf 109 on 28 May, a Do 17 and two Bf 109s on 29 May (one confirmed, one unconfirmed), two Bf 110s and a Bf 109 on 31 May, and two Ju 87s (and a further two unconfirmed Ju 87s) on 1 June.

Other members of the squadron, including Stan Turner, Pilot Officer Plinston, and Pilot Officer Bob Grassick, had also attained the illusive ace status.[8] Turner had claimed seven kills, and he and Bill were friendly but competitive with each other about their scoring totals. The two kids from Canada had done pretty well for themselves. They were the first and second scorers of Dunkirk.

No. 242 Squadron had been in dogfights for the ages, with the contrails and the innards of their enemy's aircraft flung all over the sky. The young pilots had kept their wits about them, learned quickly and adapted to conditions under life and death circumstances. They had fought their way out of traps, experienced friendly fire, and gone nose to nose with experienced enemy pilots flying superior aircraft. Their actions had saved lives, both their own and those of the vulnerable men who had been waiting on board the ships or on the beach, counting on the RAF for protection.

Following in the proud hometown tradition of the First World War aviators who had become legendary for their accomplishments – McCall, Palmer and May – Alberta, Canada, now had a new ace for a new generation who had wiped the sky with his adversaries.

There was another pilot who had had a modestly successful showing over Dunkirk, and he would play a starring role with No. 242 Squadron in the months to come. For now, he was flying Spitfires with No. 222 Squadron out of Duxford. During Operation Dynamo, Flight Commander Douglas Bader had shot down one enemy aircraft and was credited with damaging two more. Over the coming weeks, he would be selected for a leadership opportunity. While his path hadn't crossed with anyone from No. 242 Squadron during Dunkirk, a month in the future would see all their lives entwine in a meaningful way.

First, there was the briefest of pauses, an interlude for a moment of celebration – both for the troops who had been rescued and who were once again safely home in England, waiting to fight again on another day.

As for Bill, he was going to meet the King, because on 4 June, he learned that he had been awarded a Distinguished Flying Cross.[9]

His entry in *The London Gazette* read: 'One day in May 1940, this officer destroyed a Messerschmitt 109 and on the following day, whilst on patrol with his squadron, he shot down three more enemy aircraft. The destruction of the last one of the three aircraft occasioned a long chase over enemy territory. On his return flight he used his remaining ammunition, and caused many casualties, in a low flying attack on a railway along which the enemy were bringing up heavy guns. Pilot Officer McKnight has shown exceptional skill and courage as a fighter pilot.

'Distinguished Flying Cross – Pilot Officer William Lidstone McKnight.'[10]

Meet the King, Pay the Price

Dunkirk may have been a miracle, but it was anything but a victory. The British Expeditionary Force soldiers who had made it to the port had been saved and Bill and the rest of the pilots of the RAF had played a considerable role in that nearly incredible liberation. The fact of the matter was that the entire situation had been a race against time and against a foe that had just demolished Norway, Belgium, and the Netherlands and was on their way to seizing control of France.

The Canadian Prime Minister, Mackenzie King, delivered an address to his nation on 7 June during one of his regular radio broadcasts to Canadians. King's talk was titled *New Situations and Responsibilities*. He was unequivocal as he outlined the Canadian outlook towards the months to come, and towards the dangers that they all faced. He was utterly resolved:

> I speak from the heart and mind of our country when I say that every fort will be another Calais, and every harbour another Dunkirk, before the men and women of our land allow the light and life of their Christian faith to be extinguished by the powers of evil, or yield their liberties to the tyranny of Nazi brutality.[1]

King also told Canadians that they must be prepared for the vast sums of money being spent to expand and update their army, navy and air force, responsibilities he said that Canadians were proud to accept.[2]

Britain, Bill McKnight and the rest of No. 242 Squadron were not stepping up alone to face the enemy. They had the political support of the Canadian Prime Minister. However, not everyone in Canada was cheering for No. 242 Squadron or even for the Allies. But taking note of the fact that France was done for, or that the British Army had barely escaped – and stating it aloud – was being treated as the real problem.

For example, a man called André Verdier, the head of Verdier Aircraft Corporation, was on trial in Ottawa under the Defence of Canada Act. Verdier had been listening to a radio broadcast with friends. When he heard about the number of tanks the Germans supposedly had, Verdier had allegedly declared, 'The Germans have the greatest mechanized army in the world.'[3] Now, he was attempting unsuccessfully to walk back his comments. Verdier was swiftly sentenced to six to twelve months in prison.[4] It was a national news story.

No. 242 Squadron had played a substantial role at Dunkirk. They had performed well in Operation Dynamo, and it was not just Bill. Others had had a strong showing; Bill's pal, ace Stan Turner of Toronto, had an excellent record, shooting down seven aircraft. But Bill was the star. He had a personal best, shooting down eight confirmed enemy aircraft, and he was awarded a Distinguished Flying Cross and met the King.

There was only a little time to bask in the glory of the solemn and distinguished occasion. It almost seemed like one of the invented stories that he had once upon a time bragged about to his friends back home. Polished shoes, quickly combed hair, the donning of the dress uniform – who could have ever dreamed when he purchased it that it would be used for such a grand and exciting event – but after the ceremonial handshake it was straight back into the Hurricane. The Canadian propaganda squadron were not pen-pushers by any stretch of the imagination. They were doing the job. Meet the King in the morning, face danger and death in the afternoon. All in a day's work for Canada's most celebrated and accomplished ace.

No. 242 Squadron had an impressive record, but it had come at a terrible cost. Most of their losses came in the weeks prior to Dynamo. That was understandable as they had not been battle-tested prior to arriving in France, and initial outings against such a powerful and prepared foe were always going to be costly. Clearly, those who were left were fast learners, quickly gaining both confidence and experience.[5] But the price they had paid on the way to becoming useful and experienced combat pilots was terrible. Perhaps the biggest cost was that due to the heavy fighting of May and early June, every No. 242 Squadron pilot of Flying Officer rank apart from the adjutant or above were no longer there, with the squadron leader relieved of command and the others either dead or in hospital.[6]

Most of the leaders were gone.

Enemies in France

As it stood at the beginning of June of 1940, Britain was itself desperately under-resourced. France was a lost cause, its fall absolutely guaranteed, and the next attack would be occurring in the skies over Britain itself. As it became increasingly clear how critical aerial resources were, France was imploring its ally for additional aircraft support.

Britain now had 280 Spitfires and 244 Hurricanes on its home soil.[1] None of those aircraft and no additional squadrons were going to be supplied, apart from the three squadrons that were still in France. One of the squadrons was Bill's. And as if chaos and mortal danger were not enough, Bill, Stan Turner and the rest of No. 242 Squadron were now going to be caught between politicians and managers who didn't like each other.

Bill recorded flying a patrol of Canterbury on 4 June. On 8 June, the day after he received his Distinguished Flying Cross, he recorded in his logbook that he was being sent from Royal Air Force Station Biggin Hill to Le Mans. On that date, No. 242 Squadron flew back to France to reinforce the struggling squadrons there and to protect the remnants of the British Army that were retreating to the Atlantic ports. Not everyone had escaped through Dunkirk, and France was still fighting. But what the Allies were really doing was preparing to leave France for good.

No. 242 Squadron Leader Fowler Gobeil later claimed that he had been promised much-needed downtime after Dunkirk. He had lost fifteen pilots and aircraft, and the pilots who were left were utterly drained. Their Hurricanes also needed repairs and replacement. Instead, they were sent straight back into a conflict that was just as dangerous as Dunkirk, and even more hopeless. The fall of Paris was days away, and the withdrawal of the remainder of British troops on the Continent was rapidly becoming a rout.

The misadventures of No. 242 Squadron began immediately. While on route to Châteaudun from Le Mans on 8 June, Gobeil stated that his aircraft developed mechanical trouble. He returned to Le Mans, landed his Hurricane, and once it was repaired, took off after his squadron, but he became lost and was separated from them.[2] In 1940s war-torn France, it was, of course, impossible to locate someone by texting them; at Châteaudun on 9 June, Gobeil did not know where the rest of No. 242 Squadron had gone and he could not contact his adjutant, Peter MacDonald.

To state the obvious, the rest of No. 242 Squadron did not know where Gobeil was either, and in the absence of their squadron leader, they should have been reporting to his flight commanders. The problem with this of course was that Flight Lieutenant Sullivan had been killed the month previously, and on 9 June the squadron encountered another difficulty when Flight Lieutenant Don Miller had what was at the time referred to as a nervous breakdown and had to be invalided back to Britain.[3] Whether Bill knew the details of what had happened to Miller is not apparent, but what was clear was that the resources of No. 242 Squadron were becoming increasingly threadbare at the worst possible time, and the calamities were going to continue.

Snowballing the utter turmoil, on 13 June a fire caused by careless smoking destroyed much of the squadron's equipment and belongings, including their clothing.[4] The Canadians were meant to be escorting Battles that day, but given the circumstances, No. 73 Squadron was commanded to cover the mission instead. The weather was not conducive to flying in any case, but there was one army that was having considerable success, because that evening, the German advance was getting uncomfortably close to Châteaudun. The squadrons posted there were ordered to fall back at 9 p.m.[5]

The big picture was growing blacker.

Paris had fallen.

Such stressful and strained conditions would inevitably bring out the worst in anyone, and the political and personal undertones were beginning to emerge not as cracks but as abrupt ravines. Gobeil's adjutant was Pilot Officer Peter MacDonald, and it was the impression of some observers that the two of them did not like each other. In fact, Gobeil had described MacDonald's performance as 'most satisfactory' – but that was when he was at work in the relative safety of England.

'Boozy Mac' MacDonald had been born in Canada, and he had fought in the First World War. By 1940 he was a Conservative Member of Parliament from the Isle of Wight, already in his fifties. In the sheer chaos that was France in June 1940, Gobeil stated that MacDonald 'seemed in a daze at all times' and struggled to carry out his responsibilities.[6] Gobeil also said that by the time he had noticed how much MacDonald was struggling, it was too late to have him replaced. And this was about to have very serious consequences, because on 15 June, under circumstances of almost unimaginable confusion that proved very difficult to reconstruct, the No. 242 Squadron ground crew were evacuated out of Brittany.

The activities of the ground crew should have been the adjutant's responsibility. In the detailed inquiry that was to come, Air Marshal Barratt, Commander in Chief of the air operations in France, noted that he was satisfied that a responsible officer had prematurely told the ground crew of No. 242 Squadron that they were no longer needed and ordered them to evacuate.[7] The problem was, whoever had given the order for this to happen, it was not Gobeil, and it was apparently not MacDonald either. Gobeil learned from MacDonald at 08.30 on 16 June that the ground crew had departed for England sometime in the middle of the turmoil of the preceding night. Barratt levelled this damning accusation at Gobeil's leadership and at the squadron itself:

> I am, however, still of the opinion that in a properly trained and conducted squadron there would be no question of the airmen moving off ... without first reporting to their senior officers. The incident reflects the poor standard of organization and discipline within the squadron, under its present Commanding Officer.
>
> Air Marshal Sir Arthur S. Barratt,
> Commander-in-Chief, British Air Forces in France
> (c. June 1940; quoted in *Bartholomew and Barratt: The Creation of Army Co-operation Command*)[8]

Gobeil pointed out that the squadron would then continue to fly for six days without essential routine maintenance provided to their aircraft because the ground crew had been dismissed too soon. By 18 June, there were only four operational Hurricanes available.[9] This early dismissal of the ground crew became the subject of a thorough investigation by the RAF, and it was treated as a very black mark on Gobeil's record.

MacDonald, who undoubtedly had his own political reasons and his own hide to protect, sent in a blistering report, unreservedly throwing Gobeil under the bus. So did Stan Turner. Noel Stansfield had spoken out in support of Gobeil, stating that he believed Gobeil to be a solid, middle-of-the-road sort of leader. Nothing glowing, but nothing damning either. As for Bill, he was to fill out one single, solitary report dated 30/9/40 stating that to the best of his knowledge, Gobeil had shot down one aircraft over Dunkirk.

That combat report credits Gobeil with being the first member of the Royal Canadian Air Force (RCAF) to shoot down an enemy aircraft in the Second World War, as Gobeil was part of the RCAF as well as the RAF.[10] RCAF personnel such as Gobeil served in the RAF when necessary, meaning that the latter was populated with crew hailing originally from the colonies, places such as Australia, New Zealand or Canada. Meanwhile, Bill, although Canadian, had bypassed his own country's air force entirely; he was not a member of the Royal Canadian Air Force.[11]

Enjoying Himself Thoroughly

At least they had been reunited with their squadron leader. But now that No. 242 Squadron's pilots no longer had their ground crew with them, they had to fuel and rearm their own aircraft. Gobeil recalled that the pilots were scrounging through abandoned lorries to collect ammunition and were refuelling their aeroplanes with 4-gallon tins found at the dump at the Le Mans aerodrome. When Gobeil asked two non-commissioned officers of another squadron for their help to find fuel, they told him to 'go to hell and get it yourself'. No maintenance work could be done on the Hurricanes at all.[1]

Gobeil had reportedly refused to send his squadron into missions against such a fearsome enemy when their own aircraft were not serviceable. At some points, the German army was only 35 miles away. The nerves of everyone involved were at a point of failure. The pilots were also destroying aircraft to prevent them from falling into enemy hands.

The circumstances for the pilots were hectic and exhausting, but during this short, confusing, and frantic period Bill recorded in his logbook shooting down two more Bf 109s on 18 June,[2] one confirmed and one unconfirmed. While the combat report for this fight is missing, Bill later depicted a battle with a huge cloud of Bf 109s, and it may well refer to 18 June. In a letter to Mike dated 19 July 1940, he described it as 'rather a funny thing':

> … we were chasing a hun bomber – five of us – when we lost him in some bad cloud – however, right after this we saw about nine ME.109's so we jumped them thinking we'd get a couple then slip off into the clouds. Right after this however the sky just poured 109s.[3]

A waterfall of Bf 109s meant that the German fighters had the advantage of height and had possibly lured the Hurricanes into one of their traps with the bomber as bait. Or perhaps it was a crime of opportunity. Needless to say, the adventure was not over:

> … and some bloke, who must be the personal ace of the Luftwaffe jumped me and succeeded in shooting away nearly all the machine except where I was sitting before I managed to dive into a cloud.[4]

Bill had previously mentioned the decision to insert strategically placed armour on the Hurricanes. Metal plates had been added to protect the engines, and another was placed behind the pilot's seat, protecting their critical mass. With an elite Luftwaffe Bf 109 pilot spraying his Hurricane with bullets, that armoured plate had saved his life. Bill McKnight should likely have been dead in June 1940, guarded only by a metal plate on his back. By sheer random chance, the bullets had not travelled down to his legs, where the plate would have been useless. He had kept his head and disappeared into the clouds. It was a wild way to start the day and not everyone returned home from that battle. Bill reported the postscript in the letter:

> Well anyway after we got after we got home (three out of five) we found out that about eight Jerry squadrons had pooled their resources for the morning and we'd tried to jump about 80 machines. We laughed like hell when we think of it now but it wasn't so funny then.[5]

A cloud of Messerschmitts was, if nothing else, a target-rich environment. It was a dangerous situation, but a single squadron on their own against a host of eighty aircraft was not quite as awful as it sounds. It made it easier for the RAF fighters to go wild, firing nearly at will while the Luftwaffe had the conditions created for a lot of friendly fire accidents.

This letter gives a look at a day in the life, and the feral life and death, predator and prey situations the squadron found themselves in. The tale was fit for a letter to Mike, rather than a disinfected, PG-rated missive to parents and grandparents. It was a heart-pounding adventure that could have ended very differently, and Bill knew it. The group of young men who climbed out of their Hurricanes and stood in a circle, hearts pounding, shaking and laughing, had been terrified. Laughing was whistling in a graveyard, a coping strategy for an unbelievable situation that had dramatic elements of a flight and fight. Life was a blockbuster action movie, a comic book, and the comedic element was as grim as a Reaper crouching on a fuselage.

On 15 June, the *Calgary Albertan* reported proudly on the latest accomplishments of the city's hometown hero: CALGARY PILOT MCKNIGHT WINS DISTINGUISHED FLYING CROSS, proclaimed the large black letters. The article restated the line from Bill's citation, saluting his 'exceptional skill and courage as a fighter pilot'. The story also revealed that Bill had been in touch with his parents, but the letter was one of the shortest he had ever written to them. Bill told his family that he was flying back and forth between bases in England and that he could be on duty for twenty-four-hour posts. His travels had again taken him across France and Belgium, and he had left his belongings scattered across the Continent, remarking ruefully that he needed to gather them up and send them to his aunt in Scotland for safekeeping.

The nomadic lifestyle that characterized the period was going to have implications for other things that were left behind – including squadron records and documents. On 12 June for instance, three He 111s were shot by unknown persons in No. 242 Squadron. Whether because the fighting was so intense and bewildering that no one knew exactly what happened or because the records were left behind, there are no known existing combat reports for either of Bill's kills on 14 June. His logbook revealed a spiderweb of postings, from Le Mans to Châteaudun to Marigny to Haver, back to Marigny, back to Châteaudun – all between 8 and 9 June.

'Though he [is] getting little sleep, he was enjoying himself thoroughly,' the *Albertan* story had summarized, characterizing the whole desperate situation as a high-spirited adventure.

Just a light-hearted game of touch and go, with some Nazis thrown in for added excitement.

The same story in the *Albertan* then noted that Don MacQueen was missing.[6] Don had survived the first round of the Battle of France, and he had survived Dunkirk, but he himself had noted that he had some very lucky escapes; even he had thought that it was perhaps realistic that his luck would run out. He was killed in action on 9 June 1940 when a superior force of enemy aircraft flew out of the sun. Bill's logbook noted that there had been a dogfight, so it is also possible that the battle he had in mind when he wrote his 19 July 1940 letter to Mike happened on this day. Witnesses reported that Don's plane was shot down before he had a chance to make any evasive maneuvers. Stan Turner radioed MacQueen to bail out but received no reply; Turner immediately shot down the Bf 109 that had attacked Don's Hurricane. Don is buried in St Memmie Churchyard, Courisols, Marne.

Margeaux

On 10 June 1940, Bill's logbook makes a reference to a pleasure trip. Was it a day off? And what was he doing that day? What pleasure could possibly be found in a land that was collapsing and being overrun with enemy soldiers? In fact, Bill would look back on the brutal month and say that he had enjoyed his time, and it seemed that there was a girl to thank for it.

While there were no additional details mentioned in that logbook, somewhere amid all the dogfighting and death and drama, Bill had apparently met a beautiful young Frenchwoman, a *modeste* called Margeaux, who had fled from Paris. Somehow, in all the madness, the couple had time for a brief relationship, although we have very few of the details.

What we do know came from Bill, and his version of it sounded in some ways more like a story for a locker room than a romantic movie. According to him, the pair had taken a flat together in Nantes, using a car that had been abandoned by the brass hats that were escaping the country. He and Margeaux set up housekeeping, with friends dropping by every night, entertaining in 1940s fashion by listening to the radio, and there was even more fun to be had when everyone else had left for the night. Margeaux was a 'first class femme' in Bill's colourful assessment.[1] He evidently had a type, and he appreciated clever and ambitious women, for in addition to being beautiful, Margeaux had been attending university in Paris. It recalled Marian Glover's business ambitions.

As France collapsed around them, Bill had attempted to smuggle Margeaux out on one of the last RAF bombers leaving the doomed Continent. Unfortunately, the air force did not take a romantic view of the situation, and the young woman was left behind. Bill had an 'it's too bad, and oh well' attitude towards his doomed romance. While he did say it had been fun and he missed the little attempt at domesticity, it seemed his heart wasn't really in it, and he mused that he may have be fated to be a bachelor. In his own words, 'I can't fall in love anymore like I used to, I get all worked up for about an hour then I just lose interest.'[2]

Sex and an attempt at falling in love had managed to compel Bill to say that he had enjoyed his month in France and even to describe it all as 'marvellous'. No wonder he had no time to write to his father! Romance and Nazis, what a combination.

Interestingly, in the fine-tooth comb the RAF used to go through the activities of No. 242 Squadron during the month of June 1940, the incident of a member of the squadron attempting to sneak a girl onto a bomber was not mentioned in any of them. Doubtless, it would have just been one more example of the complete lack of discipline prevailing in No. 242 Squadron, but it was not discussed by anyone except Bill in the single, solitary letter to Mike Peglar dated 19 July 1940.

Decades later, Bill's nephew was well acquainted with the tale and was matter of fact and accepting of the story. Rather congratulatory of his uncle for scoring a sexy, smart French girl, in fact. But aside from the Peglar letter, Bill never mentions Margeaux again as far as we know.

Gobeil

On 14 June, Bill's logbook recorded two flights for No. 242 Squadron. There was also a raid on an aerodrome and another attack while patrolling the Seine to Paris. In the ensuing dogfight, Bill claimed two more Bf 109s.[1] It was not only the pilots' clothing and other belongings that had been left behind in aerodromes all over France. Critical paperwork such as Bill's combat reports are unfortunately missing from this period.

On 18 June, he recorded an escort of a reconnaissance aircraft that lasted for two hours. At 11 a.m., Gobeil and Pilot Officer Stansfield set out for a return flight to England; the entire squadron were told to prepare to leave France. They flew away in small groups, hoping that this would not attract enemy attention in the way a larger group might have done. Gobeil stated later that he believed when he took off for England that he was the last member of No. 242 Squadron to depart from France.

Bill never saw Gobeil again. He and seven other pilots in his squadron, including Stan Turner, flew for two and a half hours from Nantes to Tangmere, where they stopped to refuel. Then they returned to RAF Coltishall.

When Gobeil arrived in England, he reported that he managed to contact Peter MacDonald by telephone and was allegedly told by him that all the pilots who had been stationed in France were to have two days' leave. Gobeil left his address and telephone number with MacDonald in case he needed to be contacted and proceeded to take his own two days' leave, which he said was critically needed.[2]

Gobeil's decision to take that break would lead to the growing picture that the RAF was collecting of him and of his squadron. Wing Commander Cyril Walter said on 24 June 1940, 'This unit has been most unreliable. The CO was never available when required, could never be found and took absolutely no interest in his squadron.'[3] Gobeil was the only squadron leader that Bill and the rest of the pilots had known during their time in their all-Canadian squadron. Gobeil had been involved in a flying accident in 1931 in which another pilot was killed. At the time, everything had been explained away in great and enormous detail.[4] Had the events of that past trauma caught up with him at a critical time, impairing his judgment and decision-making?

The RAF understood that what had happened in France had been a fiasco, and they were looking to assign blame. In this thankless situation, middle managers such as Gobeil were particularly vulnerable. But what emerged during the coming investigation was a very damning picture of Gobeil's leadership.

Mere weeks before, the little squadron that had been created as a largely political propaganda exercise had turned in a ferocious performance, punching very much above their weight, with Gobeil highlighting in his reports that one of his young pilots had received a Distinguished Flying Cross (he did not reference Bill by name). His squadron had produced the first and second highest-scoring aces over Dunkirk. Their performance had been recognised by the RAF and by the King himself. They had lost friends and teammates, and they had killed other people.

Now, days later, not only Gobeil but the whole squadron was being viewed as undisciplined and poorly organized. It seemed that not one shred of understanding was shown for the adverse circumstances that they had been facing. The feedback was dismissive and merciless.

Only one voice had complimentary things to say of No. 242 Squadron and their efforts now. It was Gobeil's. Of his squadron he said:

> All the loyal support and co-operation possible was accorded me by the entire personnel of the squadron as always, and their work and devotion to duty at all times and under all circumstances would have made every Canadian citizen proud.[5]

All the back and forth aside, Gobeil was to be relieved of command. His reports must be seen through the lens of him fighting for his reputation and for his professional life.

Relieved of Command

With minimal explanation given to his squadron, Gobeil was packed off back to Canada. Many were pointing to his management as a failure. This may not be a fair assessment, as the opinions of his leadership were rather mixed.[1] And, clearly, Gobeil's achievements will always be compared to those of his successor.

Gobeil's formation style may have been somewhat dated, especially when compared to the up-to-the-minute tactics and aircraft of the Luftwaffe, but that was true of most of the conservative RAF manoeuvres at the time. It was their protocols and standards that he was following. The French, the British and their allies had just come up against what was arguably the most modern and prepared army of the time. Gobeil's young and untested squadron had been flung into a conflict against this machine when they were new to war. Losses under his command had been terrible, but to be fair, the test had also been dreadfully hard. He had commanded the first and second-highest scoring aces over Dunkirk, and one of his aces was a decorated pilot. He had shot down an enemy aircraft of his own. His squadron had performed well in the trial by fire that was France, and the evacuation of Dunkirk had proved that they were tough and outstanding pilots.

It was Gobeil's leadership in France after Dunkirk that was being painted as a failure. He had trained and prepared his squadron successfully judging by their performance over Dunkirk, but between 4 and 18 June he had become increasingly embattled. Peter MacDonald, the adjutant for No. 242 Squadron, was also a Conservative Member of Parliament with enough influence to be problematic if he chose to be. It was MacDonald who should have been responsible for the logistics in France, and for organizing the activities of the ground crew and staying in touch with them.

It has been suggested that what Gobeil was really being accused of was having been overheard drinking in a pub and participating in defeatist talk.[2]

We have seen that in Canada that charge could trigger swift and harsh consequences. The attitudes in Britain were comparable.

What is clear that the RAF wanted nothing more to do with Gobeil by the end of June 1940. While it is necessary to examine this one man for examples of the faulty leadership that led to him being fired, there were political, systemic and structural elements at work that were having an impact on all the leaders.

Bill's logbook noted that Gobeil had been relieved of command. For the other civilians in the audience, that wording may not quite convey that this is in fact a serious situation in the RAF. It was not so much a laying off as a firing, indicating the removal of someone who has done something grossly negligent or even criminal. It must have been stressful and demoralizing all around for the members of No. 242 Squadron, who had fought under such stressful circumstances and had now lost all their leaders. They were burnt out, physically, emotionally and mentally.

An important gap in the perspectives that we have related to this clearly political but murky chapter of No. 242 Squadron history is the perspective of the ground crew. Their insights were incredibly valuable, and they may have been the very people with the answers to the questions that we are asking. I've often wished that in the promotional photographs taken of No. 242 Squadron the lens of the camera pointed at Bill, George Ball and Douglas Bader posed in front of their muscly Hurricanes could be zoomed out to show Noel Barlow and the other ground crew standing just a few feet away. They too were in a fight for their lives, they too had stressful jobs, cleaned up horrible messes that wordlessly told the tales of dramatic battles and conflicts, and nursed ailing aeroplanes back to health. And they were Canadians far from home, with eyes and ears that took in the interpersonal and political dynamics impacting their squadron. If anyone had asked them, they could have told you exactly which leaders they thought were popular and respected, which pilots truly did not like each other, and which relationships were stretched thinly over a very tight layer of dislike, disrespect or political infighting.

For his part, Barlow observed that No. 242 Squadron felt ignored by the RAF.[3] The ground crew had been through hell and instead of being thanked or commended, they were being – it seemed – dismissed. They were competent, professional Canadians whose contributions to the war effort have been overshadowed. But behind the glamorous daredevil pilots who were the face of the RAF and indeed the Second World War, there were the fitters, riggers and armourers who spent hours around the aircraft they were responsible for having ready to fly at a moment's notice.

Barlow described what had happened to Gobeil this way. 'To the disappointment of all, especially the many Canadians on the squadron, the C. O. was transferred back to Canada on urgent business.'[4] It was clear that Barlow did not know or did not say that he knew that there were political forces at work.

We are left making educated guesses. Air Chief Marshal Trafford Leigh-Mallory's report of 24 June 1940 called Gobeil 'irresponsible and quite unfitted', and stated that he had made no effort to contact any unit from the time of his landing until he reported to him on 23 June. It was a damning indictment. In his book, *Fight for the Sky*, Douglas Bader noted that No. 242 Squadron had been 'decimated in France'. He was also warned by Leigh-Mallory that the squadron was 'tough, ill disciplined and bloody-minded'.[5]

Leader of the Squadron: Stan Turner

This turns the question to what Bill thought of Gobeil as his squadron leader. Gobeil's approach to managing his squadron shaped and impacted No. 242 Squadron and had consequences for Fighter Command itself. It also influenced Bill, although he never mentioned Gobeil in his letters. But during the stressful proceeding month, there had been an opportunity created for a member of the squadron to step into a leadership role, unofficially for the time being.

That person wasn't Bill. He appears to have been well liked and respected, and his skill as a fighter pilot was by now without question. However, when he had been promoted to section leader the previous February, he had described his duties this way:

> I lead one formation of three machines in the flight (there are six in a flight) and it sure is good fun except I'm not so keen on the responsibility. It's alright but I'd sooner be No. 1 in a formation any day where you've got the best position and only half the responsibility.[1]

Overseeing other people, particularly when he was answerable for their safety, was not his cup of tea.

So, who was the person that Bill looked up to and respected? When I asked historian Hugh Halliday who the 'real' leader of No. 242 Squadron was, he replied instantly, 'Stan Turner'. And Stan Turner was someone who Bill did mention with respect.

Bill had been trying to belong among friends ever since the Calgary days. The regard of a slightly older peer who he looked up to would have been very meaningful to him. Stan Turner fit the bill, and Bill described their dynamic this way:

> We two are the high scorers in the squadron so far having got twenty-three between us – nine for Stan and fourteen for me – so we have a pretty keen competition going on. And neither of us likes to be off duty when the other one is on as we're both afraid we'll miss a chance to get something.[2]

Gaining Bill's respect and cooperation had proved illusive thus far for his parents, his teachers, and for other so-called leaders.

Turner came across as a confident, self-assured person. He was willing to step up to be the main character in the story, even when it was hard and thankless and scary. He was tough, curt and had an extremely straightforward manner of speaking. Praise from him was grudging and rare, but when asked about Bill, he said that he had dark hair, then added that Bill was handsome and short. 'A Napoleon in the Cockpit.'[3] It was a backhanded compliment, a pointed reference to Bill's height – Bill was not a big guy. But the accolade was in there; Napoleon was one of the greatest military leaders in history.

Short, and the best.

Some of the intangible but important qualities of a leader include someone who speaks up for and inspires others, and who is consistently THERE; you can count on them. That describes Stan Turner. He was a skilled pilot, and an ace himself. The squadron's adjutant, Flying Officer Peter MacDonald, had mentioned that Turner had really stepped up in France.

As for what became of Gobeil, he continued his career in the Royal Canadian Air Force. Back in Canada, he was assigned to a bombing and gunnery school, where his students spoke highly of him. He became an aircraft accident investigator and was later attached to Ferry Command. In July 1943, he returned to Britain, ferrying a glider across the Atlantic Ocean in a difficult, four-stage mission that required a skilled and competent pilot, and he completed that mission successfully, earning the Air Force Cross.[4] Gobeil was awarded a Queen's Coronation Medal in 1953, retiring as a Wing Commander from the Royal Canadian Air Force in 1956. He spent his retirement working for the Queen's Scholarship Trust Foundation and Canadian Heritage Scholarship Trust. He had a solid and respectable track record, blackened only by a single, hectic ten-day period in June 1940.

It had been a violent, transformative month for No. 242 Squadron, and understandably morale was not in a good place. They felt abandoned by the RAF, too. Members of the squadron questioned why they had been sent to France when it was already known that it was impossible to save it.

On top of everything else, their work was far from over. The Battle of France was over, and for those who had survived it, the Battle of Britain was about to begin.

Meet Bader

'Legs or no legs, I've never seen such a blankety blank mobile fireball as that guy.'

Stan Turner

For the squadron 'erks' at least, their tasks were clear. They were testing engines, changing wings, refitting guns and attempting to nurse the wounded Hurricanes back to health.

The ground crew had their opinions on the circumstances facing their squadron too, of course. The word on the street was that a new commanding officer was on his way, and rumours had been circulating that he was missing his legs. This was not exactly what anyone had been hoping for.

On the morning of 20 June, Noel Barlow had just finished performing a thirty-hour inspection on an errant aeroplane. He noticed a low car sweeping up the driveway and across the airfield. It parked directly in front of the machine he was working on. The opportunity having presented itself, Barlow couldn't resist temptation and climbed out of the Hurricane he was fixing. Manufacturing a reason to amble nonchalantly past the car, his strategy paid off; he was asked to escort the newcomer into the office.[1] Barlow recalled that the man had a peculiar step, but he did not think he looked like he was missing his legs.

For some readers, the man who walked beside Barlow into the office is someone for whom no introduction is needed. Others may have never heard of Douglas Bader before.

Bader was described by people who had met him as having a great deal of 'life' and 'verve' and his very presence could be heartening for those around him.[2] He shared a few key background traits with his new squadron's highest-scoring member. Neither he nor Bill had been great students. In school, whenever trouble was afoot, Bader had either been the ringleader or supporting the ringleader. He also had a demonstrated history of disregard for safety – both his own, and the safety of others. Unlike Bill, Bader was teetotal and did not like the taste of alcohol.

And in contrast to Gobeil, Bader was an establishment candidate who was well connected with the higher ups in the Royal Air Force. Today, he would likely be cancelled for his attitudes towards women and people of other races. The Edwardian class system he was raised in had both limited him and given him opportunities and privileges. It had inevitably shaped his worldview. The Canadians he was meant to command had little understanding or respect for the arbitrary structure that had created him.

While out of touch in many regards, Bader certainly understood what it was like to live through loss and pain. He was a charming, cheerful and brave person who had come by his courageous outlook at great personal cost, and he had fought his way through private battles that gave him great legitimacy when he was around people who were afraid or depressed.

In photographs it is not usually possible to tell, but Douglas Bader had indeed lost both of his legs, which had been amputated after a flying accident in 1931. He now used prosthetics and had resumed not only walking, dancing and golf but flying. He had spent years fighting the powers that be for opportunities to try out his own abilities and ideas and had met resistance and dismissal from the people in charge.

He was about to find himself in the interesting role reversal of being everything that was wrong with the world to a group of youngsters. They perhaps saw him as a symbol for every crushing thing that had happened to them. Wing Commander Woodhall had informed Bader of what he could expect, warning him that his new squadron had been through a rough time in France, and that their morale was at an all-time low. Bader's biographer, Paul Brickhill, described the No. 242 Squadron pilots as, 'Wild Canadians, the least tractable young officers [Bader] had ever seen, and most allergic to commanding officers!'[3]

When Bader recalled meeting his new team, the story he told sounded like a fictional situation that had been invented for a play. He clearly understood that he was the face of the joke in the scenario, although it was really not a laughing matter. It was a big moment for him. He thought the young men might get deferentially to their feet, eager to impress their new boss.

It almost sounded as though he was approaching a herd of exotic – to him – moose in the Canadian Rockies, gazing at them eagerly through binoculars and making notes in a field diary. But rather than climbing warily and respectfully to their feet at the sight of their new leader, the group was draped in attitudes of deep inattention across the furniture around the room. Some were reading comic books, the 1940s version of handheld devices, which were lowered an inch or two when Bader walked in. They regarded the newcomer with world-weary disinterest for a few seconds. Evidently, the new recruit had been weighed in the balance and found wanting, because a few moments later, the comic books were raised again, and reading resumed. No one got up.[4]

Instead of pilots dressed in smart, neatly pressed uniforms, this gang could have been off-duty truck drivers or mechanics. They were clad in roll-necked knit jumpers (sweaters if you're from Canada) or wrinkled uniforms. Their hair was long and greasy, as though no one had showered or had a haircut in quite some time.[5] Cutting his losses for the time being, Bader asked Peter MacDonald to assemble the pilots in his office the next day.[6]

Accordingly, the next morning they all presented themselves.

Having lost the chance at a great first impression, Bader felt that he had prepared an inspiring and reasonable little speech, outlining his goals and expectations for the squadron. 'Or so I thought,' he later said ruefully.[7] He asked if anyone had anything to say. A poignant silence followed. Then a strong voice with a Canadian accent rang out.

'Horseshit.'

Loaded pause.

'Sir.'[8]

It was Stan Turner.

The second impression, it seemed, had gone no better than the first.

It was so horribly unexpected and dreadfully funny all at once. As if the addition of the word 'sir' could make up for what had just happened! Except that it did! 'For some reason which even now I cannot define, this made the monstrously insubordinate interjection from Stan Turner entirely acceptable,' Bader conceded, as though he was still trying to work out for himself why.[9]

But he recalled it all with a sense of humour. Possibly it was because in Turner, Bader had just met the real leader of No. 242 Squadron, the one person who would never put up with, or be impressed by, his 'horseshit', and would call him on it. But from Bader's point of view, he and Stan also became fast friends for the rest of their lives.

Praise or thanks from Turner, however reluctant? Not until years in the future, of course. But as Turner himself later admitted, he needed Bader at that moment, too:

> We were an awfully "scruffy" bunch, at that time; so scruffy that the Tangmere Station C/O wouldn't let us go into the Mess, made us stay down on the airfield and sent food down to us, and we sat

> under the wing, before we proceeded to our new base and had our meal.
>
> Where we got into more trouble until Douglas arrived on the scene, he got us straightened out from then on, things were pretty straight forward.[10]

Not only were the Canadians of No. 242 Squadron almost entirely without the cultural class system that would have intuitive to a group of young Englishmen, but they were depleted and demoralized. They had all lost friends. They had been deserted only days before by Gobeil under a confusing set of circumstances that had not been explained. Surely, they had their theories. It must have been unsettling and maybe even disgusting to them that while they had risked their lives every day, they were at the mercy of political games between people who did not share in the dangers and hard work that they faced. Turner had just spoken up for every person in the room who felt angry, resentful and disrespected. And probably that included the slight young pilot with dark hair and quick, sharp eyes who looked suspiciously like a kid as he took in Bader's speech.

In fact, Bader often advocated in a very empathetic way for young people, and that included the youth of successive generations. He once told the BBC on *Late Night with Douglas Bader* in 1965:

> When I was a young man, we were always taking the mickey out of the older generation … I'm all for the young, I'm all for them doing the things they want to do and saying the things they want to providing they don't irritate other people and disturb the peace.

But irritating other people and disturbing the peace was exactly what young people do. Bader was only thirty years old himself, and a complex person; whatever else could or could not be said of him, it appears that he was not interested in being a team player – unless he was the leader of that team.[11]

It almost seemed as though No. 242 Squadron had been specifically designed to keep all the troublemakers together.

Grounded

Now that he was safe for the time being, Bill was facing the horrible toll that had been exacted since the beginning of May. For No. 242 Squadron, and for him. Six pilots had been killed. Others had been captured, wounded and injured in accidents.

Bill had distinguished himself and his country at Dunkirk and during the Battle of France. He was a credit to his squadron, to his country, and to himself. It was an astonishing performance for the kid from Calgary. Finally, there was praise and gratitude from the people around him, perhaps for the first time in his life, with the King himself saying, 'Thank you.'

He was a badass ace pilot, a hero, and a celebrity, especially in his own city. 'His record is now climbing to a point where Mr. Hitler must be wishing that Canada did not produce such fine pilots,' the *Calgary Herald* proclaimed proudly under the headline 'Calgary's Air Ace Bag Twelve Huns'. But the same story had also reported that Bill, who was typically a dutiful correspondent, had not written to his family in weeks. Bill's father said that 'he knew Bill was busy' and had not been worrying over the lack of communication.

If he had witnessed the condition of his son, he might have changed his mind.

If every action has an equal and opposite reaction, the previous two months of killing and dying caught up now. The impact on Bill's young mind, body and spirit was that he now began to die. Days after meeting Bader, he was admitted to the hospital. His last recorded flight was 7 July, when his logbook recording a day of aerobatics and an engine test. He was so exhausted that he was not even permitted to write letters at first. It would be 30 July before he was well enough to return to action.

He would spend most of the coming month in the hospital.

Sick and Tired

It has been given many names over the centuries. In the American Civil War, it was called battle fatigue. The First World War term was shell shock or combat stress. Today, we know it as Post Traumatic Stress Disorder or PTSD, and we know scientifically what the people who have been around soldiers involved in deadly conflict have known for centuries – that when exposed to unrelenting stress and trauma, the mind and body will become distorted and dysregulated, sometimes to the point where the person is unable to function.

Bill reported that his stomach, ears, throat and eyes were all in revolt.[1] In other words, a total system failure. He said that he had lost 27lb in two months. The question is: from where? He was not a big guy to begin with.

The dramatic weight loss was being attributed by the doctor to two months of no sleep and almost no food.[2] For instance, while the squadron was racing for their lives away from Châteaudun on 13 June, the priority had not, understandably, been on supplying provisions. They had been scrounging for food just like everything else, and it was not only the Hurricanes that needed fuel. Someone had thought to bring along two sacks of carrots, totally insufficient to feed a veritable herd of young men.[3]

Clothing pooled rather comically at the wrists and ankles, belt cinched up – not enough notches. Sharp cheekbones, eyes rather too large and too dark. The loss of 27lb from his already slight frame had the effect of making Bill appear even more childlike than he already did.

Bill spent four days so ill that he was not permitted to write letters and was being threatened with a further four or five days in the hospital when he wrote a letter to Mike Peglar postmarked 18 July 1940. The interesting diet prescribed by the doctor forbade Bill to drink anything but beer, a very thought-provoking remedy for a stomach that had all but quit.[4] For the treatment of two months of flight, fight and trauma, the answer was alcohol. The letter he tried to write was interrupted and completed on a different date as the doctor did not think he was up to writing any more.

The letter Bill wrote when he was the next thing to dead reflected on the proceeding two months. Writing to his old friend always seemed to have a therapeutic element, although he tried to select anecdotes that he thought Mike would be amused and entertained by. He told Mike about Margeaux. His admitted that he had been trying to fall in love with her, but it didn't last. The words were shadowed perhaps with a certain weary numbness. The cruel and brutal weeks in France had not been an auspicious time for love, and perhaps he couldn't fall in love anymore anyway.

Lying limply in a hospital bed like a little ragdoll, drained of animating spirit, Bill's thoughts returned home to Calgary and his old friends. If his own love life had stalled for the moment, had Miss 'M. G.' hit a bumpy patch in her own? For someone who claimed he did not care one way or the other, Bill had responded to some gossip about his ex. 'I won't say anything as it would sound too much like "I told you so" but damn it all I did say something like that,' he wrote cryptically.[5] We don't know the other half of that story with its juicy details, so all is speculation.

There were suggestions that colonial officers might be sent back home to Canada on leave. At this stage, Bill was open to it and thought that it might be nice to spend some time in Calgary among his family and friends.[6]

The carefree young person who had written to his friend a scant year before outlining his dramatic and largely imagined adventures of partying, flying Spitfires, and terrorizing his commanding officers and the innocent local civilians was now a decorated pilot. While he described some of his battles to Mike, his only mention of his decoration in this letter is a single, solitary line. Now that he could brag and show off, he did not.

He was growing up. Or growing old.

To So Few: the Battle of Britain

The Battle of Britain began immediately. Germany was now in control of most of Europe. The trench-style warfare of the First World War was not going to materialize for the foreseeable future; the expanding battlefield was the sky. The Luftwaffe reportedly had 4,000 aircraft stationed off south-eastern England, ready to attack. The RAF's Fighter Command had only 500 aeroplanes, and they could not fly themselves. They needed pilots.

Britain was now isolated; the next step was for Germany to invade Britain, and so far they had made their conquest of Europe appear remarkably straightforward. The military superiority that Germany had spent the 1930s consolidating was by now breathtakingly obvious. France and Britain – and Canada – had not been prepared.

Now that its army was completely withdrawn from the Continent, Britain would focus on its own defence. Rather than feeling panicked or helpless, for some there was a sense of relief. Douglas Bader would recall listening to the BBC on 22 June 1940. The broadcaster announced solemnly that the French government had surrendered. One of the other commanding officers listened soberly, then said, 'Thank God, now we're on our own.' Bader said that brief statement reflected how everyone was feeling.[1] Now for the chance to focus on one thing only, the protection and defence of an island that was surrounded by a formidable natural moat.

There was a personal investment to defending one's own people and country that had been missing from the defence of France. Bill felt this, and Bader described it this way: 'Suddenly, I was angry. "Who the hell do these Huns think they are, flying like this in their bloody bombers covered with iron crosses and swastikas over our country?"'[2] Bracing for the Blitz himself, Bill thought that the young men who were joining up from Canada would be steered into the army, although he wondered what good an army would be with only an island left to defend.[3] It was a pointed observation.

Fighter Command was divided into groups, 10, 11, 12 and 13, each responsible for the air defence of a specific region. As a part of 12 Group, the territory that No. 242 Squadron would be tasked with protecting was the Midlands, with its crucial infrastructure and industry – and airfields. The squadrons stationed at RAF Coltishall were also responsible for providing air protection to the critical supply chain of transport ships.[4] Air Officer Commanding Leigh-Mallory administered Group 12 and while he was a veteran of the First World War, his appointment was rather surprising given that he had no experience with fighters, either during that war or in the time between the two conflicts.[5]

Bill's hospitalization meant that he sat out the first few weeks as No. 242 Squadron flew practice wing exercises with a Spitfire unit, No. 66 Squadron.[6] This was not the single-squadron formations that Air Chief Marshal Dowding had planned for, and it shows that Bader was already moving his squadron in a different direction.

In the 1920s and '30s, the standard formations for fighters were beautiful, close groupings that looked impressive at air shows, but they had serious consequences for the RAF when the war began. Among other challenges, the tight formations meant that the wingmen had to not only be on the lookout for enemy aircraft but watch carefully to be sure not to crash into their leader.[7] Bader believed that insisting on the obedient application of the dated 1930s strategies was a hopeless and suicidal prospect.[8] He planned to return No. 242 Squadron to First World War tactics: dogfight styles that included the pilot and wingman formation, leading one or two men at a time, ensuring there would now be more eyes watching for danger.

Bader would also emphasize other classic First World War tactics, such as climbing a to high altitude and then soaring out of the sun, one to each side of a target, then breaking away abruptly, forward and beneath, to scatter the rows of fighter-escorted German bombers before they ever had a chance to drop their bombs. Rather than flying in rigid formations, Bader thought that pilots should select their targets independently, getting close and then attacking. He also believed that fighters striking from all directions would be more lethal than the pretty-to-look-at but useless formations.[9] Bader's approach was going to be a fit for Bill's style, since he was already doing quite a few of these things anyway.

Bader was also advocating for a tactic of fighters diving into groups of bombers and breaking up their formations. Once the bombers were separated from their protective fighters, they were essentially sitting ducks, or fish in a barrel. Breaking up bomber formations was something that Bill had already been doing at Dunkirk, before he ever met Bader. His style was going to be a good match for his new boss.

The new program had commenced on 29 June. First up for the group was a tough regime of practicing formations and aerobatics. Bader wanted his pilots to be familiar with being sideways or upside down as they would be in rolls and loops in combat, and to be just as comfortable firing their guns upside down and backwards as they were sitting right side up.[10] Relaxed, watching the sky sliding away as you went into a roll, or the ground mapping itself strangely as one climbed into a loop, and calmly firing a weapon while it happened, was all part of Bader's curriculum.

Hurricane rollercoasters (no tracks) and guns!

The entire squadron had practiced aerobatics for ten hours and twenty minutes over eight days, with Bill recording an hour each of aerobatics flying on 28 June and on 5 and 7 July. As for the pretty, tight formations that looked so well in airshows, they were done for because they had proven not only ineffective but deadly in battle. Bill's logbook also reported over eleven hours of formation flying from 27 June through 7 July 1940.[11]

Bader recognised patterns that the veterans of the First World War had noticed first – that the people who had the higher 'ground' and the element of surprise could control the battle. This meant that dropping down from a great height and ideally from the position of the sun was part of his tactics. Finally, fighters would be trained to hold their fire until they were close to their target; these strategies were not revolutionary at all but had been learned by aces in the First World War.[12] There was a mindfulness to the strategies Bader was encouraging. He advocated slowly overtaking a target and to calmly begin firing. 'You will never get him in a hurry,' he rationalized.[13]

On 9 July, Bader proclaimed that No. 242 Squadron was fully operational, and he said himself that it had not taken him long to get it into first-class shape.[14] All the pilots could fly the Hurricane proficiently and most of them had fired guns at the enemy. Perhaps rest for the pilots and the chance to repair the aircraft, replenish the gear and kits that had been lost, destroyed or left all over France, and recruiting new crew, pilots and especially new officers to bring the squadron back up to operational strength that had been vehemently advocated for by Gobeil were exactly what had been needed all along.

It was not only the pilots but the aircraft that had taken a beating – eighteen new Hurricanes were supposed to be on back order, but in a turn of events that must have had Noel Barlow and the rest of the groundcrew shaking their heads in disbelief, there were no spare parts or tools to repair the aeroplanes they did have, so that was yet another situation for Bader to deal with.[15]

The squadron had reassembled at Coltishall, re-equipped and with their new officers. Flight Lieutenant G.E. Ball replaced Don Miller as the commander of Bill's A Flight. The new sergeants were Armitage, Brimble, Meredith, Porter and Terras. They were all establishment candidates, which is to say, British, like Bader.[16] While Flying Officer George Christie and Pilot Officer Norris Hart, both Canadians, also arrived to shore up the Canadian content, the all-Canadian squadron was beginning to take on a distinctly thinned-out quality.

Sub-Lieutenant Jimmy Gardner shot down an He 111 on 10 July while protecting a convoy patrol. The next day, Bader was credited with his first kill as squadron leader on 11 July, when he shot down weather reconnaissance Dornier Do 17P off Cromer,[17] but No. 242 Squadron saw limited action through out July and early August, which greatly irritated Bader. When Bill returned to action at last, No. 242 Squadron was flying mainly out of Coltishall. The Norfolk base was out of arm's reach for the more intense fighting that was going on in southern England, but nevertheless, the battle was making its presence known in East Anglia.

The squadron was charged with flying nonstop protection patrols, and that meant the ground crew were busier than ever, keeping the Hurricanes operational.[18] They had worked out a pattern of shifts, working from 8 a.m. until noon one day, 4.30 p.m. until 8 a.m. the next day, and from 2.30 p.m. until 4.30 p.m. on the final day. It meant that there was always a crew available for what was becoming a non-negotiable, twenty-four-hour a day job. No matter how badly damaged that aircraft was, it needed to be running when the next order came to scramble. No wonder Noel Barlow would turn out to be such a valuable member of the ground crew. Not only was he a skilled mechanic, but as a licenced pilot he could test fly the aircraft he was working on to make sure it was operational.[19]

Their Big Wings were waiting.

Waiting for the Big Wing

Bill was officially back in action on 30 July. His logbook for early August recorded protective patrols over East Anglia and the Midlands, with fighters dispatched to intercept and investigate unknown aircraft, and convoy patrols, protecting cargo ships over the North Sea. There were a few brushes with the Luftwaffe to report, but no real excitement. Bill recorded that his fellow Canadian, Flight Officer 'Pat' Christie, had been awarded the Distinguished Flying Cross on 13 August.

The uneasiness must have been intense. The day before Bill returned to duty, on 29 July, there was a panicky moment for Coltishall when all available squadrons reacted to a raid on a convoy off Harwich, Essex. No. 242 Squadron made no contact with the attackers, and the action left the airfield defended by only one flight of fighters.[1] Bader may have believed that having equal numbers was ultimately more effective and economical than sending up a single squadron of fighters against a large group of German fighters and bombers[2] but in this instance the strategy had left the Coltishall airfield virtually unguarded.

A morning routine for a pilot that fateful summer began at sunrise, striding across the airfield to where the ground crew were running up the engines of the Hurricanes in a dawn chorus of bellowing Rolls-Royce engines that overpowered any songbirds that may have been chanting to greet the dawn. The parachutes were being carefully laid out and packed, meticulously folding the straps. No one wanted a situation where a bailout went wrong because a strap got caught somewhere on the aircraft and the pilot was tethered to a crashing aeroplane, so those straps were fed in carefully.

Nothing less like the carefree previous summer of 1939 could have been imagined.

As if in apology for the deplorable conditions at Dunkirk and the terrible winter of 1939–40, the Battle of Britain boasted a string of clear, bright, blue-skied days that rather recalled a typical summer back in Calgary. The summer vibes background was a bizarre contrast with the fight for survival and existence that they were facing.

Sunny, with a chance of Hurricanes.

A typical day for the pilots and airmen of No. 242 Squadron included sunbathing outdoors in reclining chairs next to their aircraft. They were, of course, permitted to use the bathrooms, but an entire day could be spent in a circle next to the Hurricanes, waiting for the telephone to ring.

Lunch would be brought to them, newspapers could be read. The hot and cold contrast from utter boredom to ferocious intensity would occur instantly with the jangling of the telephone. A state of high alert ensued – which could prove to be a false alarm. With the command, 'SCRAMBLE!' the scene instantly became the site of warp-speed activity with pilots and ground crew racing for the Hurricanes and starting the engines, pilots dashing along the wings of their aircraft and swinging themselves into the cockpit, chocks being removed from under the wheels as the growling Hurricanes began charging down the runways and launching themselves, snarling, into the sky. Establishing a formation, and then turning into hunters, searching for prey. No one wanted to be late taking off. There were other predators in the sky, and an aircraft lagging behind its squadron was vulnerable to attack.

Whether Bill had any specific 'game day' rituals or superstitions is unknown, but he did talk about what the battles were like to experience. He found hunting bombers fun and easy, 'like picking apples off a tree' in his own expression.[3] When the German fighters showed up, it was a different matter, and he firmly attributed survival to speed and 'greased lightning' reactions. As for the battles, he admitted that they frightened him, but he observed that his nerves troubled him only beforehand. The butterflies evaporated once the fighting started.

'It's a funny thing this fighting in the air before you actually start or see any of the Hun you're as nervous and scared as hell but as soon as everything starts you're too busy to be afraid or worried.'[4]

The battles were over quickly, sometimes in a matter of five minutes from the time the enemy was first spotted. The sky could be teeming with enemy aircraft one moment, but the battles were after all happening at 300mph. Shoot at something or be shot at, make a turn back to the fight only to discover that it had vanished. Over. Time to compare notes, tally up the dead and missing, track down the carcasses of the crashed aircraft.

While the official dates for the Battle of Britain are from 1 July to 31 October, there were distinctive phases to the fighting. From 8 to 18 August, German bombers, escorted by fighters, were attacking shipping and ports in south and south-east England. They were trying to paralyze the Royal and Merchant Navies, the legendary flotillas that supplied and guarded the famous moat that ringed Great Britain. By 15 August, the Germans had realized that the cakewalks they had experienced as they seized control of Norway, the Netherlands, Belgium and

France were not going to be repeated with Britain. The RAF was outnumbered, but it was proving itself much tougher than expected.

It was the second half of August that would see the battle's intensity dial up over southern England.[5] As the Luftwaffe increasingly realized that it was the RAF that was standing squarely between them and their objectives, their battle plan was adjusted. The Royal Navy, the ancient guardians of the Empire, were rapidly giving way before the relative newcomers of the air force who protected the sky – and the critical transport ships that supplied Britain. It was clear that if a successful invasion of Britain was to happen, the airfields would have to be the main targets. Before the enemy ships could arrive, carrying the men and equipment needed to launch the ground attacks, the RAF would have to be disabled. This approach was going to exact a heavy cost for the Germans.[6]

On 15 August, a huge predatory force assaulted Scotland and northern England from German bases in Norway. Crossing the North Sea was beyond the range of a Bf 109, so Bf 110s escorted the bombers. Between 100 and 150 aircraft also crossed the Channel throughout the afternoon. No. 242 Squadron was stationed too far south to be of assistance[7] but the blows were falling closer.

The day 18 August 1940 has come to be known as 'the Hardest Day'. The Battle of Britain saw the peak of losses of both personnel and aircraft, with both sides sustaining heavy fatalities.

Undoubtedly fortunately for Bill, he was not flying between 15 and 18 August. He was still hurt, referencing an injured knee that may account for the gaps in his logbook. He did not specify whether the injury had been caused in combat, but going forward he would miss out on other critical dates in the Battle of Britain; his doctors were advising surgery as they thought there was a fifty-fifty chance that his injury would become chronic. Bill had refused the surgery and was periodically laid up because of it.[8]

On 19 August, he was flying again. He flew two interceptions, and that date brought home for No. 242 Squadron the realities of the enemy tactic of targeting airfields because Coltishall itself was shot up and bombed by a lone He 111. That individual aircraft caused considerable damage, and three servicemen who had been working at the airfield were killed.[9]

In sky after sky, Bill sailed along a fine and delicate line between dying himself at any moment and wiping the atmosphere with the remnants of his German adversaries. He had been hospitalized a mere month before and had been limited in the fighting to date. Now he was about to become the leading Canadian ace in the Battle of Britain.

30 August 1940 - Hat-Trick

On 30 August, the Luftwaffe dialed up the intensity of their attacks yet again.

That day, No. 242 Squadron was ordered from Coltishall to Duxford, within arm's reach of London. For weeks, they had been following the action, but now they were expecting to be summoned to the big fight themselves. To Bader's complete exasperation – probably mirrored by everyone else in the squadron – while en route to Duxford, they were required to stand down and ordered to return to Coltishall.[1] Bader telephoned Ops and gave them a piece of his mind. The tension, disorganization and continual plot twists must have been incredibly stressful and frustrating. An hour later, No. 242 Squadron was ordered back to Duxford. After all the endless waiting and irritating false starts, they now had every chance of being called to the battles raging in the south.

Late that afternoon, No. 242 Squadron was scrambled to North Weald as an incoming threat had been reported to the aerodrome there.

At approximately 5 p.m., Bill reported that while on patrol a host of between 70 and 100 assorted Bf 110s and He 111s approached them north-west of Hatfield in tidy lines of four and six abreast. The bombers were flying at between 12,000 and 18,000ft. Another swarm was stacked on top of them at 15,000 to 20,000ft.[2] With no other British fighters on hand, No. 242 Squadron was on their own with a huge swarm of enemy bombers. Never before had Bader or his squadron seen anything like it. Maybe nobody had.

There was no time for a tidy, pretty battle and that was not Bader's style anyway. He had the sun at his back and the advantage of height, just the way he liked it. He flew straight up the middle, scattering the Bf 110s and leaving the bombers unguarded.[3]

As Bader's wingman, Bill was right beside him and he slid behind an Bf 110. A Bf 110 was no real problem for a Hurricane, and a shot from behind was the easiest of all, although the Bf 110 did have a single rearward-facing machine gun that sometimes caught overconfident fighter pilots off guard.

But not this one. The short-burst kill was something that Bill was an expert at.

He slid up to 100 yards behind his victim and fired in a short burst of three to five seconds. Bill, as we have seen, was a deadly shot to start with, and dropping in close to his victims, he fired from the stable gun stand of the Hurricane's thick, heavy wings. It was an automatic score for Bill McKnight. That aircraft burst into flames and plummeted towards the ground. Bill whirled back into the fray and next confronted an He 111.[4] He had long recognised that the bombers were virtually defenseless once they were separated from their protective fighters. The aggressive tactic of challenging an enemy aircraft within 100 yards of it was not only completely unnerving to whoever was flying it, but it also assured accuracy.

Another short spray of bullets saw one of the He 111's engines die and the aircraft began to smoke. As the fading bomber turned belly up and began sinking towards the earth, a Bf 110 made the courageous but horrible decision to attack the guy flying the Hurricane with the skeleton painted on the side of it. Bill immediately curved towards his opponent and got behind the other aeroplane. He had set himself up yet again for the easiest shot in aviation. A madcap chase ensued, with the Bf 110 turning steeply in desperate late-stage evasion tactics and diving from 10,000ft to 1,000ft. This was where patience mattered; Bill followed until the aircraft straightened out again. The battle had turned into a knife fight. Then he shot at his target from 30 crazy, unnerving yards.[5] Thirty yards on a big, wide, Canadian Football League field is in automatic field goal range. Two moving aircraft should not be that close to one another at any time or for any reason.

The Bf 110 was clearly in trouble; one of its engines had stopped and it promptly burst into flames, falling into a large reservoir – the Enfield Sewage Farm no less.[6] We have all had shitty days at work, but trying to take on Bill McKnight and getting chased into a sewage farm for your pains must have to rank in history as one of the very worst there could possibly be.

It had been a great afternoon for No. 242 Squadron, and they were euphoric. Bader was thrilled with the performance of his squadron and reported that they had a successful battle. It was not only Bill who had exciting news to share. Christie, Stansfield, Ball and Hart all had their own kills, shared or solo, to toss onto the pile for No. 242 Squadron. In all, they had claimed twelve, and Bill's headcount represented a quarter of grand total. Bader himself claimed two aircraft.

The story that follows has come down through Canadian lore. It is one of the definitive moments of our history, a tale that should be etched into the minds and hearts of Canadian children, along with other great moments in Canadian history – Vimy Ridge, the driving of the Last Spike, the invention of the Noble Blade – and other images from our collective history.

The legend goes that after Bader had followed the last of his prey to make sure it had been shot down, he noticed a lone Hurricane flying out to greet him as he returned to his squadron. The sun was beginning to set, and it glinted off the side of the approaching Hurricane, revealing the sneering image of the Grim Reaper crouching along its flanks. It was gesturing at Bader. Bader held up two fingers to let Bill know his score; Bill beamed and held up his own fingers … three.[7] Surely it was a moment that Bader carried with him for the rest of his life, for it was only he who could have recounted the story to his biographer, Paul Brickhill.

This account inspired the current Canadian artist Michael Martchenko, best known for his illustrations of children's author Robert Munsch's books. He created an image called *McKnight's Hat Trick*, and it portrays a triumphant, almost tender moment between the pair, with the two Hurricanes soaring next to each other, the pale patchwork of the English countryside stretching below. The hoods of both aircraft are drawn back, and Bill is leaning towards Bader, three fingers held aloft. Beneath Bill on the fuselage, the Reaper floats quietly, sated for the time being.

Although Bader never had any children himself, throughout his life he often demonstrated progressive and respectful views towards the concerns of younger people. He seemed to understand that the things that they cared about felt new and real to them, even if their parents had seen it all before.

Bill now had a boss who he cared about impressing, and who he wanted to celebrate with, someone who was proud of him and made sure that he knew that he was appreciated. Bader would later say that Bill was a dedicated person and that the achievements of the entire squadron could be symbolized by this one steadfast and loyal young pilot.[8] Bader also said that he always felt a sense of confidence and security whenever he recognised the Reaper insignia travelling beside him. The leering, campy, creepy image meant the presence of a skilled and loyal friend.[9] This must have felt good to Bill after a lifetime of irritating his teachers and frustrating and disappointing his own father beyond all measure.

The outcome of the battle must have been extremely vindicating for Bader. No. 242 Squadron had not lost a single Hurricane. The enemy aircraft had been headed for the North Weald aerodrome, and they had not reached it. It was a day for No. 242 Squadron to be proud of, and they were congratulated by the Chief of the Air Staff, the Under Secretary of State for Air and Leigh-Mallory.[10]

No complementary or grateful telegrams arrived from the Canadian officials, however.[11]

A reporter who was on hand when the famed warriors returned to Duxford noticed that the high-spirited young pilots seemed more excited about what was for supper than the battle they had just come through. It was also noted that the most dangerous man in the room, Willie McKnight, sat quietly whistling to himself as he completed his combat reports, 'looking for all the world like a high school boy doing his homework'.[2]

Infancy and Childhood

Right: Photograph of William Lidstone McKnight as an infant. (McKnight Family Archive)

Below: Exterior of the family's Calgary home. (Shelly McElroy)

Growing Up

Left: Bill McKnight as an air cadet, dated 25 July 1935. (McKnight Family Archive)

Below: Air show at Renfrew Airport, Calgary, Alberta, circa 1920s. (CU1100719, Glenbow Library and Archives Collection, University of Calgary)

Right: Bill and Ted McKnight, 25 July 1935.

Below left: Raymond (Ray) and Ted McKnight, undated. (McKnight Family Archive)

Below right: A portrait with an uncertain identity; Bill and Ray were remarkably similar in appearance. (McKnight Family Archive)

Family Moments

Above: Bill's stepmother Doris and younger brother Ted on a family outing, possibly in the Rocky Mountains. Undated. (McKnight Family Archive)

Below left: William Campbell McKnight with Ted. Undated. (McKnight Family Archive)

Below right: Portrait of Ted as a youngster. Undated. (McKnight Family Archive)

Education and Early Ambitions

Above: Class photo from Crescent Heights High School, 1937. Marion Glover is fifth in the front row; Bill is seventh in the second row. (*The Crescent Bugle*, 1937, p. 39)

Below left: Bill, inscribed to his father on 16 January 1939, just before joining the Royal Air Force.

Below right: Dedicated to Doris McKnight, 'To Mother, lots of love, Bill,' same date. (McKnight Family Archive)

Military Service: No. 242 Squadron

Above: The original No. 242 Squadron, late February/early March 1940; Bill is fifth from the left in the back row. Fowler Gobeil, first squadron leader, is sixth in the front row. (McKnight Family Archive)

Below left: Bill, cropped from a group portrait, spring 1940. (McKnight Family Archive)

Below right: Undated photo, believed to be Bill McKnight, possibly experimenting with a moustache. (McKnight Family Archive)

Celebratory moment. (McKnight Family Archive)

There were new officers for No. 242 Squadron following the fall of France. Bill McKnight, with Squadron Leader Douglas Bader and Flight Lieutenant G.E. Ball (September 1940). (McKnight Family Archive)

Squadron Life and Camaraderie

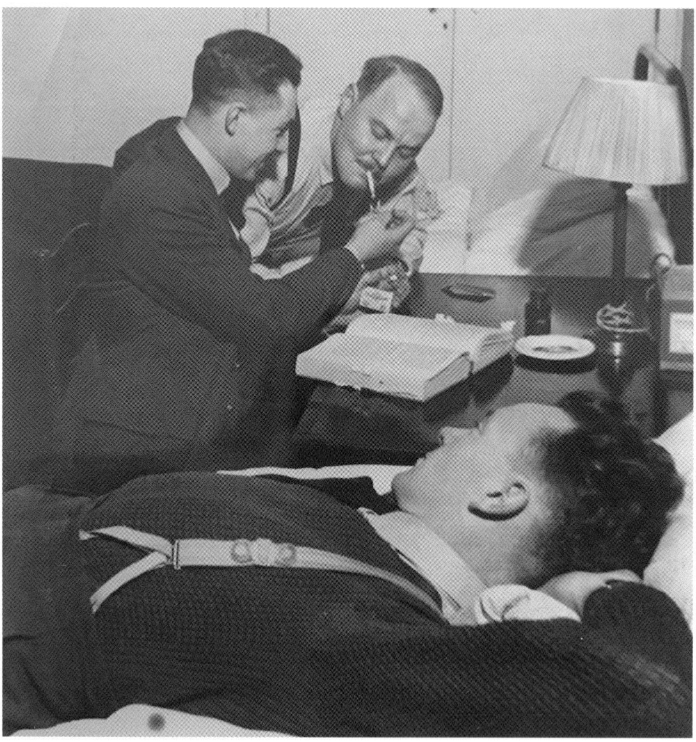

Above: Pilot Officer William 'Willie' McKnight outside Duxford's officers' mess, September 1940. Photograph by Stanley Arthur Devon. (McKnight Family Archive)

Left: Bob Grassick, Bill McKnight, and Stan Turner relaxing. (Turner Family Archive)

Right: Portrait of Bill McKnight. (IWM, CH 1321).

Below: No. 242 Squadron's pilots: Bill McKnight, Douglas Bader, and G. E. Ball (September 1940). (IWM, CH 1342)

Stan Turner, Bill's close friend and ace, September 1940. (IWM, CH 1376)

Douglas Bader with his Hurricane, September 1940. (IWM, CH 1406)

No. 242 Squadron in formation, October 1940. (IWM, CH 1406)

End of 1940

No. 242 Squadron pilots, December 1940; Bill McKnight is seated first from the left in the front row. (McKnight Family Archive)

All No. 242 Squadron personnel, December 1940. (McKnight Family Archive)

Above left: Bill with his LEA Hurricane, painted with the Grim Reaper insignia. (McKnight Family Archive)

Above right: Close-up of the Grim Reaper insignia, believed to be designed by Bill – possibly inspired by his medical training. (McKnight Family Archive)

Winter 1940–1941 and Legacy

January 1940. Pilots Edmond, Bader, McKnight, Ball, and Brown enjoying snowy weather. (McKnight Family Archive)

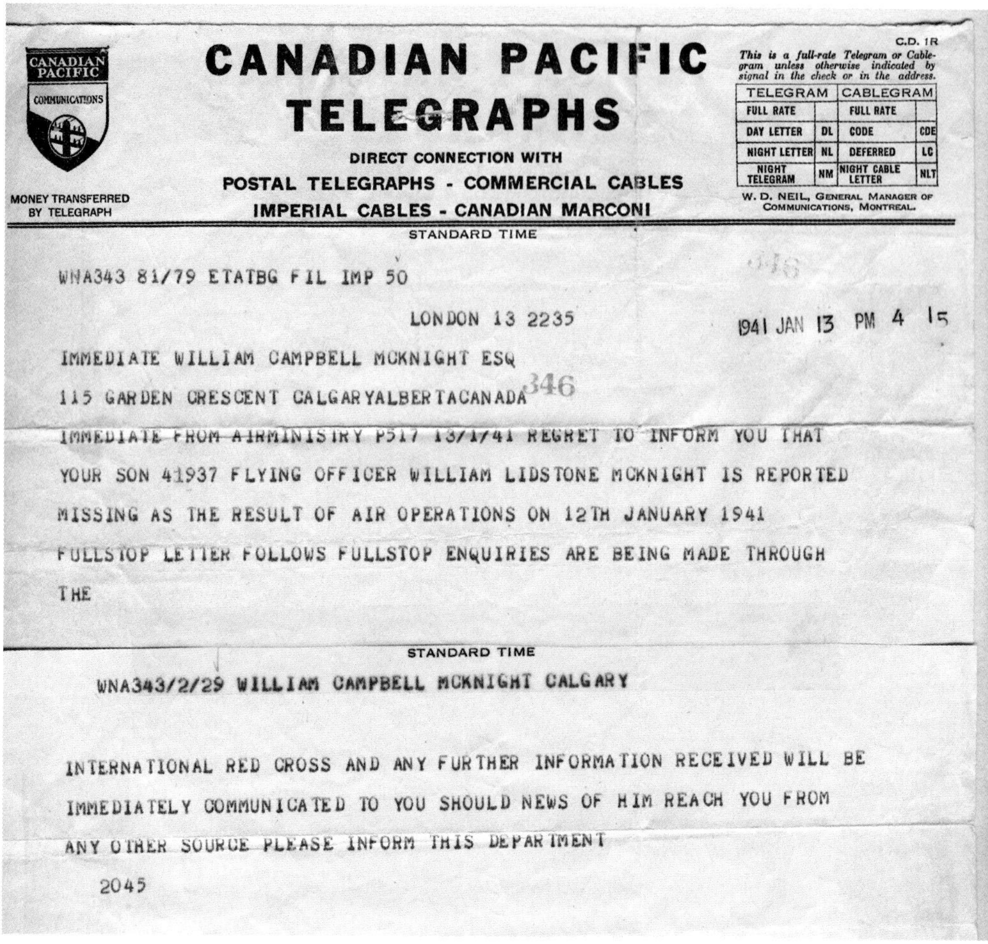

CANADIAN PACIFIC COMMUNICATIONS

MONEY TRANSFERRED BY TELEGRAPH

CANADIAN PACIFIC TELEGRAPHS

DIRECT CONNECTION WITH
POSTAL TELEGRAPHS - COMMERCIAL CABLES
IMPERIAL CABLES - CANADIAN MARCONI

C.D. 1R

This is a full-rate Telegram or Cablegram unless otherwise indicated by signal in the check or in the address.

TELEGRAM		CABLEGRAM	
FULL RATE		FULL RATE	
DAY LETTER	DL	CODE	CDE
NIGHT LETTER	NL	DEFERRED	LC
NIGHT TELEGRAM	NM	NIGHT CABLE LETTER	NLT

W. D. NEIL, General Manager of Communications, Montreal.

STANDARD TIME

WNA343 81/79 ETATBG FIL IMP 50

LONDON 13 2235 1941 JAN 13 PM 4 15

IMMEDIATE WILLIAM CAMPBELL MCKNIGHT ESQ

115 GARDEN CRESCENT CALGARYALBERTACANADA 346

IMMEDIATE FROM AIRMINISTRY P517 13/1/41 REGRET TO INFORM YOU THAT YOUR SON 41937 FLYING OFFICER WILLIAM LIDSTONE MCKNIGHT IS REPORTED MISSING AS THE RESULT OF AIR OPERATIONS ON 12TH JANUARY 1941 FULLSTOP LETTER FOLLOWS FULLSTOP ENQUIRIES ARE BEING MADE THROUGH THE

STANDARD TIME

WNA343/2/29 WILLIAM CAMPBELL MCKNIGHT CALGARY

INTERNATIONAL RED CROSS AND ANY FURTHER INFORMATION RECEIVED WILL BE IMMEDIATELY COMMUNICATED TO YOU SHOULD NEWS OF HIM REACH YOU FROM ANY OTHER SOURCE PLEASE INFORM THIS DEPARTMENT

2045

Above: Telegram delivered to the McKnight home in Calgary on 13 January 1941, marking a life-changing day for their family.

Opposite above: Douglas Bader's friendship.

Opposite below: Bader maintained a close relationship with McKnight's family, signing copies of his biography for them and Bill's youngest brother, Ted. The books were made out to 'Bill's' family – not 'Willie's.'

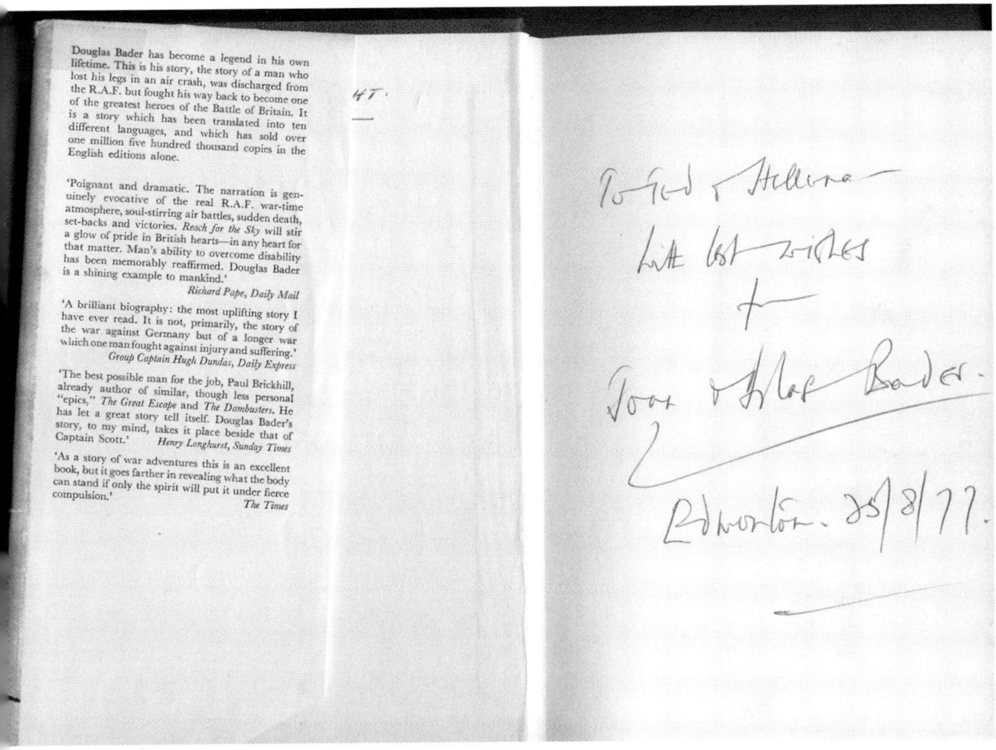
Douglas Bader has become a legend in his own lifetime. This is his story, the story of a man who lost his legs in an air crash, was discharged from the R.A.F. but fought his way back to become one of the greatest heroes of the Battle of Britain. It is a story which has been translated into ten different languages, and which has sold over one million five hundred thousand copies in the English editions alone.
'Poignant and dramatic. The narration is genuinely evocative of the real R.A.F. war-time atmosphere, soul-stirring air battles, sudden death, set-backs and victories. Reach for the Sky will stir a glow of pride in British hearts—in any heart for that matter. Man's ability to overcome disability has been memorably reaffirmed. Douglas Bader is a shining example to mankind.'
Richard Pape, Daily Mail
'A brilliant biography: the most uplifting story I have ever read. It is not, primarily, the story of the war against Germany but of a longer war which one man fought against injury and suffering.'
Group Captain Hugh Dundas, Daily Express
'The best possible man for the job, Paul Brickhill, already author of similar, though less personal "epics," The Great Escape and The Dambusters. He has let a great story tell itself. Douglas Bader's story, to my mind, takes it place beside that of Captain Scott.'
Henry Longhurst, Sunday Times
'As a story of war adventures this is an excellent book, but it goes farther in revealing what the body can stand if only the spirit will put it under fierce compulsion.'
The Times
Douglas Bader
25/8/77

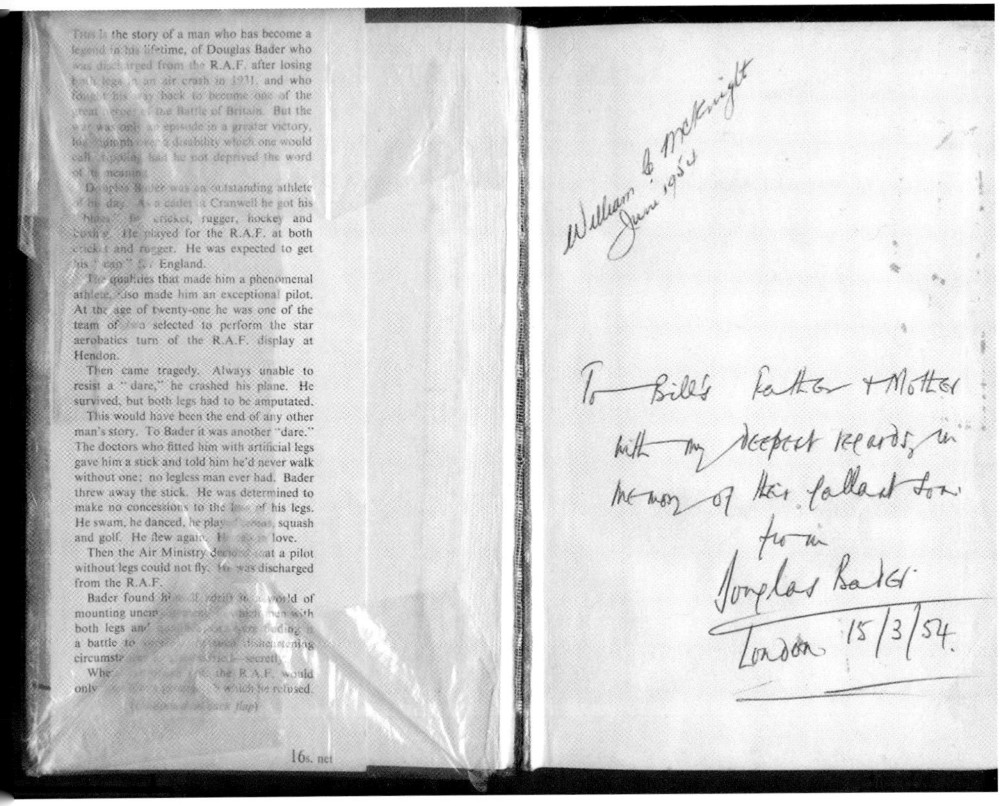
This is the story of a man who has become a legend in his lifetime, of Douglas Bader who was discharged from the R.A.F. after losing both legs in an air crash in 1931, and who fought his way back to become one of the great heroes of the Battle of Britain.
Then came tragedy. Always unable to resist a "dare," he crashed his plane. He survived, but both legs had to be amputated.
This would have been the end of any other man's story. To Bader it was another "dare." The doctors who fitted him with artificial legs gave him a stick and told him he'd never walk without one; no legless man ever had. Bader threw away the stick. He was determined to make no concessions to the loss of his legs.
16s. net
William B McKnight
June 1954
To Bill's Father + Mother
with my deepest regards, in
memory of their gallant son.
from
Douglas Bader
London 15/3/54.

Left: Bill's portrait by Eric Kennington, chosen for the cover of *Drawing the Royal Air Force* (1942), now in the Canadian War Museum. (Artifact Number: 19710261-6088)

Below: Bill's nephew, also named Bill McKnight, photographed in front of a Hawker Hurricane Mk XII at Calgary's The Hanger Flight Museum. (Shelly McElroy)

Overclaims

And then the historians arrive to ruin it all.

Before we go any further with this biography, unfortunately there are caveats. We must pause to review a certain unhappy reality of the glories of war – claims, confirmations, the frailty of memory, and overclaims.

As anyone who has ever been involved in a serious car accident – or even someone who was one of the first on the scene of one – knows, when it comes to dramatic and traumatic incidents, memory and impressions can be extremely unreliable. Certain parts of the event may seem radically overstated and sharp, while other details that are just as important are impossible to recall or appear in a vignette shadow on the periphery. The most honest thing that anyone can so often say when it comes to history, even after a careful and thorough examination of all the evidence, is 'We don't know.'

If a pilot believed that they had damaged or shot down an enemy aircraft, they were required to fill out a combat claim describing what they had seen and what they believed had happened. Unlike a logbook, the combat claims had to be filled out on the same day as the engagement to capture the most accurate picture of what had happened before conjecture and speculation had time to muddy the waters. However, being confident of what had happened when surrounded by dangerous and chaotic events happening at warp speed, with threats to life above, below and around you, witnessing the danger and death of friends and enemies alike, could make it difficult or impossible to state conclusively what had happened.

Overclaims happened from both sides. Inexperienced squadrons were especially, if forgivably, prone to this. Flooded with mega doses of their own adrenaline, pilots who had little combat experience were unreliable reporters. For instance, a diving aircraft trailing smoke, even if you lost track of it through clouds or confusion, seems like the reasonable assumption of a write-off. However, if the skeletal remains of the aircraft are never discovered, the likelihood must be examined that the wounded aircraft actually got away.

An experienced combat pilot learned that when hunting Messerschmitts, a trail of black smoke did not mean the enemy was done for at all. It was more likely that the aircraft's dragon lungs were hauling in a deep breath so it could drag itself out of its drop and lift itself back into the sky. It was the coughing of white smoke – more likely steam from a coolant leak – that meant engine failure.

Historian Dilip Sarkar pointed out in his book *Fighter Ace* that despite carefully examining the evidence, he does not believe that the bombers No. 242 Squadron confronted on the afternoon of 30 August were broken up. The He 111s did reach their target – a Vauxhall factory – and fifty-three people there were killed. That facility manufactured Halifax bombers, and the damage to the production lines was fortunately so slight that manufacture was not affected. But the idea that the formation had been utterly dispersed was not true.[1]

As we know by this point in our association with Bill, he had an ever-so-SLIGHT tendency to exaggerate himself. He made three combat claims on 30 August. The only German loss that can be verified is 4/ZG 76, the German aircraft that crashed into the sewage farm. And that aircraft could have also been engaged by Squadron Leader Pemberton, who was also involved in the encounters that day and who had also taken on a Bf 110 bomber.

But it gave Bader, Leigh-Mallory and Wing Commander Woodhall a reason to do what they wanted to do anyway: launch their Big Wing squadrons, against the direct orders and strategy of Hugh Dowding and the other Royal Air Force brass. It appeared that no one could control Bader; if he was told no, he found a way to do what he wanted to do. Was the plan going to prove to be a cutting-edge approach that was needed to win the desperate battles that loomed?

Time would be the judge.

Big Wings

The very next day after their big battle, Bill and No. 242 Squadron were back in action – if by action, you mean on patrol. Bill's logbook noted rounds to Cranwell and London on 1 and 2 September. English airfields were turning into very busy and international places, with Czech and Polish squadrons flying out of them. The global flavour by now included the Royal Canadian Air Force, also flying their squadrons in the Battle of Britain. No. 242 Squadron, the original Canadian propaganda project with the RAF, was all but forgotten by the Canadian government.

Bader was being given more responsibilities, and the chance to try out his Big Wing. It was known as 'the Duxford Wing' and '12 Group Wing'. Nos 19 and 310 Squadrons, in addition to No. 242 Squadron, were now operating out of Duxford. Those squadrons flew Spitfires, and it turned out that Hurricanes and Spitfires were good partners. The graceful Spitfires were faster, but the tough Hurricanes were better at climbing, clawing at the air to gain altitude. It was a new experience for No. 242 Squadron, and after such a terrific start, they had growing confidence in their new commander. Winning feels good.

A disadvantage of the larger patrols was that they were supremely difficult to organize. To coordinate multiple squadrons to be fueled and in the air at precisely the same time surely must have had the texture of herding cats. However, the larger patrols were being tested because the younger members of the RAF knew that even with the Big Wing formations, they were severely outnumbered by the Luftwaffe. The conservative strategies of their commanders seemed pointless to them.

The Luftwaffe and No. 242 Squadron would not meet again until 7 September, and during this time, the Germans had shifted their strategy yet again. The third phase of the battle focused on London itself. On 24 August, the RAF had attacked Berlin. While no one was killed and there was minimal damage to the city, that raid was an embarrassment for Goering, who had bragged that Berlin could never be bombed with the Luftwaffe standing in the way.

That RAF bombing raid was the justification given for what was about to happen to London.

Pubs, churches, and people's homes would be destroyed as civilians were drawn into the war in a personal and deadly way. While the main objectives may have been to demolish the shipping infrastructure in east London, the bombs did not discriminate for hospitals, babies, or old people. The raids increased in intensity, with the extremity reaching a pitch during an unbearable string of days in early September: the 7th, 10th, 11th, 12th, 13th and 15th were a nerve-shattering series of attacks against infrastructure and ordinary people. The fearful progression had an intentionality and purpose, and surely it could be sensed, even if it was not known, that 17 September was the date circled on Hitler's calendar for the invasion of Britain to begin.

On the afternoon of 7 September, the Duxford Wing crossed paths with a group of seventy to ninety enemy aircraft at around 5.20 p.m. Those aeroplanes were soaring far overhead at 20,000ft. If those who controlled the height controlled the battle, the 12 Group Wing was in trouble. The assorted aircraft included Bf 110s, He 111s, Do 215s and escorting Bf 109s. The battle was joined over the Thames Estuary and North Weald. No. 242 Squadron had been ordered away from Duxford around 4.45 p.m. When they noticed anti-aircraft fire to the east, they went to the rescue, but they were cruising at 15,000ft, significantly below the enemy. Having to climb at full throttle to reach them completely ruled out the element of surprise. Nos 19 and 302 Squadrons were accompanying them, and they were all having trouble climbing up to the enemy in a stealthy way. The Hurricanes couldn't do it, and straggled behind, but they dutifully singled out their individual targets. Dogfights broke out all over the sky.[1]

While Bill didn't have any claims to report that day, the totals for the rest of the squadron stated that there were ten aircraft destroyed, two probably destroyed and three damaged. There had been narrow escapes all round, with Bader himself having an explosive bullet slice through the side of his fuselage. It had grazed his map case. Sub-Lieutenant Cork got glass splinters in his eyes when a Bf 109 shot at his aircraft and hit the bulletproof glass of his windscreen. It had turned out that the glass wasn't so bulletproof after all. And at the end of the day, No. 242 Squadron was reporting that Pilot Officer John Benzie was missing. It was later confirmed that he had been killed.[2]

9 September 1940 – Two More for the Reaper

On 9 September, No. 242 Squadron was scrambled from Duxford to protect London as a huge group of more than 100 enemy aircraft approached it from the north – a major attack was on the way. Bader's Big Wing dreams were coming true, because No. 242 Squadron were again accompanied by the two additional fighter squadrons. Bader was in command of them all. No. 19 Squadron climbed higher, past the 20,000ft mark. It was their job to take on the German fighters so that 310 and 242 Squadrons could tackle the bombers.

It was 5.45 p.m. The Bf 110 and Do 215 bombers were escorted by Bf 109 fighters, soaring at 22,000ft. Bill stated that No. 242 Squadron launched their assault from behind on the left flank, and he broke left to confront the enemy fighters. By now, Bill had his signature tactics down to a science, which was to circle behind his target, get as close to it as he could (100 yards or less), and then spray it with bullets in a three- to five-second burst. That was what he did now. It was textbook McKnight; the bomber glided away, wrapped in flames.[1]

Bill immediately found himself confronted by two more enemy fighters. His aggressive 'f*** you' strategy was to get between them and shoot at them in his signature bursts of bullets from 100 to 50 yards.[2]

The enemy pilots had weapons too, of course. Bill said, describing 'the big do' later: 'Then just to finish it this bloke put a few machine gun bullets through [my] cockpit practically smashing everything in it but missing me.'[3]

His Hurricane rocked and bucked as enemy bullets slammed into it, ripping away his left aileron; the Reaper's fingers spun wildly as it selected its victim. Bill had his hands full trying to regain control of his aeroplane as he dropped away from the fight. As he did, he noticed one of the fighters he had shot at plunging out of the sky, burning.[4]

When Bill returned to base, he was met with the details of the rest of squadron's experiences. The engagement had been effective for No. 242 Squadron, because Latta and Tamblyn had also scored. Three Do 215s, four Bf 109s, and three Bf 110s had been reported as destroyed. But two Hurricanes had also been wrecked, and Pilot Officer Schlanders had died. Between being shot at and having his own Hurricane damaged, Bill had escaped narrowly with his own life. 'All I got out of it was a few shrapnel splinters in my left hand.'[5]

15 September 1940

On 11 September, No. 242 Squadron stayed at Coltishall. The following day presented dreadful weather, a dreary rain and cold combination. After the dramatic events on 9 September, Bill's aircraft must have been in for repairs, because he was flying a Magister and another Hurricane during the downtime.

The date 15 September would be known to history as the day the tide turned as the Luftwaffe did their worst, throwing, it seemed, every available aircraft they had at Britain. The outnumbered Royal Air Force and the Luftwaffe were going to go toe to toe, and it was a do or die situation. That morning, 700 enemy fighters rose into the air, escorting 220 bombers. They were headed straight for London. The fatal destruction of the British resistance and key infrastructure were the objective.

By now, Bader commanded a huge collection of predators: his Big Wing dream had come true. The 12 Group Wing contained two squadrons of Spitfires and three of Hurricanes, including, of course, No. 242 Squadron. The Spitfires had been trained to attack the Luftwaffe fighter screens, while the packs of Hurricanes would trail the bombers and their escort fighters.

By noon, the sun was glittering off the armour of the colossal foe amassed in the sky over Kent. Wave after wave of RAF squadrons flung themselves into the fray. While the Luftwaffe had the power of numbers, they had to manage fast-dwindling fuel reserves as they flew across the Channel. The German pilots were glancing nervously at their watches and fuel gauges; they had enough reserves for approximately twenty minutes over Britain and then, unless they wanted to land in the Channel, they had to turn for France. That critical moment of turning for home was when the fresh wave of Big Wing fighters hit them, including No. 242 Squadron. The squadron participated in vicious battles throughout the day, and they were indeed death grapples.

At a moment of what must have been simply unbelievable tension, Churchill would turn to Air Vice Marshal Park and ask what fighter reserves the RAF had available. He was told, 'There are none.'[1] As far as Park knew, everything and everyone the RAF had was in the sky, and on the line.

Except for Bill McKnight! Their celebrated Canadian pilot was not in action, maybe due to the ongoing effects of his knee injury. On 15 September, Bill recorded flying passenger trips in a Magister in his logbook. He was going to be missing out on this very significant day for the RAF, for the Luftwaffe, and for history – probably luckily for him.[2]

By 12.15 p.m., the unbelievable happened. The prospect of a peaceful lunchtime interlude stretched ahead. The Germans had been halted – for now at least. It had the unsettling quality of a half-time, an armistice, a pause. At Duxford, Guy Mayfield reported talking to 'the boys' of No. 242 Squadron as they came in for lunch, chattering about the terrific air fight that had happened over London.[3] The battle would go on for many weeks to come, but by teatime that afternoon there had been a tangible shift in momentum. The greatest number of enemy aircraft had been destroyed[4] and in the years to come, 15 September 1940 would be recognised as the day the Battle of Britain had been decided – by 12.30 p.m.!

By 2 p.m., a fresh enemy wave was breaking. It was another target-rich environment, and by day's end nearly everyone in No. 242 Squadron had scored, except for Bill, who wasn't there! Stansfield, Hart, Latta, Tamblyn, Campbell and Turner all reported victories. Stan Turner had a hat-trick (that's three scores, just in case you don't watch sport) of his own to celebrate.

It had been a frightfully busy time but in fact Bill would say a few days later that he had 'thoroughly enjoyed'[5] the Battle of Britain. He liked flying with his Big Wing team and proudly reported the (overinflated) claims for his squadron – he tallied the grand total at over 130! His own confirmed status – according to him – was at twenty-one kills.[6]

Interestingly, in Bill's opinion, the Luftwaffe pilots he clashed with in the Battle of Britain were not as good as those he had respected and feared when he had met them over Dunkirk and during the fall of France. The wariness and admiration with which he described the enemy pilots in July was gone. It was not only the RAF that had dealt with horrific casualty rates.

Bill speculated, 'Either we've killed all their real good pilots and they're using new young ones or else they are losing their nerve. They haven't got the same guts they used to have and except in a few cases try to avoid a real scrap.'[7]

Photogenic

While the Canadian government was far less interested in the fortunes of No. 242 Squadron now that they had their own Royal Canadian Air Force squadrons flying in Britain, the propaganda and promotional aspect of Bill's job had not changed. He was the squadron's leading ace, and he was, frankly, a very photogenic person himself.

Stanley Arthur Devon was an official RAF photographer, and he visited Duxford during September 1940. He took photographs of the Big Wing in action from an aeroplane himself. He also captured portraits of Bill outside the officers' mess at Duxford during his visit. The photographs taken included posed images of Bill with Douglas Bader as the squadron leader and Flight Lieutenant George Ball, as well as group photographs with the other pilots in the squadron.

Bill is not awkward in the photographs. His expression does look in some of them as though he would just as soon be somewhere else, but usually he is poised and professional. A person doing his job. Nevertheless, there is a star quality to the images. He was a celebrity, he was an elite pilot, and it did not hurt that he was a very handsome person into the bargain. He looked great in the resulting photographs. While Bill was performing his job at a very high level, there is a certain 'halo effect' that sometimes surrounds people who are seen as beautiful and attractive by others. Bill had miles of receipts to back up his claims, but he looked like a movie star. He was an excellent subject to point a camera at.

For such a good-looking pilot, it stood to reason that Bill would need a photogenic aeroplane to match. For anyone wanting to identify Bill's Hurricane, there are several ways to do this. First, LE was the squadron code for all No. 242 Squadron aeroplanes, and each individual aircraft had its own single-letter identifier. The aircraft that Bill was most strongly associated with was LE-A. That Hurricane's serial number was P2961, painted on its rear fuselage. Bill did fly other Hurricanes in addition to LE-A; if it needed maintenance or repairs then he would fly other available aircraft. In the engagements at Dunkirk, he had not flown LE-A at all. His first flight in his Hurricane was recorded on 9 June. It was to become his signature aeroplane.

Finally, this seems like a good time to discuss the artwork on the fuselage of Bill's Hurricane. Most of the nose art that adorns the fighters and bombers of the era does seem like exactly what you would expect men in their early twenties to come up with. Popular images included Disney cartoon characters, sexy images of their girlfriends, or somebody's girlfriend, and insulting caricatures of the enemy – unless they were luckless enough to have a pearl-clutching squadron leader who did not allow for such creativity. Or one who insisted upon professionalism, however you want to make the argument.

Bill's logbook indicated that the initial impressions of him as a pilot in spring of 1939 were that he was above average. Categories included average, above average, and exceptional. Receiving any designation higher than average was rare. The unique things about Bill that other people had noticed back in Calgary were seen early in the evaluation of the RAF, too. Only now, they were valued. Bill had remarkable eyesight. Those keen eyes would have also been a tremendous asset to a surgeon. His nephew commented that someone with eyes like that might have identified diseases or issues that others may have missed. Douglas Bader remembered that Bill often spotted enemy aircraft before anyone else did.

It was not only LE-A that had been through a war. Bill's eyes, as he faced the cameras pointed at him in September 1940, were too old for a twenty-one-year-old's face. There was the scar over his right eye from the long-ago tobogganing accident. They were bright, alert hunter's eyes, like the eyes of the tough little prairie hawks that soared over the Bow River Valley in Calgary. But they had been world-weary and exhausted for a long time, really. Probably ever since he lost his mother. Now there were dark shadows under them that spoke of hunger, lack of sleep, flying for his life, and killing other people. And calling it 'fun'.[1]

There were things about life that Bill evidently saw differently too, including what he wanted to present to the enemy … what he wanted them to see when they looked at him. So, his Hurricane didn't look like anyone else's, and it is believed that he designed and drew the art that decorated his fuselage himself.[2]

Bill's Hurricane was adorned with a cruel, uncanny, and ghoulish image. The skeletal figure of the Grim Reaper appears in profile, sickle in hand, looming along both sides of the Hurricane. It is pointing straight at whatever it is he is chasing. Pointing at you. While some have linked the inspiration for the grinning skeleton to Bill's brief medical training, what cannot be denied is that there is a different sort of mind in there. We don't know when exactly Bill's Hurricane was painted with his signature Reaper, but Noel Barlow thought it might have been in early September 1940.[3] Douglas Bader stated that the Reaper's sickle was painted with a bloodstain on it[4] but it is hard to tell in the few black and white photographs that exist.

The eyes through which Bill saw the world and possibly himself show us that perhaps he did see things sooner, and differently. He saw the world as a threatening place, and instead of mocking death, or taking a light-hearted approach to it, his artwork leaned into the cruelty and brutality. We cannot escape. Sometimes, in the face of something truly frightening, you are driven to transform and become something startling, fearsome, and terrifying yourself.

Meanwhile, there was more portraiture to come.

The Portrait

Douglas Bader's portrait was to be included in artist Eric Kennington book's *Drawing the Royal Air Force*, and as his wingman and a decorated ace, Bill was included as a high-profile representative from the Commonwealth.

The Governor General of Canada was Vincent Massey, and Bill had met him in December 1939 and during Operation Dynamo as part of scheduled media appearances. He had also stayed with Massey and his wife, Alice, on some of his leaves. Massey had a prominent role with cultural institutions in England as he would become the trustee of both the Tate Gallery and the National Gallery from 1941 to 1945.[1] I am not certain whether it was Bader's influence or Massey's that led to Bill's selection as a subject for Kennington and for eventual inclusion in his book. However, the decision to put Bill McKnight's portrait on the cover must surely have been the artist's.

Kennington was an official war artist in both the First and Second World Wars. His works are today housed in Tate Britain, Scotland's National Galleries, the Imperial War Museum and Canada's War Museum, among others.

During the First World War, Kennington had served in the 13th Battalion of the London Regiment. By 1915, he had been invalided back to Britain, but it was not the end of the time he would spend at the Western Front. In 1917, he returned to the blood-soaked battlefields as an official artist.[2] Sir Ronald Storrs described him as 'a soldier painting soldiers'. Kennington recorded many scenes of Canadian soldiers, including during significant battles such as Vimy Ridge, so he had been acquainted with Canadian regiments (including Calgarians) in the war. Battalions from Calgary had been instrumental in securing Vimy Ridge, including the infamous 'Pimple'. So, Kennington knew Canadians, and he likely knew where Calgary was on a map of the Dominion.

Between the wars, Kennington created images that were used in T.E. Lawrence's *The Seven Pillars of Wisdom*. Lawrence proved to be a strong influence in Kennington's life. Lawrence had chosen to make the switch to the RAF from the army, and Kennington followed him.[3] When the Second World

War broke out, it led Kennington to create the RAF portraits that included his likeness of Bill McKnight.

Kennington originally produced a series of pastel portraits of officers in the Royal Navy. The works were created to be used in a Women's Army Auxiliary Corps (WAAC) exhibition in the summer of 1940 at the National Gallery in London. Given Kennington's existing links with the RAF, the portraits that followed that captured the pilots populating the air force were a natural progression.

As we have seen, Bill had participated in several high-profile official photo ops for the RAF. His image had been used for promotion and propaganda alongside others in No. 242 Squadron. Now, he was being selected for the exclusive honour of having his portrait drawn. For Bill to be included alongside such high-ranking personalities as Air Commodore A.H. Orlebar, or wing commanders such as F.V. Beamish and squadron leaders like Douglas Bader was a significant honour.

Portraits took multiple sittings to complete. Kennington's artistic process included the continuous background noise of the radio, which was left on all day to 'kill the silence'.[4] As many of the subjects were pilots who were on active duty, they could be summoned to action in the middle of a sitting. No matter how exclusive the company seemed to be, the men being painted were risking their lives in the dangerous duties that they had taken on. The tension is evident in many of the portraits; the subjects appear distracted, as though their minds are elsewhere. In some sittings, the pilots were waiting to have their machines repaired so that they could return to work, and their minds could not reasonably have been expected to remain in the room.

The portrait rooms were filled with cigarette smoke – everybody smoked at the time. The young men had shortages of cigarettes, earlier shopping hours and closures of cinemas to contend with.[5] War had not only endangered their safety and ended the lives of their friends, but it included inconveniences and disruptions. The little ordinary pleasures of life were harder to come by. Simply living was more difficult in ways seemingly insignificant, but the young men in the sittings referred wistfully or resentfully to those small and outwardly trivial losses.

During the First World War, Kennington's works showed the influence of impressionism, but the works he created for his RAF subjects had a different tone. Artists are influenced by the world around them, and the years between the wars had seen profound changes in the artistic sphere. Artists were questioning and exploring where art itself came from, and this led to explorations of expressionism and surrealism. Was art at its most pure in our early years?

Did it come to us in dreams? Was art at its purest and most original in so-called primitive art created by indigenous artists?

The years between the First and Second World War also saw changes in popular artwork marketed to the masses. The period saw the beginning of twentieth-century consumerism and included in this was mass entertainment. Cinema had become a popular form of enjoyment. Animation and cartoons were introduced in movies from studios like Disney and comic books featuring indestructible heroes became popular with young readers.

In Kennington's RAF portraiture, the influence of comic books is noticeable. Comic book illustrations and cartoons feature exaggerated features, heavy outlines and a separation of the face from the body. Often, the results are overly masculinized or overly feminized. In short, the subjects – like Batman, Superman and their accompanying villains – were not portrayed as human beings. Kennington was creating his moody portraits to appeal to a new audience, a generation of young men who went to animated movies and enjoyed comic books. The aesthetic would appeal to their most heroic and protective instincts. Nevertheless, the portraits do have a personalized look, highlighting the most unique features of the subjects. Each of the men are clearly individuals who have a backstory, as though they had each walked out of a comic book of their own.

Bill does not mention sitting for his portrait in the letters we have. In fact, he also rarely discussed with Mike Peglar the important political figures he had rubbed shoulders with. As the portrait is not dated definitively, it could have been drawn anytime during the dangerous summer and autumn of 1940. An afternoon, frozen in time, and then straight out the door into fire and danger and a world burning, to defend a cause that was far from certain of succeeding.

18 September 1940 – 1 Kill, 1 Shared

No. 242 Squadron and 12 Group Wing patrolled London three times on 18 September. The first two patrols were not noteworthy. It was on their third trip, at approximately 5 p.m., when they were part of a massive group of five fighter squadrons, that they engaged a group of approximately forty enemy Dorniers and 'Junkers'. 'Junkers' seemed to be Bill's all-purpose word for aeroplanes produced by Junker Aircraft and Motorworks; these were Ju 88s, a versatile twin-engine aircraft that were used successfully as night fighters and dive-bombers. The Dorniers, Do 17s, were twin-engine light bombers. The flock of bombers were approaching Hornchurch and undoubtedly en route to the Tilbury Docks. The enemy aeroplanes were flying at 17,000ft when No. 242 Squadron confronted them. Without any escorting fighter protectors, the bombers were easy pickings. The enemy aircraft were attacked from above and behind, the perfect set-up for a bloodbath. Bill's first victim was a Do 17; he circled behind it and closed to a length of between 50 and 70 yards before spraying it with bullets in his classic, three-second-burst style. As an engine ignited, the crew promptly bailed out.[1]

Bill then teamed up with a Spitfire to harass one of the Ju 88s. They shot at it and watched as both engines failed.[2] Again, the parachutes ballooned as the crew abandoned their disintegrating aeroplane. It was a sight that had become increasingly common as pilots and crews of enemy aircraft were deserting their crumbling aeroplanes in a wild gamble for survival. If they made it back to earth, they faced the prospect of capture and imprisonment for a very indeterminate period.

And that was if they made it to the ground at all. This didn't always happen. During a Ministry of Information broadcast, Douglas Bader spoke of witnessing the consequences when parachute jumps went wrong:

> One unfortunate German rear-gunner baled out of the Do 17 I attacked, but his parachute caught on the tail. There he was,

> swinging helplessly, with the aircraft swooping and diving and staggering all over the sky, being pulled about by the man hanging by his parachute to the tail. That bomber went crashing into the Thames Estuary, with the swinging gunner still there.[3]

It was horrifying to picture a man being hauled to his death, fully conscious, in a most terrifying and painful way, a way that surely no human ever deserved to die.

It was not only the Germans who had to bail out. How to bail out of a Hurricane? Well, the most common way was to strip off the oxygen mask and radio equipment, undo the seatbelt, open the breakaway door located next to the right elbow, kicking it out of the way if necessary. Stand up on the seat, and – jump on out of there. The tail of the Hurricane was directly behind. Travelling at 300mph, all one could hope was not to hit it on the way past. This did happen. But if all went well, you and your aeroplane parted ways, the growling of the Merlin engines falling away as you separated into the loud, silent cold of the sky, potentially with other people's aircraft still darting around you. Now you were airborne, floating, or hurtling, towards the ground, or the sea. A strong, reassuring, but aggressive jerk as the parachute filled with air behind you.

This is the most positive scenario, not accounting for the fact that the pilot was leaving that aircraft for a reason. The rumour was, if you bailed out and your parachute didn't open, you would stay conscious until you hit the ground, knowing until the last possible moment that you were going to die.

Sometimes the pilots were wounded, as well as the aeroplane. Conceivably the engines had failed, and quite possibly they had caught on fire. Fuel tanks on the Hurricane were located in the wings, and they were sealed with a foam that would expand to seal leaks if a bullet should happen to pierce them. This sort of worked. There was another fuel tank located in the fuselage, just above the pilot's feet, just below their face. The cockpit could fill with fire instantly. No time to do anything. Burning, burning, burning to death. Extinguished by the cold, final slap of the waves of the Channel. Or, somehow, if survived, the face erased, describing wordlessly what had happened. Hair, eyebrows, eyelashes that never grew again. Ears burned away. The texture of the face a smooth, expressionless parchment.

Human faces have forty-three intricate muscles that convey a tremendous amount of information to other humans. They are flirting with us, and we are flirting back. A scowl; they disapprove. The words are harsh, but there is a quirk at the corner of their mouth that tells us that they are trying not to laugh. Some of our expressions have been passed down to us for generations, a unique signature of our family, even if we don't recognise it. All deleted by a few seconds of inferno.

The 18 September battle was claimed as another terrific performance; almost every enemy aircraft in the formation was reported as destroyed.[4] In addition to Bill's wins, Campbell, Tamblyn and Hart all had conquests of their own to celebrate, and in rolled the congratulations for the Big Wing's performance. But there were other squadrons working just as hard, and they were not receiving the same amount of admiration or thanks for their work.[5] The propaganda squadron was doing its job.

The 18 September 1940 marked the date of the last joint kill for Bill and his Hurricane LE-A .

Meanwhile, the squadron adjutant, Peter MacDonald, was up to his old tricks of throwing his leaders under the bus. He had nothing to say in support of Squadron Leader Gobeil when he was embattled. This time, he was prepared to stab Air Chief Marshal Dowding and Air Chief Marshal Park in the back, using his influence as a sitting Member of Parliament to seek an audience with no less a figure than Winston Churchill. MacDonald laid out his arguments about the ineffectiveness of the cautious battle plan that was being managed by Dowding and Park and pointed to the enormous, apparent successes of the Big Wing. Churchill was listening. MacDonald's interference was going to have consequences both for the leaders and for those doing the fighting – including Bill himself.[6]

On 19 September, Bill's logbook reported one sweep over London along with the rest of the Big Wing. It was uneventful.

The German invasion of Britain had failed. The plans were shelved for the moment, put off until the spring that Bill would not live to see. However, modern warfare had introduced a new and cruel concept that dictated that it was not essential to win battles to win wars. The other thing that could happen was that the price you exacted from your enemy could be so terrible that they would no longer be willing to fight you. That meant that while the Germans had given up on an invasion – for now – their tactics had switched to night bombing raids that were meant to exhaust, terrify and cause great numbers of civilian casualties. The RAF had not yet developed radar that could be fitted into aircraft, and they were nearly defenceless against the night bombers and their nocturnal raids of terror.[7]

German aircraft were intentionally and indiscriminately targeting men, women and children who were going about their ordinary lives. It seemed that a new low had been achieved in the shameful traditions of war. Ironically, it seemed that both sides were prepared to target each other's civilian populations, and indeed, Bomber Command would continue to do this until the very last day of the Second World War.

'Until the end ... Or the other end'

Bill wrote his final letter to Mike Peglar on 22 September 1940, speaking with respect for the courage and resolve of the English people. He talked about how meaningful it was to protect them; they were his own people, more or less. He stated that he had 'thoroughly enjoyed' the fighting. (Contemporary gamers tell us that zooming around and shooting at things is fun; it sounds like it can be rather fun in real life, too.) Bill did not mention Douglas Bader by name but did reference that his squadron commander has been awarded the Distinguished Service Order.[1] A Distinguished Flying Cross was also being awarded to Flight Lieutenant Ball.

Professionally, morale was vastly improved since the previous letter in July, written while Bill was in hospital. Perhaps it was the Bader Effect. A leader who projected assurance and confidence had brought success and high praise to the squadron. Bader did possess an authoritative presence that felt paternal and reassuring – in a supportive way. Pilot Officer Denis Crowley-Milling had once remarked, 'You always felt perfectly safe when flying with Douglas Bader.'[2]

Advancements for both Bill and Stan Turner were incoming; they were both being promoted to flying officers. Bill didn't mention his own award to Mike, but a bar was being added to his Distinguished Flying Cross. He sounded businesslike and proud of the solid accomplishments of No. 242 Squadron. The fact that their casualties had now been minimized must have gone a long way towards the lift in his spirits after the brutal losses at Dunkirk and during the fall of France. He reported that the squadron had lost only two pilots in the last three months, in contrast to most of the squadron being decimated earlier in the year.

However, he admitted that the close calls had continued. They had included Ball being shot down in flames, Crowley-Milling's engine being blown away by cannon and two other pilots bailing out. Bill concluded his recounts of Ball and Crowley-Milling's misadventures with the phrase 'but [he] got away with it'.[3]

Bailing out over home soil was a different story from the guaranteed captivity awaiting the Germans who had to bail out over enemy territory. Losing machines was one thing, losing people was another. As for himself, Bill reflected that Lady Luck must be his permanent passenger, an essential addition to the cockpit of the Hurricane that had absolutely no room for travelers. He then went on to reference being shot up on three occasions. They were terrifying stories that emphasized the razor-thin margin between existence and disaster. The very, very close calls that he personally had experienced. He was lucky, yes, but immediately one thinks, Bill, that luck is going to run out, it is inevitable. It does not sound like luck. It sounds like it is just a matter of time.

While Bill didn't brag about his own achievements, he did not exactly downplay them either, reporting his own twenty-one 'confirmed' kills.

He gossiped about mutual acquaintances, and he talked a great deal about Calgary. He mentioned that he only heard regularly from two old friends. His life as influencer and a celebrity meant, as some influencers today have also discovered, that sometimes, even when it seems like everyone knows who you are, you are alone. Bill had met the King, but what he needed and wanted was a bundle of letters waiting for him every night.

Bill was reflective and thoughtful as the Battle of Britain was winding down. He had choices to make as he had been offered a job as a flight instructor back in Canada if he wanted one, but he said that he intended to stay in England.[4] He knew that he would not be a good fit for civilian life after the victories and thrills of his dangerous job in the RAF.

Bill could indeed have left the dangerous work that he was doing for a job as a flight instructor, and he could have potentially gone back to Calgary. The Department of Transportation had taken control of Calgary's airfields after Canada had entered the war the previous September. No. 31 Elementary Flight School was already open at the Calgary Municipal Airport, using Tiger Moths as their trainers.[5] The British Commonwealth Air Training Plan (BCATP) was expanding in western Canada, with four more airfields being constructed near Calgary during the tail end of the violent first summer of the Second World War. Flying schools were being officially planned for High River and Penhold, with other locations yet to be selected.[6]

Bill McKnight would have been welcome as an experienced combat pilot, and a celebrity no less, at any of them. After leaving Alberta under rather dubious circumstances, he was now a catch for any job with aviation that he wanted to do, either in Canada or Britain, and there were many roles available. He had legitimate choices, and they would all be honourable, good for his career and valuable for the war effort. He had proven his courage, his worth and value. But offered the chance to return home – to relative safety, and a chance at a new life – he said no.

Not everyone is cut out to be a leader, and getting to know your interests and strengths is an important part of young adulthood. And while leadership is a skill that can be acquired, Bill did not have the interest. Perhaps this aversion accounted at least in part for turning down the offers for employment as a flight instructor. Bill's entire career had amounted to being a little brat among a gaggle of other little brats, all committed to making life hell for The Man in charge (the teacher or the unfortunate middle manager who had little to no power themselves). And while he had grown up considerably over the last six months, perhaps the prospect of standing in front of a room of twenty or thirty new recruits would have cast Bill in the role of The Man. It had no appeal for him. He had long said he was happiest flying as a number one – and in the position he liked, he was the best of anyone.[7]

Bill's parents and siblings had moved earlier that year, leaving the childhood home full of memories in Crescent Heights. They were now living on Garden Crescent in the fashionable Elbow Park neighbourhood of Calgary. His friends and classmates were getting on with their lives. He was discovering that he did not have many close relationships. Life, as it does, moved on. Changed. Leaving things, and him, behind. There was an observable pattern of people moving away from him. Bill's was a story winding down before it really had a chance to get going. He was choosing not to move forward. He did not see a future, a path to continue.

As for Calgary, 'the old burg', he claimed that he was avoiding being 'nostalgic' and 'homesick' when in fact he was a little of both. He hankered for a slice of Ma Riley's chocolate cake, promised to come to Mike and Olive's wedding, fantasized about taking in a football game, and imagined driving along the newly opened Banff to Jasper highway through the loveliness of the Rocky Mountains.[8]

He was open to, even looking forward to, the visit.

But a visit was all it was going to be.

Because he did not fit in in Calgary, and he never had.

Bill had arrived in Britain seventeen months before, fleeing a failure at university, the stepmother he did not like, the anger and frustration of his father and the end of his relationship with Marian. Quiet, civilian life had not suited him at the time. He saw that people were profoundly transformed by war and by the constant 'dicing with death'. If he were to return to Canada, his fractured relationships and the ennui of life in a little prairie town were waiting for him.

A year before, he had figured out zero per cent of his life. Now, a year later, he had his career sorted, and it had brought promotions, medals, success and even celebrity. But he was the same old Bill, with all the same old problems. He had it all looking from the outside, but he knew that it didn't matter. His tone, aside from describing what was happening with his squadron, was flat. There was no momentum to his story that could lift it or change the trajectory. He was someone who acknowledged that his career path was potentially suicide, and he seemed to be okay with that.

It is ominous to witness the increasing maturity of this man, and his simultaneous heartbreaking youth, expressed in the longing for friends, and cake, and home. But offered the choice between life and death, he chooses death.

It was the last letter to Mike, and now the story accelerated, with Bill committed to remaining in Britain 'until the end … or the other end'.[9]

8 October 1940 - Bar to the DFC

Bill spent the rest of September flying a succession of Hurricanes that were not LE-A, and a Magister. LE-A was evidently in the Hurricane version of the hospital for some much-needed medical attention. Bill missed the excitement of 27 September entirely, when the rest of the Big Wing took on a vast flock of German fighters over Dover and Canterbury.[1]

Bill reported local flying on 28 September, but poor visibility created the conditions for an uneventful outing for everyone, and anyway, he was flying the Magister. LE-A was back in action the next day, but between the bad weather conditions and the Luftwaffe's daylight raids being drastically scaled back, October was rolling in with a different quality to the frenzied do or die momentum of the two preceding months.

It was not only LE-A that needed a break. Bill was given time off, recording no flights between 9 and 26 October. Perhaps his injured knee was the reason for the downtime.[2]

Bill reported over 700 logged hours of flying as September wound down; half of those hours had been spent in Hurricanes. The aircraft that he had airily dismissed as obsolete in the summer of 1939 had earned his respect and he now ungrudgingly called them 'the best fighter in the service'.[3] '[N]ot even barring the "much talked about but never there when needed" Spitfires,' he added ruefully.

This should have been downtime, but the period was remembered as the most exhausting phase of all. Just when everyone was at their most fatigued and the end seemed to be in sight, additional gears had to be found. Anyone who has watched a football game where it seemed that one team has definitively won a game with three to five minutes left on the clock can relate to how badly wrong that can go, with the losing team suddenly digging deep and staging an impressive and terrifying comeback. Guarding against this, the repetitive and boring standing patrols were endless.

Bill remarked that the damage the Luftwaffe had been able to inflict had ultimately been quite negligible given the thousands of pounds of bombs that they had dropped. As for the morale of the people, he thought that the different classes of English society had actually been drawn together by the raids rather than separated as had perhaps been the enemy's intent.[4]

There was an echo of Gobeil for Bill early in October. The Royal Air Force and the Royal Canadian Air Force were still following up on the events that had led to Gobeil's dismissal, and 1 October 1940 saw Bill and other No. 242 Squadron pilots – those who had known Gobeil who were still living, at least – filling out paperwork that asked them to recall if Gobeil had shot down any enemy aircraft. Bill filled out the form stating that to the best of his recollection his former commander had shot down one aircraft over Dunkirk.

In the meantime, in the very midst of all the drama and trauma and destruction, there came big milestones to celebrate. Bill – and others of No. 242 Squadron – were going to meet the King (and in the case of Bill, meet the King again). His citation published in *The London Gazette* read:

> Bar to Distinguished Flying Cross – October 8th, 1940
>
> This officer has destroyed six enemy aircraft during the last thirteen weeks. He has proven himself to be a most efficient section leader, and has consistently given proof that he is a most courageous and tenacious fighter.

Awards and accolades were incoming for other members of the squadron as well.

'Ace Scores Again!' reported the *Calgary Herald* triumphantly on 4 October in advance of the honours. 'Calgarian believed first for the D. F. C. Bar', added the sub-heading. 'Canadian Aces Honoured for Daring!' caroled the Toronto *Star,* proudly saluting Turner, Stansfield and Bill. On 5 October, the *Daily Mirror* in London had some fawning praise for Turner who, while he could be notably prickly, richly deserved it. 'Although his own fighter plane was knocked out of control by a cannon shell, Acting Flight Lieutenant Percival Stanley Turner got his gunsights on to a German machine and shot it down,' it reported admiringly, adding, 'Acting Flight Lieutenant Turner, whose "bag" is now ten enemy aircraft, figures in the latest list of R.A.F. awards. He gets the Distinguished Flying Cross.'[5] The same story also acknowledged Bill, mentioning his bar.

Ball, Stansfeld, and Stan Turner were all decorated with their Distinguished Flying Crosses on 8 October, while Bader was awarded the Distinguished

Service Order. And there was another honour for Bill, a bar to attach to his Distinguished Flying Cross. It must have been a proud day for Bader as he reflected on the accomplishments and hard work of his squadron. They were proud of him, too.

Once Bill was back in action, on 29 October the three-squadron Big Wing was prowling over Maidstone on patrol; they flew over twice, without incident. Then they were scrambled at 4.15 p.m. to intercept two parties of raiders headed for Sheerness. Two 11 Group squadrons were also scrambled, but the targets at North Weald were bombed before anyone could intercept them.[6]

Two days later, the Battle of Britain unofficially – and officially – ended.

Bill had made it. He had survived.

5 November 1940 - Final Victory

In Calgary, the November society pages noted that there were multiple bridal showers being held in honour of Miss Marian Glover, who was to be married to Carl Jones at the end of the month.[1] Carl was the chief ground instructor at the Lethbridge Flying Training School, No. 5 EFTS. The couple were planning a Vancouver honeymoon, returning by aeroplane, and were planning to live in Lethbridge after their marriage.[2]

Bill had known about the engagement for weeks. He had been blindsided but claimed that he had lost interest months before. He still remembered Marian as the most beautiful girl he had ever seen. He also knew that she had profoundly influenced his life. He had come to Britain because of her, or so he would claim. He thought that he was a more well-rounded person, more broad-minded and educated, because of his experiences. In a mature and measured way, he had asked Mike Peglar to give Marian his congratulations and good wishes. More of the threads that connected him to Calgary were being sliced away, and his indifference to the job offer to train other young pilots had taken on yet another dimension.[3]

The official date that historians agree on for the end of the Battle of Britain was 31 October 1940, when the Luftwaffe shifted their tactics to miserable night bombing raids. As November began, duties for No. 242 Squadron meant regular patrols, with Bill recording beats near Maidstone and Sheerness early in the month. The night bombing raids neutralized the effectiveness of the Hurricane squadrons; they could provide protection for the daytime forays, however. The Luftwaffe were trying to use their Bf 109s to bomb the British coasts, but they were more of an irritation than anything.[4]

It was while on patrol on 5 November that Bill scored his final victory during precisely such a raid, shooting down a pilot called Erhard Scheidt while making the rounds near Thames Estuary. The battle occurred around 6.15 p.m. when a group of approximately thirty enemy aircraft, flying very high at 26,000ft in small groups of three, were spotted by the 12 Group Wing.[5]

Bill responded immediately, climbing sharply to alert the leader, and then tried to scramble up to the enemy's height. He reported that he was unable to do so.[6] The fact of the matter was that the Hurricane's many strengths were being severely tested by this stage of the war. The Mk I was an extremely tough and reliable aircraft that had abilities and skills that the graceful and swift but more delicate Spitfires did not possess. However, the new height requirements of battle were now stressing the Hurricanes to the point of failure. As the war went on, they simply could not mount up to the summits of 25,000ft that were becoming the standard requirements. The Hurricanes were becoming the underdogs. 'Attempted to climb up to carry out attacks but was useless,' Bill wrote in his Combat Report for that day. Bill also reported that his windscreen was alternately icing and fogging up, causing understandable difficulty in aiming.[7]

Then a Bf 109 unwisely decided to pick on the guy flying the tired old Hurricane and dropped out of the sky to confront him. Bill shot at it from 150 yards and saw smoke rise from the aeroplane; Bill's Hurricane was sprayed with oil leaking from the disintegrating fighter. Bill waggled his wings at the pilot, signalling him to land.[8] Instead, Scheidt bailed out and was captured shortly afterwards, spending the rest of the war as a prisoner.

The events of that day were officially awarded as a half claim for Bill, shared with Flying Officer L.A. Haines of No. 19 Squadron. The Big Wing had developed into a good team.

The battle had been ferocious, and it had proven costly. Squadron Sub-Lieutenant Gardner was forced to land his badly injured Hurricane after it had been shot up, and Pilot Officer Hart had been killed.[9]

Every engagement concluded with calculating the tallies.

The wins.

The losses.

19 November - Emergency Jump By Parachute

There was still work to do. There were convoy patrols almost every day, and local flying. Between the battle on 6 November and writing off an aeroplane, Bill managed to have an eventful month. The day after the battle in which he had shot down his last Bf 109, Bill and the rest of No. 242 Squadron were playing darts at Duxford with Guy Mayfield.[1]

The next step for the Luftwaffe was to continue the exhausting night bombing raids, but there wasn't much No. 242 Squadron could do about that. The Hurricanes were not suited to flying in the darkness and night fighting was not a skill their air force had acquired yet. They were hawks; now the battle needed owls. Only Bader, Stan Turner and Ball were night operational.

Overnight on 14–15 November, assisted by radio wave technology, the Luftwaffe stalked over 12 Group territory – and they bombed the city of Coventry to bits. The raid lasted eleven hours and involved nearly 500 Luftwaffe bombers. It was the most concentrated aerial assault on a British city during the Second World War. During the raid, the Luftwaffe deployed 500 tons of high explosives, 30,000 incendiaries, and 50 landmines, and they tested out a new device: the exploding incendiary.[2]

While the primary objective was to incapacitate Coventry as a centre of war production, the city suffered extensive losses, including the destruction of St Michael's Church, along with the central library, market hall, numerous shops and public buildings. Casualty estimates indicate that approximately 568 people lost their lives, and a further 863 were seriously injured. In the aftermath, German propagandists introduced the term '*coventrieren*' to describe the complete and utter destruction of a city.[3] The bombing of Coventry would be used as justification by Bomber Command to target civilians in German cities for the next four and a half years.

Bader, Turner and Ball were patrolling that night. They knew that predators were moving about them through the darkness, but they didn't spot the enemy bombers.[4] Bill had mentioned how much he did not like flying at night. It seems that even Bill McKnight drew a line at dangerous stunts, and it came with flying at 300mph in blackout conditions.[5]

Bill's Hurricane LE-A must have been in for badly needed repairs and maintenance again after months of unbelievable strain, because he spent most of November flying Magisters and other Hurricanes. It was not only the pilots who had taken a serious beating over the last six months of battle, hard and near continuous work. The aeroplanes needed serious attention, too. In fact, for his last kill Bill was flying Hurricane LE-E, not his renowned LE-A teammate.

On 19 November, the day after his twenty-second birthday, Bill finally did write off an aircraft, a Magister, when he had to bail out, an emergency jump by parachute for which he was reprimanded. Ironically, the dramatic event did not occur in a violent battle, but because of bad weather, and perhaps his own overconfidence. He had recorded five and a half hours of flying in the Magister that day and the notation from his logbook for 19 November 1940 reads: 'This officer was guilty of carelessness 19.11.1940 in that he failed to obtain a weather report prior to taking off for to return to Duxford with the results that he had to bale out and the aircraft destroyed.'[6] He had lost visibility and could not find Duxford, nor any other place to land.

It was 26 November before Bill was reunited with his old friend, LE-A, the leering image of death itself sneering along the flanks.

For the moment, he was alive and unharmed.

The Reaper is always pointing, selecting, only ever delaying, never deterred. Someday, its ghoulish exacting finger will turn to you.

For now, it bided its time.

Meanwhile, the blue and red and green Christmas lights were blazing through the darkness of the late autumn evenings in Calgary when, four days later, clad in shimmering satin and lace, Marian Glover married Carl Jones on 30 November. Over 100 guests, including out-of-towners, travelled to Saint Michael's church for the ceremony. A reception was held at the American Women's Club afterwards.[7]

I had to go to London town,
To buy my girl a London gown,
So merrily I strode along
And passed the time away with song,

I sang my way to London town
With 'London bridge is falling down.'

In London town the houses stood
Like skeletons of brick and wood:
Dead houses with the bones picked bare
By hungry vultures of the air.
And not a child in London town
Sang 'London bridge is falling down.'

The bombs, that fell so thick and fast,
Ripped off the trappings of the past;
While prince and peasant side by side
For England's freedom fought and died
In London town, in London town,
Lest London bridge should tumble down.

I could not buy my girl a gown
In London town, in London town.
But I shall send to her a snood
Of bandages for spinsterhood –
A snood to bind her tresses brown,
A crimsoned snood from London town.

For I shall stay among the crowds,
Where Death dives shrieking from the clouds
On London town to snatch away
From children's lips a song so gay,
And I shall die in London Town,
To keep the bridge from falling down.

Charles G. Crellin

Winter

Fast away the old year passes. Even the violent bloodbath that had been 1940 was temporary, it turned out.

On 29 November, No. 242 Squadron hosted a party at Duxford. Stan Turner tried to make merry, drumming in the halls; the party purportedly made more noise than any real excitement.[1] Instead of dispersing to enjoy their various Christmas holiday plans, two days later everyone was still at Duxford, stranded by the downturn in the weather.

Bill reported limited flying during the month of December. He had blocks of well-deserved leaves to rest, relax and heal as the final weeks of 1940 faded into oblivion. The logbook recorded the infinite, inevitable patrols when he was airborne, but his flying hours were limited. Somehow, he had against every odd and every chance and every danger kept himself alive through one of the deadliest years that human history had ever recorded. By wits and by luck he had made it through the Battle of France, Dunkirk, the fall of France, and the Battle of Britain. Fortune had seen him through; his own instincts and reactions had protected him. It was the political machine, and the next decisions of the people in charge, that were going to shape his fate now.

No. 242 Squadron relocated to Martlesham Health in Suffolk on 12 December; Bill recorded a flight with LE-A 'to Duxford and return'. There was no way he could have known that the clock had started on the last month of his life.

Martlesham Health put No. 242 Squadron in the heart of 11 Group territory. Now that the Battle of Britain was over, they were the bullseye. This was a nod to their boss. Bader had impressed his commanders. And they were new bosses – Dowding had been replaced as Commander-in-Chief of Fighter Command, and Leigh-Mallory was now the Air Vice-Marshal. The new leaders were very familiar with the Bader Big Wing, and they intended to put it to use. So far, the conservative old guys had been plotting the course of the war. Now the younger officers wanted to put their ideas into practice.[2]

Bill recorded no flying on 20 December, but something happened that day that, while it seemed unrelated to him, was going to have an impact on his life, and ultimately his death. Two pilots from No. 66 Squadron spanned the English Channel under orders to try out a new offensive strategy, a sweep along the coast of France.[3] The nuisance raiders were now going to be coming from the RAF, and they were under orders to harass the enemy in France and in Belgium. The new operations were called 'Mosquitoes' and later 'Rhubarbs'.

More photographs were taken; this time Bill posed with LE-A. The Hurricane behind him in those images was beat up, the paint stripped off it in places. It looked good, but only if you didn't look too closely. The Hurricane looked like it had been through one of the violent prairie hailstorms that passed through the Calgary area. Balls of ice the size of marbles, golf balls and occasionally even baseballs dented solid metal, smashed glass, gardens and crops and stripped away paint in a matter of minutes, and then floated away, leaving devastation in their wake.

Hailstorms versus Hurricanes. And, of course, there hadn't been a hailstorm.

We don't know where Bill spent his last Christmas. Possibly with his father's Scottish family as his Aunty Jean lived near Glasgow. While *Tuxedo Junction* by the Glenn Miller band and *I'll Never Smile Again* by Tommy Dorsey had been chart toppers in 1940, Bill loved the sentimental music of Bing Crosby and owned every record. Crosby had a smash hit with *Only Forever* in 1940. Crosby was The Weeknd or Taylor Swift of his generation; he was a hit machine and his romantic songs and poetic voice were often heard floating through the rooms where Bill McKnight was reading comics, filling out his paperwork or otherwise enjoying his downtime.

Understandably, there were some who felt that there was nothing to sing about at the New Year Party to celebrate 1941. *Auld Lang Syne* rang hollow when so many acquaintances were lost. Who could remember, and who could forget. Even for people who never doubted for a moment that they would ultimately prevail, hearts were heavy as they contemplated the future. Because there could be no doubt or denial now. There would be a terrible, ongoing price to be paid. Spring would be a time of renewal – of horror, and now there were rumours that the Germans would use gas.[4]

Even before the Battle of Britain, Bill had noticed changes in his own outlook. There was a maturity to his words and thoughts in July 1940 as he lay helplessly in a hospital, sick himself and reflecting on the fate of his young friends from the original No. 242 Squadron. And really, the losses had been total, because even the young men who were still physically alive were not the same people they had been before the combat started.

> We've only got five of the original twenty-two pilots in the squadron left now and those of us who are left aren't quite the same blokes as before. Its peculiar but war seems to make you older and quieter and changes your views a lot on life – you also find out who are the blokes worth knowing and who aren't and I haven't met one yet who wasn't worth knowing.[5]

Anyone who has sat with an older person who has recently attended a string of funerals has felt the heaviness of witnessing someone who is saying goodbye to a lifetime's worth of friends. The social events of the seasons have progressed from graduations, weddings and christenings to burials, and the unavoidable reality is that this person's own funeral is in the not-too-distant future. It is a certainty of aging, a developmental norm for an eighty-year-old. Bill was experiencing this at twenty-two. He was older and quieter and there was a gentleness in his tone as he remembered the good people who had been lost.[6]

The words of the Scottish poet Robert Burns that welcomes in the New Year all over the world must have had a particular poignancy as 1940 died away. *Auld Lang Syne* can be rousing and boisterous, but the old song also has a wistfulness. It reflects on old mates who have separated by great distances and by long periods of time. To drink the health is meant to be to a reunion with the person across from you, instead of a circle of invisible, absent friends.

> Should auld acquaintance be forgot,
> And never brought to mind?
> Should auld acquaintance be forgot,
> And auld lang syne!
>
> For auld lang syne, my dear,
> For auld lang syne.
> We'll tak a cup o' kindness yet,
> For auld lang syne.

As the New Year dawned, the first few days of 1941 introduced one of the coldest starts to a New Year on record, with a high-pressure ridge sloping down from Scandinavia, bringing snow and bitter cold. A temperature of -20 doesn't really do anything in Canada; everything keeps right on running in those conditions.

It is just … Tuesday. But even for the Canadians, these temperatures had to be respected. The pilots shrugged into their thick winter bomber jackets and turned up the collars, the grounding scent of lanolin from the warm sheepskin accompanying them as they walked out into the frigid mornings.

January brought its own tasks; however cold it was, after the holidays, it was time to get on with things.

And there were things to look forward to including a rather big occasion; the King and Queen were expected to visit Duxford for lunch on 16 January.

For the pilots, there was the new offensive Mosquito strategy to be implemented more widely.

Bill had twelve days left.

12 January 1941

It is my strong feeling that the RAF would have had the toughest time getting Gobeil to participate in Mosquitos. At this point in this narrative, my readers will likely realize that usually means that something senseless and predictable is about to happen.

Mosquitos were Leigh-Mallory's idea. The lesson learned at the Luftwaffe's expense in the Battle of Britain was that flying fighter-escorted bombers deep into enemy territory – even if you vastly outnumbered them – was costly and unsuccessful. Now that the German invasion had been thwarted, the RAF was contemplating how it could continue to fly in a meaningful way as it waited and gathered strength for an eventual invasion of its own. For now, low-level ventures into occupied enemy territory to shoot up arbitrary targets by pairs or small groups of up to four fighters were being pitched.

If it has the look and sound of a suicide mission, does that mean it is a suicide mission?

It is the bomber that is the offensive tool of an air force. Fighters are defensive weapons. Offensive missions are not their strength, nor was it the forte of their pilots, who were also defensive players. During the Battle of Britain, the Germans had been the ones who had to cross the Channel, managing their fuel resources carefully, and they had been the ones to take the risks of having to bale out over enemy territory, facing indefinite imprisonment if they were captured. However, those risks had been taken as part of their offensive battle plan to occupy Britain. Now, the RAF had decided to replicate some of the offensive conditions for their own pilots, but without the same strategic goal. And, unlike the Germans, who aside from the 'nuisance raids' had usually been airborne in large hunting packs, the Mosquito patrols were to be composed of small groups or pairs of fighters, flying alone and isolated over enemy territory.

As someone entirely outside of military history strategy, I cannot fathom why Mosquitos were ever permitted. They sound as though they were extremely perilous, and they had no real observable purpose, aside from messing around with the Germans. They involved flying at low altitude along the Belgian or French coast. There was no specific information being gathered or targets that were selected. It was low-hanging fruit that was being looked for. The reality was that it was the pilots flying these missions who were the low-hanging fruit.[1]

This dangerous mission appealed to Leigh-Mallory; the Royal Air Force was shifting into an offensive strategy, and it tempted Bader, too. Bader was a brave man, and he could not tolerate boredom. He was willing to get his hands dirty; he was doing the job; he was not a pen pusher sitting in the safety and climate-controlled conditions of an office. He flew the first of No. 242 Squadron's Mosquitos, for it was he and Sargent Richardson who went to raiding to France on 9 January. They returned safely, but also without having done any damage to any enemy targets.

Bill flew out on an offensive patrol to Calais for the first time on 10 January; he did not report any attacks made.[2]

Mosquitos would quickly prove how deadly they were. By the end of the day on 12 January, the date scheduled for the true roll-out of the new offensive strategy, they would all find out. And that day's events generated a lot of paperwork for the people who survived them.

Three Mosquitos were organised for No. 242 Squadron. Bader and Stan Turner flew out at 10.20 a.m. that morning from RAF Martlesham Heath, through cloud hovering at around 600ft, forcing them to fly close to ground level on the French side of the Channel. They headed for the French coast east of Dunkirk, where they attacked an E-boat twice, then returned to England, the patrol taking a little over an hour total, from 10.20 a.m. to 11.30 a.m.[3]

While Bader and Stan Turner flew out for the first Mosquito of the day, Bill was getting ready to fly out on his own patrol. He tossed his logbook on the table; it was later updated for that day, recording a Mosquito patrol. '"E" Boat and troops strafed with PO Brown' was written in a different hand.

Bill gathered his belongings. For the last time, he banged the lid shut over his heavy Royal Air Force trunk, the annoying shelves intended to hold shoes and toiletries threatening, as always, to tumble out before the top swung closed. He shrugged into his sheepskin-lined bomber jacket, turning the collar up against the cold. He and Marvin Brown could see their breath clouding in the air as they walked out into the courtyard. Waving goodbye to Noel Barlow, they strode across the frozen tundra of the grass airfield to where four Hurricanes had been assembled. Pilot Officers Hugh Tamblyn and Bruce Rogers were coming along. Bill was wondering vaguely what supper would be. Perhaps there was the hopeful prospect of a decent bowl of soup and fresh bread to look forward to instead of the house speciality – the unlimited, lifetime supply of cooked to death vegetables smothered in ketchup. He pulled his goggles down over his eyes. His feet, attached to the short, aching legs, walked along the strong wing of LE-A. The sturdy wings of the Hurricane that had supported and lifted him for so long did not vibrate rhythmically with his footfalls. They were too heavy to move under the weight of a man, and a rather slight man at that. They throbbed to the Merlin engines thrumming them in non-musical growls.

With the Rolls-Royce Merlin engine roaring, the Hurricane hurled itself down the runway. Bill gunned its engine, aiming into the headwind. The solid wings and powerful engine lifted it into the sky as Bill drew back on his stick. The ground fell inevitably away.

The Reaper had long waited quietly, sensed, but silent. Unseen by anyone, it had turned its exacting, irresistible, selecting finger at last.

Mosquito

The weather was rather good for a cold winter day along the French coast by the time the second group flew out on their patrol, with fine visibility. Below the Hurricanes, the slate grey water of the Channel tumbled, with silver highlights slanting from its cold, rough surface. Off Gravelines, Tamblyn and Rogers broke away. They turned north, flying east of Dunkirk, where they found and shot up a large flat boat and a small trawler with a machine gun mounted to it. There was no observable effect, so they turned back for another sweep past Dunkirk and then headed for home.[1]

The last person to see Bill alive was Marvin Brown.

After the pair separated from Tamblyn and Rogers, they had turned south and attacked an E-boat; their bullets hit it, and Brown saw that it was heading for the shore. He also reported that they were being sprayed with 'accurate and effective' flak coming from other ships moored offshore. Both Hurricanes turned away and crossed the coast at Gravelines. They strafed at a concentration of enemy troops that were near the beach, although they didn't notice whether the attack had any effect. Bill was flying 800 yards ahead of Brown when a Bf 109 dropped down behind them from a height of about 200ft. Brown immediately evaded and turned for home, flying over the enemy troops for a second pass on his way out.[2] Brown said that he had looked over and Bill was flying ahead of him. The next time he looked, Bill was gone.[3]

Having no idea what had just happened, a third flight took off for the French coast at 1.25 p.m. This time, Flying Officers Cryderman, Arthur, Latta and Edmonds were headed for the Dunkirk area. They met with 'substantial flak' and 'flaming onions' when they arrived – perhaps the enemy was increasing their anti-aircraft fire after the two previous attacks, making the sky even more deadly for the Hurricanes. As both pairs flew eastwards along the coast, Cryderman saw a Bf 109 with a yellow nose approaching. He took evasive action into the clouds; when he reappeared, he had been separated from the other three Hurricanes. Arthur stayed with the other pair of Hurricanes, and they sailed together towards Calais. Arthur saw a Bf 109 below and behind the other Hurricanes, and climbing for a better position, he soared into the clouds preparing to attack it. But when he dropped down, both the Hurricanes and the Bf 109 had disappeared. Edmonds also took evasive action once he heard the warning; he met the enemy aircraft in a head-on attack and fired at it but did not notice any result. When Edmonds returned to base, he realized that his own aircraft had been struck by bullets. At the time, he had not even noticed.[4]

Another person did not return from that Mosquito patrol when expected: John Latta. Latta was also an ace and had been awarded a Distinguished Flying Cross. Both he and Bill were experienced combat pilots; they were not the kinds of people who the RAF could not afford to lose. Neither of them had returned to base by 5 p.m.

By then, they were presumed missing, and the squadron entered a tense waiting phase of hoping against hope that the telephone would jangle on the wall, with a voice on the other end informing them that one or the other of the missing pilots – or, against all odds, both – were being held as prisoners of war or had been rescued from the cold sea.

That night, two young faces were missing from the tight-knit and rapidly dwindling members of the original No. 242 Squadron. It must have been a heartrending evening for Stan Turner, who had been through this awful experience so many times before. After the war, he remembered the day's events this way:

> Most of the boys who fought in the Battle of France are dead. There was Willy McKnight, who was my roommate. We used to do these things, these were attacks, that we were making on the French inland about five or ten miles, but only in very bad weather. The cloud base was only a couple of hundred feet and [it] was raining or something like that. We would go in twos and shoot up anything in sight.
>
> When we got over there, Willy was over there one day with his Number Two, Number Two lost him in low cloud, came out of the cloud and saw some 109s heading in the general direction where we had last seen Willy and that was the last we had ever seen of Willy.[5]

What was going through Bader's mind as he filled out the mandatory paperwork? Did he question himself in any way, or was it too soon to panic? Were losses just an expected part of this awful job, and you had to discipline yourself to expect them? Did the dark question of who was to blame for this calamity cross his mind? Or was it only the war, the enemy, and the Reaper?

The planned visit of the King and Queen now had a deep and dark shadow across it.

Official documentation was only one aspect of record keeping. Guy Mayfield had his personal journal, and it offered another perspective from the fact-based, who-what-where-when structure of the business-like combat reports. As the Duxford chaplain, Mayfield was the only mental health support, aside from copious quantities of alcohol, that was available at the time. He and the other chaplains were cast in the role of listeners, offering spiritual support and guidance to the men who were fighting for their lives every day. This dark and heavy task took a toll on their spirits as well. On 20 January, Mayfield recorded these words in his diary:

> McKnight and Latta of 242 are missing. They have been shot down over the Pas de Calais. There is a chance that they may have been rescued in the sea but this is not the weather for picking pilots out of the drink, nor is it suitable for pilots waiting in the drink to be rescued.[6]

Of Bill, Mayfield said, '[He] was short and wiry and tough. If anyone had asked me what a typical fighter pilot of Fighter Command was like, I could not have done better than to introduce MacK.'

Separated as we are by many decades, the words have yet the ring of the heavy heart of the person writing them. Two young lives were ended, two brave youthful faces were absent from the group that had been together a scant twenty-four hours before.

The other thing that had to happen was for the Latta and McKnight families to be informed of the day's events.

Two families were about to have their lives upended forever.

The Telegram

The McKnight family had relocated from Bill's childhood home in Crescent Heights to a larger house in the Elbow Park neighbourhood of Calgary. It was in that home that a dramatic scene would unfold on 13 January 1941.

After what must have been a series of incredibly frustrating years of attempting to parent a grieving, contrary and strong-willed teenager, finding himself the father of the most celebrated pilot in Canada must have been an astonishing reversal of fortune for Bill's father. And living with the reality of your son existing in what sometimes amounted to a hand-to-hand combat with the Luftwaffe – even if he sometimes appeared to be single-handedly kicking their ass – must have only added to the years Bill's father spent worrying. Once, he had hoped that his son would grow up to be a good man. Now he was simply worrying about his son growing up at all.

'We're fatalistic about it,' Bill's father had once remarked. 'If it's going to get him, there's nothing we can do about it so there's no use worrying.' And he added, 'If confidence and fearlessness mean anything [Bill will] come through all right.'[1]

In the end, of course, he didn't.

Strong, warm winds were blowing in Calgary on the Monday afternoon of 13 January. The Chinook is a unique phenomenon. The vertical north–south orientation of the Rocky Mountains is set at a precise distance from the very high-altitude city that creates regular pauses in the fierce western Canadian winters. Dramatic and rapid temperature changes are recorded regularly. So -18 C. may be the starting point on a frosty winter morning. Three hours later it is +2 C. One would presume that the warmth must be revitalizing and welcomed, a pleasant interlude from the wintertime hostilities that for months at a time seem to be attempting to kill you.

But the Chinooks have a mixed reputation, with many people dreading the 'Chinook headaches' brought on by the intense pressure changes. Chinooks generate a mild winter climate. Splashy and muddy road conditions paired with icy patches appear within hours. Calgarians setting out for a pleasant winter walk wind up in hospitals with broken bones and other assorted injuries. The icy patches are invisible, lying in wait, instantly transforming what had been a good day moments before into an emergency.

Strange, haunted shadows arrive, racing in the wind under a thick dome of cloud as the sun begins to set early on January afternoons. Most of all, while they are warm and mild, the Chinooks are only ever a pause, a false spring. They are not permanent, or a real change of circumstances, and they can end just as quickly and dramatically as they begin.

Bill's parents had spent part of the afternoon on 13 January at a radio station in Calgary. The Royal Canadian Legion had decided to create a program for family members of men in the service to connect with each other. The Legion was bearing the expense, creating a lottery draw for the lucky family members to apply to create messages that were intended for broadcasts to the troops serving overseas. That week in Calgary, some of those electrical transcriptions were being taped. Eight Calgarians had been chosen to record messages to the sons or husbands who they had not seen in months, or in the case of Bill's family, years.[2]

Bill's parents recorded their messages at 4.15 p.m. at the CFAC radio station in Calgary on Monday afternoon.[3]

Once they finished, they arrived back home at Garden Crescent. This telegram was delivered to the McKnight home:

> YOUR SON 41937 FLYING OFFICER WILLIAM LIDSTONE MCKNIGHT IS REPORTED MISSING AS THE RESULT OF AIR OPERATIONS OF 12TH JANUARY 1941 FULLSTOP LETTER FOLLOWS FULLSTOP ENQUIRES [sic] ARE BEING MADE.

Until now, I have been one of the few living people who knows what happened that day. I know it because my friend Bill McKnight told me what happened, through tears. He knew what had happened, because his father, Bill's brother Ted, was there when it did. We are going to witness it through the eyes of an eleven-year-old child. A knock came to the door. Ted was perched on the stairs. The family's maid opened the door and saw a man standing on the doorstep with the telegram. She backed away, holding up her hand as though warding off a blow. Bill and Ted's father walked up to the man holding the telegram and took it from him. He said merely, 'Thank you.'[4]

He shut the door. Scanned the telegram. And everything changed for the McKnight family.

Did you ever see your dad afraid? It must be the scariest thing in the world.

We got to see it through the eyes of a heartbroken little boy sobbing his eyes out on the stairs.

Bill is a Prisoner

Bill's disappearance was front-page news in Calgary. The next day, the McKnight family were doing their best to keep calm and carry on, while Calgary newspapers had screaming black headlines two inches high reporting on the story.

Then, the newspapers reported that Bill was likely, hopefully, safe.[1] By Wednesday, the *Calgary Herald* was already proclaiming that their correspondent, Allen Bill, had spoken to 'Bill's pals' and was saying that Bill had been seen to bail out of his Hurricane just a little inland of the French coast. According to this version of events, there was a strong likelihood that Bill was a prisoner. Allen Bill had been the former news editor of the Winnipeg *Tribune*, and he was the official war correspondent for the Southam newspaper chain.[2] Allen Bill was an experienced and respected reporter and a former serviceman himself, so his reports were narratives that readers believed that they could rely upon.

Even more promising, Bill's relieved family had received a follow-up letter on 14 January from the Air Ministry, declaring that they were hopeful that Bill was still alive, and possibly a prisoner of war in France. Bill's father commented to the *Herald* that this was 'wonderful news'.[3] It confirmed his first instinct, which was that his son was still alive.

It was a rollercoaster experience for the McKnight family – from heart-stopping anguish in one moment to a cautiously optimistic prospect the next, built on a foundation of a testimony believed to be credible and verified. 'He's bailed out twice before,' Bill's father mused. 'He could do it again.'[4]

Next to the front-page story reporting Bill's disappearance was a photograph showing Pilot Officer J. B. 'Bob' Renison, Pilot Officer Murray and Flying Officer Lepine. The three Canadians were all being held as prisoners of war. Bob Renison had sent the photograph to his parents in Toronto, and all three men were unkept and unshaven as they faced the person who held the camera. A shortage of soap was being reported as the reason for their extremely ill-kept appearance.[5] Imagine being in a position where the good news for you would be that your child is being held a prisoner by literal Nazis.

What followed were months of waiting, with no word at all, but this was taken to be rather a good sign. Four months after Bill went missing, Ray McKnight quit the Navy and joined the Air Force. He had spent eight months learning to become a sailor but now intended to make the dramatic change to the sky. It was noted that the transfer was complicated and unusual, but that the authorities were sympathetic, given the circumstances. In the *Calgary Herald* story reporting the changes for Ray, they also referenced that Bill's father had not heard definitively as to the fate of his oldest son, but that the family 'has not given up hope'.[6] It would be months before the newspapers reflected that Bill had most likely been killed.

As weeks passed with no further developments and no word from the Red Cross, Douglas Bader sent a personal letter to Bill's family, dated 15 March 1941:

> Dear Sir,
> I write to you to express, on my own behalf and that of the whole Squadron, the deep sympathy we all feel for you in the news of your son being missing. We all hope that Bill is just a prisoner of war although it is only fair to tell you that I consider this unlikely.
>
> In any case I would ask you to be proud, as we all are, of Bill and men like him who have come over from Canada to fight so gallantly for all that is worthwhile.
>
> Bill used to fly alongside me whenever we went into action and I can assure you that he well earned the D. F. C. and Bar with which our King decorated him. He was a courageous and tenacious fighter and a good shot.
>
> I realize that sympathy is useless but in your anxiety, you must get some consolation from the British Prime Minister's famous words, 'Never in the history of human conflict has so much been owed by so many to so few.'
>
> Bill was one of those few,
> Yours very sincerely,
> Douglas Bader, S/Ld.

In July 1941 a letter was sent to Bill's father confirming the view of the Air Council that in view of the time that had elapsed since Bill had disappeared and given that no one had heard from him, it had been regretfully concluded that he had lost his life on 12 January.[7]

The impact on families of missing persons creates a complex legacy. The Runnymede Memorial to the Missing commemorates by name over 20,000 men and women of the Air Force who were lost in the Second World War. The Canadian aviation historian Richard de Boer points out that the Scotiabank Saddledome in Calgary holds 19,289 people. There were enough missing Commonwealth aircrew from the Second World War to fill the Saddledome, with almost 1,000 extra people wandering around in the parking lot.

The RAF and newspapers didn't necessarily help the grieving process. To be fair, often no one knew for sure what had happened. Families of missing persons were often permitted to hold onto hope for too long, even when it was understood by witnesses that the person was likely dead. For instance, during the fall of France, Stan Turner had known that Don MacQueen had been killed right away, but the news stories reported him as missing until August 1940. The RAF chaplains had long understood that that there came a point in which encouraging people to hold onto hope became cruelty, and that they needed to be told gently not to do so anymore.[8]

As that knowledge dawned, I wonder if Bill's father ever allowed himself to remember the day his oldest son was born. If he went back to the November day that someone had passed him a warm little bundle. 'Mr. McKnight, you have a son.' Bill was a handsome person, and I am sure he was a cute little shaver from the beginning, with bright fearless eyes taking in the whole world. His father had always described him as confident and fearless. Those traits had made parenting that fiery, impulsive teenager extremely challenging at times, but it was those very attributes had made Bill into one of the finest fighter pilots that Canada had ever produced.

Bill never heard his father's voice again. The message sponsored by the Legion was too late; he was most likely in his Hurricane tomb, his coffin under the sea, for over twenty-four hours by the time it was recorded. Face and hands burned horribly? Or still perfect, with the last thing happening so quickly that he never knew it? Bill McKnight's sharp, clear eyes didn't miss much.

It was impossible to know. So, it was understandable that a family would not believe it for a while. My son is alive, he bailed out. He's a prisoner. It's good news. I believe it.

For family members of missing loved ones there can be additional barriers to healing. They match the things that Bill's nephew described to me about when he talked about his uncle. The torment of not knowing what happened. Hoping that your loved one had been mortally wounded and killed instantly. Imagining all sorts of scenarios, including some that are quite unlikely. Mourning does not properly end, or even begin, when there are no answers.

The Duxford chaplain, Guy Mayfield, had a poignant verse from the Book of Psalms that brought him comfort when he thought of those who were missing, whose families would never know what happened to them:

> Though I take the wings of the morning and remain in the uttermost parts of the sea, there also shalt Thy hand find me.
>
> *Psalms* 139:9.

Missing

The day 12 January had been a disastrous one for the RAF and for No. 242 Squadron, and a thorough and detailed combat report was completed. The inquiry into what had gone so badly wrong was under way immediately. It is easy to imagine Bader and the rest of his squadron soberly filling out their paperwork. It had the grim texture of an autopsy, solemnly recording what they had seen and done, all the while listening with everything they had for the ringing of the telephone – with details to follow, and the strangest good news ever reported, that Latta and McKnight were being held prisoner by the Germans, somewhere in France.

The telephone did not ring.

In describing the second patrol of the day, Hugh Tamblyn noted that McKnight's section was receiving very heavy flak from the ground. He also echoed Brown's statement that a Bf 109 had appeared on Brown's port side, prompting him to turn home.[1]

Flying Officer Arthur's report detailed the final Mosquito patrol of the day, and he reported that he, Latta and Edmonds had become separated from Cryderman. They were attacked by Bf 109s just off Calais and Arthur stated that the last time he saw Latta, his aircraft was taking evasive action. It therefore seems certain that he was shot down by a German fighter.[2] The reports all noted the heavy and accurate fire from the ground.

However, although Fighter Command reported the loss of two Hurricanes that day, only one was claimed by the Germans. There would have been a combat claim from the Luftwaffe flak unit to report a Hurricane shot down. There is no mention of either a Hurricane or a Spitfire, meaning that there was no case of mistaken identity with the identification of the aircraft. Aircraft were frequently misidentified by both sides, so it is certainly possible that a German fighter could have claimed a Spitfire when they had shot down a Hurricane. That is not the case in this instance.

No. 12 Group squadrons were also flying Mosquito patrols on 12 January. No. 266 Squadron and No. 19 Squadron were both Spitfire squadrons.

On 12 January, No. 19 Squadron flew with a Hurricane Squadron, No. 46, for two wing sweeps off of Norfolk. No enemy aircraft were spotted, and no Spitfires or Hurricanes were reported damaged in active operations or in combat. No. 222 Squadron were not flying any operations at all on 12 January.

At this point, I am going to venture away from the facts and take a guess at what I think most likely happened. It is possible that the Hurricane claimed on the German side by Fw. Helmut Brugelmann of 8./JG 26 was flown by John Latta, as Latta was witnessed taking evasive action by Arthur. Flak was developed to specifically target aircraft, but since the Germans did not report any aircraft shot down by flak, it seems probable in Bill's case that he was downed by the random groundfire. The Hurricanes had been flying at such a low level that they were vulnerable to fire from the ground. This was exactly why the Mosquito patrols were so dangerous.

So that is where we find ourselves. Questions and possibilities have been ruled both in and out. We find ourselves back exactly where we started: as of the time of this writing, in the winter of 2025, we still have no idea what precisely happened to Bill McKnight and John Latta, only guesses.

For a biography looking into Bill McKnight's life, it is only right that a thorough investigation into his death would be renewed. When I reached out to the author Dilip Sarkar, writer of literally dozens of books about the Second World War, including a biography of Douglas Bader called *Fighter Ace* that was a major source of material for this book, I was hoping that he would recommend some original sources for me. What he did instead was to investigate this matter thoroughly himself, consulting resources that I would never have thought of and lifting every possible stone. What he suggested to me when we spoke was that perhaps there was a way to find out what had happened to Bill after all, and that could be done by reaching out to the Second World War cemeteries along the French and Belgian coast, requesting information about unnamed Royal Air Force pilots found and buried between January and February 1941. While it would be impossible to know for sure if the person found was Bill McKnight or John Latta, it would still have offered new possibilities to Bill's family, friends and to the readers of this book.

None were reported.

So, we still don't know where Bill is. He existed. He was real, and his Hurricane was real. That means that they are somewhere. Someday, perhaps, this mystery may be solved, when the sea gives up its dead or the carcass of a Hurricane is improbably unearthed from a riverbank in France. For now, we are just as lost as ever, with no real answers and therefore no closure.

Now that so few family members are left, I feel the cold burden of a missing person resting on me. There are no satisfying answers, and I feel deeply ---------- lost.

Loose Ends

Tragically, Marvin Brown, who had accompanied Bill as his 'Number Two' on his last flight, died himself in an accident only a few weeks after Bill went missing. The Canadian content of No. 242 Squadron was already being watered down after the heavy losses in France and at Dunkirk in the spring of 1940, and we can even see that in the way that Bader replaced Gobeil. Bader was promoted and reassigned to the Tangmere wing just a few weeks after Bill vanished, in March 1941.[1] He took Stan Turner with him.

No. 242 Squadron would be transferred to combat in Sumatra. In May 1942 it was recommended that the Canadian designation of the squadron be officially dropped, just two short, long years after the squadron had participated in its very first battles in the defense of France.

Bader himself was shot down in August 1941. He spent the rest of the war in a German prison camp. He seems to have been a favourite of his guards; they permitted his prosthetic legs to be parachute dropped by an Allied plane so he could have use of them, but they had to take them away at night because he kept trying to escape.

Canada's Contribution to the Second World War

On 15 September 1945, a deafening procession of 300 aeroplanes charged across the misty London sky.[1] A fly-past had been coordinated to commemorate the return of peace. It was the fifth anniversary of the Greatest Day in the Battle of Britain. Douglas Bader, who had been freed from his German prison in April, had been asked to lead it. His wingmen for the event were both former members of his all-Canadian squadron, Stan Turner and Denis Crowley-Milling. Bader's wingmen were now wing commanders themselves, and they both had Distinguished Flying Officer and Distinguished Flying Crosses pinned to their uniforms.[2]

Stan Turner had commanded no less a person than George Frederick 'Buzz' Beurling in Malta. Beurling had finished the war in the rank of flight lieutenant and had been awarded the DSO, DFC, DFM & Bar. Beurling was the most successful Canadian fighter pilot in the Second World War. His style of fighting had reminded Turner of someone:

> Buzz was a real fine shot, very much like Willy McKnight. He was the kind of guy, it was no good trying to put him into the Squadron formation, he was strictly an individual. You would give him a #2 to keep his tail clean and he would let him go. Willy McKnight was the same guy that way.[3]

What should have been a celebration felt heavy, and serious. Everyone was older, weary, stern and grown up. The young faces had aged far more than would have been expected in a mere five years. Many faces, of course, were absent altogether. The Hurricane with the Reaper painted on its flanks had been missing for a long time.

Bill McKnight had entered the Royal Air Force as a young man searching for himself, for a meaningful place in the world. Or, if nothing else, simply for the next steps as he figured out what he wanted to do. The fact that one of the deadliest conflicts in human history had been straddling his path had not only altered his life but ended it before he had a chance to grow up.

Flight had evolved rapidly, and Bill had narrowly missed out on technological advances such as film cameras being mounted onto military aircraft to record dispassionately what was happening in the air. Had he been flying only a few months later, one might have been added to his own aeroplane, and it would have been possible today to go onto YouTube and watch the Hurricane with the skeleton on its sides attack its prey and pummel it out of the sky.

Or watch an enemy aircraft shoot it down.

The Hurricane had nearly single-handedly defended France and had been the critical workhorse in the Battle of Britain. But by 1945, even the Spitfire, the elite Royal Air Force fighter that Bill had never had the opportunity to fly, was becoming rather a dated aircraft. Hawker had developed the Tempest, a fantastic fighter-bomber that I believe he would have enjoyed flying. Surely Bill would have been amazed by the changes that had shaped and evolved aircraft.

Bill had always shunned leadership opportunities when he was alive. Telling other people what to do and being responsible for their safety had never appealed to him. Had he lived until the end of the war, however, promotions like the ones given to his old friends Stan Turner and Denis Crowley-Milling were undoubtedly in his future whether he liked it or not. Perhaps he would have discovered gifts and abilities that he never knew that he had.

Bill had missed out on the 1943 Canadian invasion of Dieppe that everyone would like to forget. He had not been present for the Canadian achievements at Juno Beach during the D-Day invasions. To this day, Canadians proudly tell each other that the Canadians were the only Allied army to meet their D-Day objectives. He also missed out on the gratitude shown to the Canadian troops who had liberated Holland. They would never be forgotten in that country. Every April finds little Dutch towns lovingly celebrating and honouring the Canadians who liberated their communities with an appreciation and respect that Canada does not have for itself.

Canada itself was a dramatically different nation from the underdog Commonwealth country that had been struggling out of the clutches of the Great Depression at the beginning of the war. From the 'fleet' of seven destroyers and a random assorted collection of other vessels at the start of the war, the Canadian navy now boasted nearly 1,000 naval vessels and merchant ships.[4] As for the fighter effort, Canada had started the war with a small and unimpressive collection of Mk I Hurricanes. The Royal Canadian Air Force had boasted enthusiastic young pilots with no combat experience whatsoever from No. 1 Squadron, plus some auxiliaries in No. 115 Squadron. As the war ended, those fighter squadrons had expanded eightfold. Canadian squadrons were flying Spitfires and Hurricanes by day and radar-enhanced Beaufighters and Mosquitos by night.[5] Canada had ended the war with the world's fourth largest air force.

When the future had appeared the darkest and most formidable, Canada had stood beside Britain. Its farmers and ranchers had fed Britain, and its miners had helped to supply its energy needs. Canada had trained pilots and other aircrew from all over the Commonwealth. It had voluntarily paid $1.6 billion CAD of the total cost of $2.2 billion for the British Commonwealth Air Training Plan.[6] Out of a population of only 11 million people, 47,000 Canadians serving in various branches of the Canadian army, navy or air force had been killed and 58,000 had been wounded.[7]

Not many people today know that Canada had gifted Britain $1 billion early in 1942. Before the war came to an end, Canada had contributed an additional $3.5 billion in gifts and even more in low-interest loans.[8]

In fact, Canada had been a good metaphor for Bill in 1939. It had good bones but had been through depleting traumatic experiences and had a lot of things to figure out. It had stepped up immediately and made an outsized contribution that is largely unknown to the world and to itself. Its position in the Second World War was promptly forgotten or was never fully known by the ally that would shape its future.

Canada had closely supported Britain when it was not in its own interests to do so. As the war ended, it was perhaps inevitable that Canada would begin to work even more closely with its massive southern neighbour than it already did. For better or for worse, going forward, Canada would increasingly link its economic, cultural and diplomatic interests to the United States.

As for Bill McKnight, and those like him who had fought, died – and still lived – in the Commonwealth, Canada had a new task as it forged ahead.

Whether they had been celebrities like Bill or ordinary members of the armed forces, it was time to forget about them.

McKnight Boulevard

When peace returned, Douglas Bader became Managing Director of Shell Aircraft Ltd. It allowed him to pay many visits to Alberta over the coming decades. Bill was not his only link to Calgary. Barlow Trail in Calgary was named for Noel Barlow. As we have seen, Barlow had challenged himself to become an expert fitter, with specialized knowledge of Rolls-Royce engines. The fact that he was a licenced pilot meant that he could also take the machines he worked on for test flights. Bader had noticed and Barlow became Bader's personal fitter.[1] Whatever hellish thing Bader's Hurricane had been through on any given day, it had been Noel Barlow who made sure that it was ready to fly out again whenever his boss was.

The McKnight family had by now relocated to Vancouver, so Bader, rather than staying somewhere grand like the Canadian Pacific Railway's elegant Palliser hotel as might have been expected, sometimes stayed with the Barlow family at Carseland, Alberta. The western Canadian hospitality meant war stories and whisky in the living room after supper. The visits were returned; in fact, Barlow's daughter stayed with the Baders for three months when she visited England.[2]

On one occasion, Bader and his wife Thelma visited Alberta early in July of 1957. They went to the world-renowned Calgary Stampede; Bader proclaimed it, 'Almost the 8th wonder of the world.'[3] The visiting McKnights arriving from Vancouver also received him, and he signed a copy of *Reach for the Sky* by Paul Brickhill for Bill's young nephew. As Bill's nephew (also called Bill) was contemplating what should happen to his family's artifacts, he commented that the book Bader had personally signed for him would stay in his own possession. The connection between them was cherished on both sides.

Visiting friends was not the only reason for the trips. Of No. 242 Squadron, Bader said:

> Any good fortune or reputation I enjoy has been due entirely to the members of the 242 Squadron. All the good fortune I have

> had during and since the war can be placed squarely at the feet of the Canadians.[4]

Because of Bader's encouragement, major roadways in Calgary were eventually named for the men who had supported and aided his successes as a leader: Barlow Trail, and ultimately of course, McKnight Boulevard.

Bader had a famously dismissive attitude to people had who worked for him, even if they had served under him faithfully, and he could be indifferent and arrogant towards anyone he thought was lower in status or class than he was. People who spent time around him and who had looked up to him were frequently taken back by his dismissive attitudes towards women, minorities and anyone else who he did not view as an equal – which could be almost everyone. It seemed that the only people he could tolerate were those who fawned over and idolized him. Today, he would probably be cancelled, as the Gen Zs say. But for all his problematic Edwardian worldview, he was also a person of tremendous personal courage who at times demonstrated a great deal of compassion for others, including those with missing limbs and disabilities. He was a complicated and difficult person, but it was clear that he had a very soft spot in his heart for Bill and his family.

As for Calgary itself, however, by the 1950s and '60s, it had long moved on from the McKnight story. Bill's parents, Ted and Hazel, had left Calgary shortly after Bill went missing, and were living in Vancouver, although Bill's younger brother Ray McKnight and his wife Alison still lived in Calgary. The war had touched many Canadian families deeply, and Calgarians can be notoriously dismissive of their own history. It was over a decade before Bader's suggestion to honour Bill was acted upon.

The story can be traced through a family scrapbook created by the sister-in-law who Bill never met, Helene McKnight, who married Ted. The curated newspaper clippings included a reference to Bader's trip to Calgary in 1957. Bader on this occasion was honoured by the Kainai indigenous peoples in southern Alberta as an honorary chieftain. The *North Hill News* had a photograph of Bader wearing a Kainai headdress after the ceremony.[5] This visit happened the year after the smash hit film *Reach for the Sky* starring Kenneth More had been released, based on Paul Brickhill's 1954 bestselling biography of the same title; Bader's star had never been brighter.

While speaking to a Chamber of Commerce luncheon, Bader used a light-hearted address to suggest to Mayor Don Mackay and to a assortment of prominent Alberta citizens such as Premier Manning, Lieutenant Governor Bowlen and members of the Royal Canadian Air Force brass that they should consider naming the roads leading to the Calgary Airport for their Second World War heroes. The new airport was under expansion, so it seemed like an auspicious time.[6]

Mayor Mackay presented Bader with a pair of silver cufflinks engraved with the word 'Onward' and the Calgary crest. He responded with supportive comments of his own, stating that there was no doubt that the city would find a way to honour McKnight, 'who had done so much for Calgary, Canada and the Commonwealth'.[7]

It seemed like a promising start, but nothing happened.

It took time, numerous visits, and consistent advocacy for 48th Avenue to be renamed.

As time passed, Bader's visits became a semi-annual tradition of arriving in Calgary and noting with increasing surprise and disappointment that a road had yet to be named for McKnight.

In 1966, the city planners proposed that a stretch of road leading past the airport be named for Noel Barlow. It cleared the final hurdle when the province declined to object to the use of the word 'trail' in the name, and Barlow Trail it became.[8] A memorial to Bill had been passed over when the 24th Street Expressway in the west of the city had been named for the Tsuu Tina chief David Crowchild instead.

It was in 1967 that Bill acquired a new champion, and this time it was Calgary Police Inspector Andy Little. Little, it turned out, had gone to high school with Bill back in the Crescent Heights days and had known him personally. Andy had left school in grade 11 to join the police force and it appeared that he was one of the people Bill had gone to say goodbye to a few days before he left Calgary. Andy had been rather surprised as he had never considered Bill to be a close friend, but he listened as Bill told him that he intended to take a cattle boat overseas to join the Royal Air Force.[9] After the pair separated that day, they never saw each other again. However, Little had followed Bill's exploits for the next two years as his high school buddy went on to become a celebrity pilot.

Little had served in the Royal Canadian Air Force for two years himself, joining up in 1943. As someone who had met both Bill and Douglas Bader, he had taken a personal interest in the back-and-forth efforts to have Bill memorialized in Calgary, and he knew that Bader had found it astonishing that someone as worthy as Bill had been so quickly forgotten by his own city. If McKnight did not deserve to be remembered, nobody did.[10]

Calgary's aviation greats from the First World War were already honoured, with their names decorating the nearby roads – Palmer Road for Jock Palmer,

McCall Way for Fred McCall. Now, from the Second World War, Barlow had been remembered. Little believed that some of the difficulty in creating the memorial had been the indecision about which road would be suitable. Little had a place in mind, a bridge along Palmer Road, and had taken up 'the memorial cudgel' in promoting the idea. However, by 1967, Little had sought out the media because after presenting his suggestion to the suitable authorities, nothing had happened.[11]

In fact, nothing appears in the City of Calgary archives referencing McKnight until 1968. Then, sandwiched between requests for changes to the parking bylaws and upgrades to the sewage facilities, it was the city planner who was ultimately informed that a council meeting held on Monday, 8 April 1968 had received a communication from the Royal Canadian Air Force. The communication, dated 27 March, requested that a memorial in honour of Flying Officer William McKnight be received and the request was granted. A stretch of 48th Avenue between Centre Street and McCall Field was to be named 'McKnight Boulevard'.[12] While the city commissioners agreed and had at last recognised their Second World War ace, the name change was being delayed until after a new city directory was compiled, to avoid confusion. However, they had decided to increase the length of the road, which now ran from John Laurie Boulevard to 68th Street North-East, spanning the entire north half of the city at the time.[13]

By 1970, the boulevard was still known as 48th Avenue. The name change was officially on the way but it was proceeding at a glacial pace. Calgary city council had meanwhile received an interesting proposal, suggesting that a road on a former Royal Canadian Air Force base be named for the First World War German ace Manfred 'The Red Baron' von Richthofen! This may likely have been inspired because of a popular film, *The Blue Max*, that had been released in 1966. The recommendation to rename a Calgary street had evidently received enough traction that Calgary's city council had formally discussed it. The enemy ace briefly had a shot at getting a road in Calgary named for him before Bill McKnight did! The ideas had been discussed in the same council meeting. To their credit, the city council promptly shot the scheme down. 'We have the greatest respect for the Blue Max and the Red Baron and all that but really, they were on the other side,' Alderman Roy Farran observed. McKnight Boulevard had been debated yet again too; council were still hemming and hawing about exactly which stretch of road it would be.[14]

An old friend of Bill's was later asked for her thoughts about the naming of the road. Marian Glover, now Marian Jones, had approved. 'I'm just sorry that people don't know who it's named after.' Marian estimated that less than 1 per cent of Calgarians had any idea who the 'McKnight' in McKnight Boulevard was.[15] She wasn't wrong – Andy Little had been making educational presentations in Calgary schools, and he noted the that local youngsters knew who the Red Baron was but had never heard of Douglas Bader or their own Bill McKnight.[16]

Once the road was finally, officially named, the Calgary Police Association sponsored a commemorative plaque that was placed at the Calgary Airport. Ray McKnight was in attendance as Douglas Bader personally unveiled the plate.[17] The major initiatives prepared to honour Bill also included a significant element of education for a new generation of young Albertans. They had not been alive when Bill's exploits decorated the front pages of their newspapers. McKnight wasn't their hero; he was some guy who their parents thought was cool.

Bader was the guest speaker on the evening of the unveiling of the airport plaque at a dinner for the Calgary Police Association. Those attending were asked to bring along a young guest so that they could learn what, and who, all the fuss was about.[18]

He Was Never Willie

Today in Calgary, across Canada and around the world, those who know McKnight will automatically refer to him as 'Willie'. Remembrance becomes more challenging as time begins to erase the personal elements of someone's life, to the extent that Calgarians, Canadians and British fans of Bill will be unlikely to know his real name.

If you were introduced to him, he would have held out his hand for you to shake and said, 'Hi, I'm Bill.' He signed his letters 'Bill'. He autographed photographs given to family members as 'Bill'. In the Canadian newspapers dating from the period he was flying he is called Bill (the British newspapers called him 'William McKnight'). His family called him Bill. In 1954, Bader inscribed a copy of *Reach for the Sky* to William and Doris, 'To Bill's Father + Mother with my deepest regards, in memory of their gallant son. From Douglas Bader, London, 15/3/54.' Bader called him Bill, too – because that was his name.

Where then did 'Willie' come from? People serving in squadrons were often given unofficial nicknames, and you didn't necessarily get a choice of what you would be called. In fact, the Duxford chaplain Guy Mayfield had referred to Bill as 'MacK'. Stan Turner called him 'Willy' though. It must have been Paul Brickhill, the Australian writer whose biography of Bader created a legend not only of Bader but of the supporting cast around him, who popularized its use. Brickhill's *Reach for the Sky* was a runaway bestseller, reportedly to the annoyance of Bader at times, when people wanted him to sign it, rather than copies of his own book, *Fight for the Sky*.

Brickhill was a very engaging writer, the sort of descriptive and expressive storyteller who makes other authors envious. He had a fascinating subject and period of history to work with, and he used up every bit of the canvas, creating vivid and larger than life heroes and an adventure story that you can't put down. It can be read through in an afternoon, and you will still be thinking about it long after you close the book. I suspect that Brickhill was the source that would simultaneously immortalize Bill and erase his real name.

Willie was propaganda.

Bill was a person.

I suspect that as Bill's biographer, I may be clarifying this for the rest of my own life … and it is probably futile.

The Reaper in Canada

While Bill McKnight is not a household name in Canada in the way that he deserves, it is also true that he does have a national and an international fan base. Among Canadians who have an interest in aviation, and particularly as it is related to the military, he is highly regarded and respected.

There is a rather hit and miss pattern to the recognition. As of 2025 Bill is not yet a member of the Canadian Aviation Hall of Fame, but although he was never associated with the Royal Canadian Air Force, they took it upon themselves to recommend that the city council in Calgary finally name McKnight Boulevard for their hometown hero. And in Gatineau, Quebec, over 2,000 miles away from Calgary, Vintage Wings of Canada took on a significant restoration project to salute McKnight.

Rather improbably, that story began in Assiniboia, Saskatchewan, where a farmer called Harry Whereatt owned a Hurricane. Harry's Hurricane was a Canadian-built Mk XII that was manufactured in the Canadian Car and Foundry plant in Quebec. Harry had a lifelong interest in aviation and Assiniboia had been one of the sites of the dozens of Royal Canadian Air Force Elementary Flying Training Schools that were dotted across Canada during the Second World War. That proximity to a local airfield undoubtedly inspired Harry's affinity for aircraft. Not only was Harry one of those infinitely capable western Canadian farmers who have a strong mechanical flare and can fix almost anything, but he was a pilot himself. As a skilled cabinetmaker, he was uniquely suited to care for a Hurricane, which unlike the almost all-metal Spitfires are partially constructed of wooden pieces.[1]

In 2006, Harry began to think about finding a permanent home for his Hurricane. He eventually sold it to Mike Potter, and after a long life spent on the western prairies, the Hurricane travelled to Vintage Wings in Gatineau, Québec. While the Hurricane needed restoration, after being cared for by Harry for most of its life, it was not destined to be a static display, because it was still in excellent condition. Still, an extensive rebuild was in its future, beginning with the wings being taken off to have new fuel tanks installed. It was decided that the centre wing section needed to be reconstructed from scratch, and the Hurricane's skin was also stripped.[2]

Since its fuselage was going to be repainted, it presented a literal blank canvas. What should be painted on the sides of this Canadian-built Hurricane? The idea of a Hurricane tearing through the clouds with Bill's Reaper crouching along its fuselage inspired the historian Dave O'Malley and others working on the restoration.[3] Great care was taken in applying the signature nose art that had decorated all No. 242 Squadron aeroplanes. It was a mischievous image of a big, black boot kicking Hitler in the butt. Then, using the few photographs known to exist of Hurricane LE-A, the image of the Grim Reaper, believed to have been drawn and designed by Bill himself, was carefully applied to the Hurricane.[4]

Faithfully following the guidance of the black and white photographs and using a film projector, the Reaper was painstakingly aligned with the rivets along the side of the Hurricane.[5] Getting the size, the colours and the orientation of Bill's icon perfectly replicated was carefully and meticulously researched, which was not an easy challenge as it had been decades since anyone had seen the original LE-A. It was speculated that previous guesses by other artists may have been inaccurate. For example, the Vintage Wings Reaper does not have blood on its sickle.[6]

The restoration took sixteen years and thousands of hours of volunteer labour to complete. On 23 April 2022, pilot Dave Hadfield took the Hurricane for its first test flight. The classic fighter sprinted down the runway and lifted itself into the sky. It was the first time since 12 January 1941 that an aircraft painted with that specific configuration had been airborne, and on that occasion Bill himself had been at the controls.

The Hurricane was a Canadian-built relative to the Mk I that Bill had piloted, and the aggressive, eerie painting on the fuselage had an emotional message for any Canadian watching it circle the airfield. The Reaper had arrived in Canada. If there were any Bf 109s in the vicinity, their cruel metal skin must surely have been crawling as the emblem of their ferocious enemy soared through the clouds and shadows once more.

Pilot Dave Hadfield has flown that Hurricane many times and he has also had the experience of flying in formations when that Hurricane has been flying beside him. He describes it as instantly recognisable.[7]

Sixteen and a half German families at a minimum have photographs of uncles and brothers and friends in their family albums or hanging on their walls, of men who Bill McKnight shot out of the sky. Their families have remembered and missed them for decades, just as Bill's family have remembered and missed him. I can appreciate that they would feel differently about the reappearance of that Reaper. For sixteen and a half German pilots, it may have been the last thing that they ever saw. Then there was Douglas Bader, who said that it brought him a sense of comfort when he saw the campy, grinning skeleton soaring beside him, because it symbolized the presence of a loyal friend.

As a Canadian and a Calgarian from a generation of people who were brought up not knowing a darn thing about Bill McKnight, a strange feeling seems to come over me and circulate through my nervous system when I think about this. Is this what you might call … patriotism? As a Canadian, I really moderate patriotism. I am ambivalent about what being a Canadian means in some ways. What are symbols of Canada that are meaningful to me? There is a maple leaf on our flag. I am from western Canada, so we don't have many maple trees thriving on the great plains. I might be more inclined to pick out a bison as a symbol of home. But these days that demented Reaper leering along the sides of that Hurricane kind of works for me, too. I personally think it would look good on money. I would not want it charging after me, that's for sure.

The fact that a museum thousands of miles away from where Bill and I were both born would spend hundreds of hours to restore that Hurricane to honour him means a lot to me.

Best of all, if you visit the Vintage Wings of Canada website or follow pilot Dave Hadfield's YouTube channel, you will be able to see photographs and video of that aircraft flying for yourself. Nothing lasts forever, but this is one example of a meaningful way that Canadians from one end of this country to the other found to remember the Reaper and to bring it back to life, in the skies over Canada this time.

On the Cover

What became of the portrait of Bill created by Eric Kennington? A well-known book created from the sittings, *Drawing the Royal Air Force*, was released in 1942. It included fifty-two Royal Air Force portraits, including an image of Douglas Bader. Most of the subjects were British, but the portraits included a select representation of pilots from the colonies, including two Canadians. One of the Canadians, of course, was Bill, who was briefly introduced with a fleeting paragraph noting that he had been born in Edmonton and gone to school at Crescent Heights. 'He has destroyed a number of enemy aircraft and has proved himself to be a most efficient section leader, consistently given proof that he is a courageous and tenacious fighter.'[1]

The information is short and businesslike; not very interesting to be honest. However, it was Kennington's striking, vivid portrait of Bill that was selected to adorn the front cover of the volume, and that was not boring at all.

In Kennington's depiction, Bill is gazing out of the canvas to the right of the observer. He is wearing his battledress uniform, and he has his flight goggles slung over his shoulder, as though he has been summoned to action and is about to walk away. His lips are parted; he is about to speak to whoever it is that he is looking at (not the painter), and the portrait has a rugged, contemporary quality. It could be used in a moody, atmospheric comic book. Bill is not portrayed with the exhaustion or weariness he must surely have been experiencing; he is calm and alert and perhaps described best in the phrase that sometimes attached itself to Canadian personnel, quietly competent.

It is a restrained portrait, fully intended for propaganda, and one can see what Kennington liked about it. This was created to inspire the next generation of fighters, a motivation to other young men from the Dominion who were thinking of joining up, and there is a maturity to Bill's pose and expression that is not always apparent in photographic portraits that had been taken of him at the same period. The pastel medium lends the portraits a theatrical air characteristic of both the time and of the narrative the artist wanted to communicate. The effect is heroic and composed, and not entirely human. The larger-than-life figures in the RAF were intended for shining pedestals as they battled the Hun and willingly gave their lives for the Empire.

The images also bestowed an immortal quality to men who most definitely were not. What happened to Bill was not uncommon. Another young man left Kennington's studio and never returned to complete his portrait, remaining ghostly and half drawn, suspended somewhere between this life and the next.[2] By the time the Second World War ended in 1945, more than forty of the men whose portraits Kennington illustrated had been killed in action.

As of October 1941, Bill's portrait hung in the Air Ministry in London.[3] Multiple copies were typically created of artworks, and one copy of Bill's portrait was sent to his family.[4] Today, there is a copy in Canada's War Museum.

Mike, Marian, Ray

Bill's old friend Mike Peglar joined the Calgary Highlanders; he became a lieutenant. After the war ended, he returned to Calgary and married his long-time girlfriend, Olive Riley. He went to work for the meat-packing firm P. Burns and Company and spent time working for the business in both Calgary and Regina, Saskatchewan. The pair had two children.[1]

Marian Glover married Carl Jones. After their marriage, Marian and Carl relocated to Lethbridge, Alberta, and then to High River, where Carl worked as a ground instructor in the British Air Commonwealth Training Plan.

When the war ended, Carl and Marian returned to Calgary, and Carl made the move into the oil and gas sector. It was an inspired and timely move. The energy sector began to boom in the 1950s and '60s in Alberta, and it created wealth and prosperity for an entire generation of Albertans. Carl became the first Canadian President of Hudson Bay Company Oil and Gas in 1970. He helped to raise funds for Calgary Zoo, and he loved fishing, skiing and hiking in the Rocky Mountains. He and Marian also enjoyed vacations in their RV all over North America. He was described as 'Quiet, modest, knowledgeable and thorough'.[2] No one less like the fiery, rebellious and occasionally conceited Bill McKnight could be imagined. Carl Jones sounds like a bomber pilot – cooperative, calm and moderate. He died in 1999, honoured by the many people who his hard work and community involvement had impressed.

Marian was still living in Calgary at the turn of the last century. Her life circled back to Bill when Calgarian reporters in the 1990s and the early 2000s began to rediscover the ace for whom their McKnight Boulevard was named. There was additional interest when Mike Peglar donated the letters that Bill had sent to him during the war to Library and Archives Canada. Not only were the letters written by a significant Canadian and Calgarian, but they were not typical letters home. Bill's sharp eyes, quick wit, and his perspectives and observations of what was happening during the early years of the Second World War were a valuable historical record in themselves, but his reflections and revelations about his own thoughts, feelings and inner state were a disclosure that set them apart. They included very perceptive comments at times.

The letters also revealed how he had felt about Marian all along.

Marian had the 'eerie'[3] experience of reading Bill's letters for herself and then speaking about what she learned. It had come as a surprise to her. After a life that she had chosen and lived on her own terms, Bill was back. He was finally telling her what he had felt. She was blindsided to realize that Bill claimed he had left to join the RAF largely because of her. 'I came over here principally because of the way I felt about [Marian],' he had written to Mike.[4] Had all the honours and big events been to impress her?

Little did Bill realize, but she had been thinking about him, too. Marian admitted that she had masked deep feelings of her own. She had been unable to speak about Bill for 'years and years'.[5] When our lives silence us, that stillness often speaks of something meaningful that has happened. Or not happened. Of love, trauma, and other profound feelings that don't lend themselves very well to language.

Marian had been astonished when she learned that Bill was going to England. The announcement had come just a few days before he left. What was she to conclude but that he was pulling away permanently from her? The on again/off again couple had most definitely been off again when Bill left to join the RAF; Marian hadn't even realized that he was leaving. But she remembered an incident that happened the night before Bill left with a new understanding; he had come to say goodbye to her family. Standing on the front doorstep as he prepared to leave, Bill had turned to Marian and said that when he came back that 'they would start up again'.[6] The strange memory finally made sense.

'[Marian] did me a good turn because it was mainly because of her I left home, and I think I'm quite a bit more broadminded and educated than I was then,' he had written.[7]

Marian objected to Bill saying that he had outgrown her, though. 'I wonder if that was really true, but that's fine, if he had cancelled it off, then that relieves me.'[8] From her perspective, she was the one who had moved on first, even before he left. 'He was like this, he told all kinds of things, and that's one reason I could never have married him.'[9]

It turned out that Bill had written to her as well. Although she had destroyed his letters after she was married, Marian remembered he had told her in one of them that the fighting amounted to 'legalized murder'.[10] 'He was killing people, so he had that on his conscience,' she mused.

She had had a deep influence on Bill. Decades later, she finally heard the goodbye that Bill had intended for her. 'I'd like you to give [Marian] my best wishes and congratulations,' he had told Mike when he learned of her impending marriage.[11] His hopes for her seem to have come true, almost as though he had said a blessing over her future.

Ray McKnight had been in the Royal Canadian Navy when his brother went missing the day after his twentieth birthday. Ray made the decision to switch to the Royal Canadian Air Force after his Bill disappeared. Losing Bill had understandably changed his outlook.[12] Ray completed two tours of operations, one in North Africa and one in India. He had reportedly bailed out of his aeroplane in the middle of the night and landed in the Libyan desert.[13] The adventure had an improbable quality, and Ray did not like to talk about it. 'Oh, that old story again,' was his dismissive remark when asked for details.[14]

Ray worked in the food industry as area manager in Alberta and British Columbia for Nestle Canada for thirty-eight years.[15] Any attempt to find Ray McKnight online or in a newspaper archive will include at least a sentence and more often a paragraph referring to his famous brother. That was quite a shadow to live in.

Bill had evolved from continually mystifying, disappointing and frustrating his family to becoming the person that all the other McKnight men had to measure up to. It was impossible. If anything, he was in the way, preventing his brothers and nephews from being themselves, even if they were proud of him.

And Ted

The McKnight family moved to Vancouver, British Columbia, in 1944, not long after Bill disappeared. Like his big brother, Ted McKnight was athletic and loved football. He played as a halfback in school and later spent time with the BC Lions. A professional football career was a potential option. According to his son, Ted would have liked to focus on his football career, but received tremendous opposition from his father, who expected his son to pursue an education and a career rather than something that he regarded as a flippant game. Had the same challenges that Bill experienced repeated itself in the way that William McKnight was trying to parent high-spirited Ted? The harsh guidance caused deep resentment against his father.[1]

What is it Like to be Bill McKnight?

For the generation of McKnights who lived after Bill, he was a heavy family legacy. Both of Bill's brothers, Ray and Ted, had sons whom they named Bill. There was a family who remembered William Lidstone McKnight for the rest of their lives. Being your own person and measuring up to a war hero was hopeless. And when a newspaper or a historian turned up in your life, they never wanted to talk to you about … you. Bill's short life cast a long shadow over his family.

I met 'my' Bill McKnight, son of Ted and Bill's nephew, in 2020 at Calgary's Central Calgary Public Library. He walked into my life with his satchel full of treasures, and I realized that he had gone to considerable trouble to track me down. How on earth did he happen to watch my story about the Calgary Stampeders and the military? Why did I tell Cami Kepke from GlobalTV the throwaway comment I had shared with her about Don MacQueen being in the same all-Canadian squadron as William McKnight – I knew next to nothing about either of them at the time – and how did Bill just so happen to be watching when I made that statement?

His mother, Helene, the sister-in-law who Bill never met, had created a scrapbook filled with never-before-seen family photographs, and a letter from Bill that historians didn't know about. There was a signed copy of *Reach for the Sky*, inscribed by Douglas Bader himself. There were the personal family stories about Bill. There was an essay, written by Bill's nephew in high school, writing about his hero, his uncle. He got an A.

These things just don't happen all the time to historians. This was a bolt from the blue, and I knew one thing – it wasn't meant for me. I immediately reached out to my colleague Anne Gafiuk, who made a referral to the Canadian aviation historian Richard de Boer. I gratefully put Bill and Richard in touch, thinking that I had played my wee footnote role in the history of this important family. That it was all in the right hands, the best of hands. I could go back to researching agriculture.

Good at His Job

Bill McKnight was the leading ace of Dunkirk. The leading Canadian in the Battle of Britain. The first Canadian in the Second World War to win a second DFC Bar. The leading Canadian fighter pilot in the first half of the Second World War. Any one of those topic sentences is great. Any of those bullet points is a significant and impressive standalone achievement. The fact that they can all be attributed to the same person indicates an extremely elite pilot. But he also has the receipts! By the most conservative possible estimate, he had down sixteen and a half confirmed kills in eight months of flying, and half of those were the toughest shots in the business, the Bf 109s, flown by elite and victorious Luftwaffe pilots who had trounced the competition in Spain, Denmark and Norway.

The question is, what was so special about him? While I don't pretend to have definite answers, I have spent years obsessing over this young man and as his biographer it is fair to say that I have some theories. At the very least, I have noticed things about him that may explain some of his outstanding success.

First, he was rated immediately by his first instructors as an above average pilot, a rare designation. Flight must have made sense to him; there were some innate abilities that were noticed early on. This designation changed to average when he was transitioned to piloting bombers, which he did not enjoy. He immediately applied for a transfer back to fighters. However, that training on both types of aircraft gave him an interesting offense/defense experience of fighting and piloting that may well have come in handy when he was in combat against both types.

Bill also started breaking up bomber formations and getting very close to his targets before firing at them before he ever met Douglas Bader, meaning that he updated the style of tactics that he had been trained in before he was told to do so. That was important, because as we have seen, the dated RAF tactics proved to be dangerously lacklustre against the Luftwaffe in the early days of fighting. The gun sighting of 300 yards was completely ineffective when shooting at a target moving at 300mph. Bill got around that by being aggressive and confrontational in battle and getting close to his target before firing. He was a 'short-burst specialist'[1] using ammunition sparingly and with deadly accuracy. Squirting the bullets in short, extremely pointed bursts prevented wasting bullets and disposed of whatever aircraft he was attacking in short order, so that he could take off and shoot at something else.

Bill had the benefit of 253 hours and thirty minutes of flying time logged before he was engaged in combat, meaning that while he lacked battle experience, he was a somewhat experienced pilot, not a completely green, scared kid who could sort of fly and to whom everything about his first battle was brand new.

I think we would all have loved it if Bill McKnight had got his hands on a Spitfire at least once so that we could have had his thoughts on its performance. But as a pilot who enjoyed aerobatics, the Hurricane was a good partner for him, as its abilities, particularly in rolling, have been rated higher than the Spitfire's according to pilots like Dave Hadfield and Douglas Bader, who have flown both.

Canadian pilot Rob Erdos, who has flown all three aircraft, has pointed out that in a gunnery breakdown between the Spitfire, the Hurricane and the Bf 109, Hurricanes come out on top. They have a better field of view, stability, and firepower.[2]

Once in the sky, an aeroplane and pilot need each other. The pilot can't fly, and the aircraft can't think. Pilots who have flown warbirds have expressed the sentiment that there is an extent to which your own machine is trying to kill you.[3] For fighter pilots, you are simultaneously exposed and claustrophobic. There is also a strong sense that no one can reach you. There is a certain focus and mental toughness that is required to cope in an environment like that, in which the pilot and the aircraft are on their own to handle whatever is thrown at them that day. Pilots also say that every aircraft has a personality and that they build relationships with the machines that they fly.[4] Some pairings are a better fit than others; if you find an aircraft that suits you, you have a good partner. For Bill, who was known as a 'flinty-eyed little deadshot', perhaps the Hurricane was exactly the right teammate, a better fit for a leading marksman than a Spitfire, and he expressed his respect for his Hurricane partners.[5]

And while the Bf 109, the Spitfire and Hurricane all have their advantages and deficits, the odds are good that the best pilot will win in any machine. Bill McKnight was an excellent pilot.

As a brave and confident person who was not afraid to defy authority, Bill had driven his parents, teachers and instructors to their wits' end, but once he was in the life and death aerial battles that could have cost him his life at any second, he did the right thing by abandoning impractical and old-fashioned training and using his own judgement instead. While he did feel afraid in the terrible situations that he found himself in, Bill reported that once the battles started, he was too busy to be afraid.[6] Feeling calm and alert rather than panicked during an aerial battle indicates that he was using his pre-frontal cortex, the 'smart part' of his brain, when he was fighting. Being able to keep hold of your nerves and rational thought during such an overwhelming experience would be a tremendous advantage, particularly if you are surrounded by opponents who are dissociating or panicking.

His exceptional eyesight was mentioned numerous times by Douglas Bader; he was often the first person in his squadron to spot danger and to warn others. Additionally, those eagle eyes were a tremendous asset with target shooting.

We have no way of knowing whether Bill had Attention Deficit Hyperactivity Disorder (ADHD) and this theory has been explored in this biography because it was recognised as a possibility by an expert. However, if Bill was impacted by this condition, it could go some way to explaining his performance as a fighter pilot during the stressful and dangerous conditions of the early war period. Today, people with ADHD are understood to have unique minds, which have been described as simultaneously being a terrible curse and an unexpected advantage. It has also been noted by researchers that while people with ADHD may struggle with paying attention during tedious, repetitive tasks that don't interest them, they also have a rare ability to do hard things – and to do them easily. When they do find challenges that are the right kind of difficult, it is increasingly understood that people who have ADHD can be creative, focused and original.[7]

Bill's unique mind was also demonstrated in the nose art for his aircraft that he is believed to have designed and drawn himself, and in the letters that he wrote to his friend Mike Peglar. Neither his nose art or his letters are conventional examples of letters home or of a design for an aeroplane. Being different had been the bane of his life when he was living in a quiet, conventional Calgary neighbourhood or attending school in university classrooms where everyone else was there to follow an unadventurous, predictable path. In battle, Bill's instincts likely saved his life on numerous occasions. He was an outsider, with an outsider's perspective and skills. In that context, it turned out to be a bigger advantage than obedience.

Far more than he was exceptional, Bill was just a guy. He wanted to belong and to be loved, like everyone else. He was a young adult who was doing his best to grow up in times that were anything but ordinary. The life experiences and developmental milestones that he should have had were coloured and shaped, like those of everyone else in his generation, by exceptional circumstances. Even going to the cinema was shadowed by threat, and death was a heartbreakingly commonplace occurrence, to the point where numbing with alcohol was an understandable response. It was still early enough in the war that death would always be a horror, and it hurt to lose friends.

Bill's skills and abilities loomed large and shone over a time of darkness. He could be an inconvenience and a menace in times of peace. It was when death and danger stalked the world that he shone a bright and radiant light.

Bill's Legacy in Canada

It took longer for Douglas Bader to see a road in Calgary called McKnight Boulevard than it did for the Allies to defeat the Axis powers in Europe and Japan. Bill's family never forgot him, although 'my' Bill worried that one day we all would. Bill McKnight and his family were high profile, but they were not an isolated Canadian story.

Both the First and Second World Wars created a devastating legacy for Canadian families. In 1943, 405 Squadron, the first Royal Canadian Air Force bomber squadron, became part of No. 8 Group, the Pathfinder Force. John Fauquier was the commanding officer of the squadron, which flew heavy Halifax and Lancaster bombers, each carrying a crew of seven. The Pathfinders flew out ahead of the bomber squadrons on major bombing raids to mark targets for the bombers. From 1943 until the spring of 1944, that squadron flew nineteen bombing raids to Berlin.

The casualty rate from those nineteen Bomber Command missions were horrible; 617 bombers were ultimately lost. The Canadian aviation historian Richard de Boer has pointed out that if each of the bombers contained a crew of seven, that means that approximately, 4,319 young lives were lost on those raids. That's 4,319 families – a minimum of 8,638 parents, plus siblings – that were affected. Many of the young men on the raids were too young to have wives or children, but let's say a third of them did. Perhaps another 1,500 people directly affected. Small communities where everyone knew each other, an extremely common situation in rural Canada, were profoundly impacted by the losses. Let's say there were three close friends for each of the men lost on the Pathfinders raids. That's another 12,000 people impacted. From nineteen raids alone, at an extremely conservative estimate, that is 30,000 people who were impacted by those losses for the rest of their lives.

But while Canadian families and communities had experienced profound losses that would stretch across their families for generations, they had also been sheltered from first-hand experiences of air raids and bombings, the daily threat of invasion, and enemy aircraft prowling through their skies. People in Canada tried to sympathize and relate to their returning veterans, but there was a gap in their capacity to understand what they had been through. For Canadians on the home front, the hardships had been butter shortages. When they returned from serving in the war, Canadian veterans were firmly given to understand that no one exhausted by the long and terrible years of war wanted to talk to them about their depressing stories. Having spent so much time dreading what the days would bring, friends and families were ready to move forward and wanted nothing more to do with war. Perhaps some veterans felt the same way. They were often characterised by their matter-of-fact attitudes towards the dangers they had faced and their adventures and accomplishments, even when they had been awarded elite honours such as medals and crosses.

The Legions were places where veterans and their families from all branches of the armed forces could gather with others who understood what they had been through. But even there, the support could be hit and miss. Anecdotally, in my family, we had an army veteran who lost an eye and his best friend during the liberation of Holland in the Second World War. He and his wife attended a social event at their Legion where there was a veteran who tried to bring up some of his less positive memories. He was firmly shut down, with my aunt commenting later what a buzz kill he had been (I paraphrase) at an event that was supposed to have been fun.

In wider Canadian society, veterans were isolated, left to live with what they had seen and what they had done, privately. Hidden in plain sight. If Bill McKnight had survived the war, a sad but awful future was possible where he turned up at the Legion, 'gone to shit' to use the colourful Canadian expression and the drunkest person there. No one would ever believe that once upon a time McKnight had been the best fighter pilot in the country. Now he was nothing but a sad, struggling man who everyone avoided, and no one wanted to talk to.

Before I ever spoke to Bill McKnight, I knew that McKnight Boulevard was named for a Second World War flying ace from Calgary, and there was a rumour that his name wasn't Willie. With those scraps of knowledge, I was already in elite 2 per cent company. As my research progressed, I encountered the names of other Second World War aces from Calgary, Bob Niven and 'Moose' Martin. Until then, I had no idea who they were.

When I am asked to promote this book in Canada, I wonder if the people asking me about McKnight will have the faintest knowledge of anyone from Canadian history, aside from John A. Macdonald, Canada's divisive first Prime Minister. For the most part, Canadians are not history people. Our orientation to time seems to be the present, and history offers a lot of complication. We are beginning to face our imperialist heritage. It isn't a bad thing not to glorify war. There are layers of Canada's history that are wincingly embarrassing, painful, divisive and uncomfortable. I do think Canadians could handle it, but we haven't been taught much about our history in school. We are a nation of people who move on quickly, focused on the present moment and daily life. That can be a strength, but it means that important things that could help us to make better sense of ourselves and make better decisions about the future are quickly forgotten.

Bill did have to spend time around politicians who were using his image for their own visibility and purposes. In March 2025, Canada had a general federal election. As I watched the debates, I could not help but think that all of the leaders vying to be our next Prime Minister could agree on one thing. Mark Carney, Pierre Poilievre and Jagmeet Singh, the front runners, would probably concur enthusiastically that Bill McKnight was a significant Canadian, with an impactful Canadian story. But none of them know who he is.

What it seems that Bill does is to focus on one Calgarian at a time. The letters he wrote to Mike Peglar were preserved for a lifetime by his old friend. Then they were protected forever when Peglar donated them to Library and Archives Canada. Those letters sparked additional interest from journalists at critical times who interviewed people who had known Bill before they too were gone. The fateful visit that Bill paid to Andy Little before he left for England inspired Little decades later to see the name McKnight affixed to a significant roadway at last.

Now it's my turn. One Calgarian at a time – and it seems that there can be only one – picks up the memorial cudgel and walks forward with it just enough that it doesn't get obliterated entirely. Bill's life will never get the coverage and respect that it deserves, but it doesn't disappear altogether either.

This is a strange fact to admit to the world. What is the lasting impact that Bill McKnight left on Canada? The truth is, he didn't leave one. Aside from his admiring and respectful fans who have an interest in aviation or military history, no one in Canada knows who he is, and probably in Calgary least of all.

It was fascinating to watch this young man doing his best to grow up. In the summer of 1939, he was partying in Scotland, seeing one girl, and using her car to pick up another (he claimed), enraging his commanders and earning a two-week 'time out' for his behaviour – twice, or was it three times? In the spring of 1940, he was expressing remorse for the way he treated his stepmother as an adolescent, reflecting on what it would be like to be back in Calgary, and longing for friends.

There is no need to set Bill McKnight on a pedestal. In fact, I think it does him a disservice. In so many ways, he was just a guy. But neither can we take away anything from his accomplishments, because in other ways he was great.

The historian Hugh Halliday sums him up thus, 'He was a very professional fighter pilot, he was doing his job. He was a good killer.' Halliday also points out that the environment has a role in creating aces. In a target-rich setting, pilots will have more things to shoot at and more chances to hit things. At the same time, the pilots in those conditions were in great danger themselves; there was a far greater likelihood of being shot down because of the density of the enemy. Dunkirk and the Battle of Britain were both prime examples of those target-rich environments. Having said that, only one in 100 fighter pilots ever became an ace. Many never fired their guns at an enemy aircraft. And if they did, they missed.[1]

Although leadership was something that Bill never wanted or was comfortable with, he was both well liked and well respected in his squadron. The qualities of leadership include an ability to inspire others. Other people also need to feel that they can rely on you. Stan Turner had more of that quality than Bill did, speaking out for his squadron when they went through a time of chaotic, debilitating political turnover in their leadership, losing every senior officer they had, including their squadron leader, Gobeil.

However, Bill was someone that you would have been comfortable to sit down with in the mess hall; he was fun, and he was funny. He had a dry sense of humour. He could be observant and self-deprecating. His letters reveal personal growth and a desire for connection. Through his letters we see that he could be generous, protective, observant and self-reflective. Physically, he looked very young. You might have done a double take if someone had pointed out to you that you were sitting next to the leading ace (killer) in the squadron.

Family lore recalled his 'modest' ambitions to personally kill Hitler as the Second World War commenced. And then he shot down more German fighters than any other Canadian in the first fourteen months of the conflict.

Bill was the leading Canadian ace at the time of his death. It has been suggested that if Bill had kept flying, there would have been one of three crosses waiting in his future. Had his luck held long enough, he was almost certainly destined for the Victoria Cross. Or the Red Cross – terrible facial or spinal injuries, permanent brain damage – for when the luck ran out. Or a little white cross, somewhere in France, for when the luck ran out altogether. In the end, he was denied them all, his name inscribed instead on the Runnymede Memorial for the Missing along with the thousands of others who vanished.

Remembrance Day

A map of Bill's world in Crescent Heights, Calgary, Alberta, includes the house on Alexander Crescent, Mike and Bill Peglar's place across the alley, Marian's house around the corner, Stanley Jones Elementary School and Crescent Heights High School. The Renfrew Airfield hangar building is still there. It was a good range for a kid with a little brother. On the edge of the neighbourhood is McHugh Bluff, which overlooks Memorial Drive. It is a tall ridge, set high above the Bow and Elbow Rivers that wash through the valley.

Surely Bill and Ray gamboled along McHugh Bluff many a time, back when Calgary looked so different. Hawks, meadowlarks and the occasional aircraft looped through the sky. Picking wildflowers for Rose? – a handful of the velvety purple crocuses early in the spring. Sunshine, the clean smell of the natural grass, the Bow River washing through the floodplain, the Rocky Mountains shining on the edge of the western horizon.

The two brothers looked down to the spot along Memorial Drive where for Remembrance Day every November since 1924, Calgarians have set up little white crosses with the names of their fellow citizens who were killed in military service. Perhaps they even attended a ceremony.

Today, Bill's name is on one of them. William McKnight.

Bill met the Luftwaffe at their best, at the peak of their training and strength. They had the most modern equipment, the best-trained pilots, superior numbers of aircraft and combat experience. They were at a heady period of their history, full of assurance and determination, seizing one victory after another. How terrifying they must have been, and how terrifying it must have been to stand up to them. They were the best of the best. And then they encountered Bill, who was officially credited with shooting down sixteen and a half of them in a little over six months of flying. He was terrified, but he was terrifying, too.

When we think about sacrifice, we remember the people imprisoned, injured, and killed. It is easy to forget things like isolation, separation, bad food, growing up too fast, grief and loss. I believe that the seeds of who Bill was and the person he was growing into were to be found in the original letter to his family in the spring of 1939. Care and concern for family and siblings. Generosity. Encouragement and support expressed to friends, along with playful teasing. Calgarians deserve to know this Bill, a multi-faceted whole person, not just the 'flinty eyed little dead shot from Calgary'.

Bill McKnight's recommendations for a great day out in Calgary (in the 22 September 1940 letter that Bill wrote to Mike Peglar):

- Go to a football game, I recommend the Calgary Stampeders
- Get your best friend's mom to make you a chocolate cake and have a piece!
- Listen to Bing Crosby
- Drive the Banff to Jasper Highway (now that it's open …)

Author's Note

It is always a delicate balance when one attempts to break the fourth wall and insert yourself into a biography. Any attempt by me to place myself into a biography about Bill McKnight's life feels inappropriate and indulgent. However, the story of how I met his family is a story within a story. I have included it at the end, so the reader can decide if they want to learn about the strange postscript of how this book came to be.

The first time that I met Bill's nephew, I received this text message from him moments after we separated:

> Don't speed, they'll give you a ticket regardless of your last name lol. I'm literally walking on air right now. It was truly a pleasure to meet you and spend time not only discussing my family but getting to know you. I thoroughly enjoyed [our] afternoon together and I'm so pleased I could be a part of sharing my family's history and treasured memories. I have all the faith in the world that you will respect it and make it live forever for everyone to know and enjoy. War sucks but these brave people need to be known for their service. I owe you a huge thank you for taking time for my uncle. You're awesome.
>
> I said this is all up to you. I'd be thrilled to have him immortalized, and the entire 242. I have little else to share but what an honour to share what I have with you. I literally had the best afternoon of 2020, which effin sucked. Calgary went into lockdown the day before my birthday so any time I get to share stories and be happy gives me great joy. I'm so happy to have met and been able to share what I have and what I know.
>
> Bill McKnight

The phrase 'walking on air' suggests to me a person who had a recovered a sense of freedom. A person who has been released from a heavy burden, and legacy treasured and cherished but that was undeniably weighty. I thought to myself, 'I know where that burden went! It's landed right onto me!'

And indeed, it felt that way. I didn't have the first clue of what I should do, except to help this story to get where it was really going. Once I made the introductions, I would be free, too.

I could make a presentation for Historic Calgary Week, but that was the extent of my ambitions. And then I didn't do it. Too busy. Too scared. It was too big for me. What weighed on me the most was the story of the day the McKnight family had the telegram delivered to their home in Calgary. It was heartbreaking. I felt that other Canadians deserved to know about that. The loss that little Ted McKnight experienced on that terrible day.

'My' Bill and I were turning into friends. We visited the Hangar Flight Museum, where he posed in front of the Hurricane, beaming. Standing next to Bill McKnight and staring at the Hurricane does seem like an ultimate Calgary experience. He also told me funny family stories, such as how getting a speeding ticket on McKnight Boulevard was pretty much something everyone in the McKnight family was expected to do.

One day he called me, weeping, because of the stories that were being widely circulated in the media at the time, bringing to light the hidden in plain view legacy of Residential schools for indigenous children in Canada. Bill, who was an advocate for women and children, and for anyone who he saw as an underdog, sobbed as he asked me, 'Did my uncle know about this? And would he have fought for this country if he did know?'

It was rather like confronting the nice guy image of Canada and our history and realizing that someone you had liked and respected was secretly an incel. It upended or at least severely undermined certainties about who the good guys are. Why were there concentration camps for indigenous children in our country until the 1990s? All I could do was listen. I didn't have answers, either.

Facing the Reaper

On a hot summer day in 2022, I was leaving work and saw that Bill, who I had not heard from in a few months, had texted me. I picked up my phone only to learn that the text was from Bill's partner. Bill had died. I spent the rest of that summer grieving for my friend. Now it also felt like I was carrying that burden alone. It got heavier.

In 2023, there was yet another plot twist. I was struck by an impaired driver on my way home from work. The only thing left of my truck was my seat. The Reaper came very, very close indeed. I needed to learn to walk again, how to live with chronic pain and a mind that no longer felt like my own. I was haunted by the idea that I could have died, and no one would have known Bill's – and Ted's – and Bill's – story. The story about the telegram could have been lost forever.

My dad encouraged me as part of my rehabilitation to think about something meaningful that I could work on as I was healing. Of course, I thought about the McKnight presentation. I started working on it, and that was when I realized how hurt my brain was. History now felt like a 50lb weight. The sharpness and agility that I needed to fact check, to write, to switch back and forth between books and screens and sources was no longer there. Things that should have taken three hours could take three days. It was also the only thing that got me out of bed sometimes.

The weight of history grew even heavier. What I did have was time, and I knew what I wanted to do. I wanted to pick up that weight and carry it. I thought that an article describing the life of this significant Calgarian was a realistic goal; that became a meaningful thing to aim for. Then the article was 9,000 words long. I was accidentally writing a book.

The McKnight family legacy is one that I do know about. 'To you from failing hands we throw.' I know that people from the United Kingdom and the United States and Bill McKnight's other international fans will read this. But I especially hope that Canadians and other Calgarians will give Bill's story a chance.

Bill was a dear person in some ways. Obnoxious in others. Clearly struggling with his mental health at times. A man who was coolly shooting down other men, observing that it was 'legalized murder'[1] even if he claimed that he was enjoying it. If he were alive today, I think that he would love gaming. He loved the romantic music of Bing Crosby; he was a sentimental person. His letters had made that so clear to me all along. The missing piece in Bill's story is his mother. What if his last thoughts, whatever they were, were of peace and love, of the person he had been missing all along – you see, I am an unreliable narrator, desperate for closure.

I do know what it is like to think that you are going to die. To see death coming, and to say goodbye to life, before your brain does the last kindness it will ever do for you. Unconsciousness. Then again, Lady Luck was my passenger that day. It was a miss for the Reaper. We have an unknown date in the future. But the underworld will have to wait, for now.

I know what it is like to have injuries. A story that is hard to talk about. To have shrapnel in your hands (I have glass in mine). To have to get into a vehicle when you are sick with fear. To be at a crossroads in your life and wonder what to do next.

The way that Bill and Bill came into my life, because of a random story about football.

Here is the strangest thing about the whole strange affair.

The road I didn't I die on was McKnight Boulevard.

Bibliography

Published Sources

Atkin, Ronald. *Pillar of Fire: Dunkirk 1940.* London: Sidgwick & Jackson.

Bader, Douglas. *Fight for the Sky.* Barnsley: Pen & Sword Aviation, 1973; repr. 2005, 2008.

Bercuson, David J. *Canada's Air Force at 100.* Toronto: University of Toronto Press, 2024.

Brickhill, Paul. *Reach for the Sky.* London: Collins, 1960.

Burnett, Thane. 'The Amazing Willie McKnight', *The Calgary Sunday Sun,* March 3, 1991, S3.

Daily Mirror. 'Fighter Hit by Shell Bagged 2', October 5, 1940.

Edmonton Journal. 'Air Development Recruits', November 30, 1938, 2.

Granatstein, J. L. 'Vincent Massey.' *Canadian Encyclopedia,* 2008. www.thecanadianencyclopedia.ca/en/article/massey-charles-vincent

Halliday, Hugh. *242 Squadron: The Canadian Years.* Stittsville, ON: Canada's Wings, 1981.

– – – . *The Tumbling Sky.* Stittsville, ON: Canada's Wings, 1978.

Hallowell, Edward M., and John J. Ratey. *ADHD 2.0: New Science and Essential Strategies for Thriving with Distraction – from Childhood through Adulthood.* New York: Ballantine Books, 2021.

Hastings, Max. *Bomber Command.* London: Michael Joseph Limited, 1979.

Holmes, Tony. *Hurricane Aces 1939–1941.* Oxford: Osprey, 1998.

Kennington, Eric. *Drawing the Royal Air Force.* Oxford: Oxford University Press, 1942.

Lange, Klaus W., Susanne Reichl, Katharina M. Lange, Lara Tucha, and Oliver Tucha. 'The History of Attention Deficit Hyperactivity Disorder', *Attention Deficit and Hyperactivity Disorders* 2, no. 4 (2010): 241–255. https://doi.org/10.1007/s12402-010-0045-8.

Matheson, Shirlee Smith. *A Western Welcome to the World.* Encino: Cherbo Publishing Group, Inc., 1997.

Mayfield, Guy. *Life & Death in the Battle of Britain.* London: Imperial War Museums, 2018.

Osterweis, Marian, ed. *Bereavement: Reactions, Consequences, and Care.* Washington, D.C.: National Academy Press, 1984.

Reardon, Terry. *Winston Churchill and Mackenzie King: So Similar, So Different.* Toronto: Dundurn, 2014.

Reeves, Kate. *Rosedale Stories: A Community Remembers.* Calgary: Two Printers Inc., 2000.

Reid, Harry. 'Ace Paid Ultimate Price', *Calgary Herald,* 1997, 11.

Rhodes, Guy. 'Calgary Boy Gets His Commission', *Calgary Albertan,* September 30, 1939, 17.

Sarkar, Dilip. *Fighter Ace.* Stroud: Amberley, 2014.

Sebag-Montefiore, Hugh. *Dunkirk: Fight to the Last Man.* London: Penguin, 2006.

Simaluk, Vern. 'Aviation Report', *Calgary Herald,* July 19, 1979, 52.

Simonsen, Clarence. 'Notes from Noel Holland Barlow on No. 242 [Canadian] Squadron Nose Art', *Lest We Forget,* November 20, 2014. https://athabaskang07.wordpress.com/wp-content/uploads/2014/11/a-street-in-calgary-named-after-him-but-nobody-knows1.pdf.

The Calgary Albertan. 'Follows Flying Trail of His Famous Brother', April 30, 1941.

The Calgary Albertan. 'Ray Joins the Royal Canadian Air Force', April 30, 1941.

The Calgary Albertan. 'Ski-Ski-siana, From the Powder Snow Country', March 22, 1940, 12.

The Calgary Albertan. 'Wartime Air Ace Proposes Honor for Calgary Hero', July 27, 1957, 3.

The Calgary Daily Herald. 'Letters from Members', 1931.

The Calgary Daily Herald. 'Wins Distinction', 1931, 8.

The Calgary Herald. 'Another City Pilot Missing', June 12, 1940.

———. 'City Pilot with 14 Planes Leads Flying "Musketeers"', August 26, 1940, 26.

———. 'Fighter Pilot Lost in France', 1941, 1.

———. 'Heros Shrine Urged', July 27, 1957.

———. 'Parents Hear Son on British Radio', February 20, 1940, 9.

———. 'Remembering the Heroes', November 6, 1991, 104.

– – – . 'Wed 50 Years, Two Grandsons in Air Force', December 24, 1940.
The Calgary Herald. October 2, 1940, 3.
The Calgary Herald. October 17, 1941.
The Crescent Bugle. Calgary: Crescent Heights High School, 1937.
The Leader-Post. 'Canadian Aircraft Corporation Head Denies War Charge', June 7, 1940, 2.
The Times Colonist. 'McKnight, Raymond – Obituary', May 23, 2002.
The Toronto Star. 'Planning to Build Bombers Here for Ocean Spanning', July 28, 1938, 3.
The Windsor Star. 'André Verdier Sent to Prison', June 10, 1940, 21.
Turner, Stan. Turner Family Archive.
– – – . *Documents.* Turner Family Archive.

Websites

Canada Remembers Program of Veterans Affairs. 'The British Commonwealth Air Training Plan', accessed June 2025. https://veterans.gc.ca/en/remembrance/classroom/fact-sheets/britcom.
Calgary Mosquito Society. 'Willie McKnight, Calgary's Battle of Britain Ace', accessed January 15, 2025. https://calgarymosquitosociety.com/feature16/feature16.htm.
Coventry City Council. '20 Facts You Might Not Know About the Coventry Blitz', accessed September 2025. www.coventry.gov.uk/coventry-blitz/20-facts-might-not-know-coventry-blitz#:~:text=The%20aim%20was%20to%20knock,on%20the%20road%20without%20light.
Dougy Center. *Developmental Responses to Grief.* Portland, OR: Dougy Center, 2021. www.dougy.org/grief-resources/developmental-responses-to-grief.
Flight Global Magazine. ' – ', July 8, 1937. www.flightglobal.com/pdfarchive/view/1937/1937-1934. Accessed September 12, 2024.
O'Malley, Dave. 'The Return of the Reaper', *Vintage Wings of Canada,* April 25, 2022. www.vintagewings.ca/stories/first-flight-of-the-reaper.
Royal Canadian Air Force Association. 'Honours & Awards', accessed September 2025. www.rcafassociation.ca/heritage/honours-awards
– – – . 'RCAF Combat Claims, 1939–40', accessed September 2025. www.rcafassociation.ca/heritage/history/rcaf-combat-claims/rcaf-combat-claims-1939-40
Simonsen, Clarence. 'Notes from Noel Holland Barlow on No. 242 [Canadian] Squadron Nose Art', *Lest We Forget*, November 20, 2014. https://

athabaskang07.wordpress.com/wp-content/uploads/2014/11/a-street-in-calgary-named-after-him-but-nobody-knows1.pdf.

WW2 Eagles Blogspot. 'Willie McKnight Canada's First Ace', October 2011. https://ww2eagles.blogspot.com/2011/10/willie-mcknight-canadas-first-ace.html, accessed September 12, 2024.

Archival Sources

- The National Archives (UK), AIR 50/92/7, *Combat Report*.
- The National Archives (UK), AIR 50/92/98, *Combat Report*.
- The National Archives (UK), AIR-50-92-108, *Combat Report*.
- The National Archives (UK), AIR 127/1471/912.
- Library and Archives Canada, ID 103020, *McKnight Letters*, 23 July 1939. https://recherche-collection-search.bac-lac.gc.ca/eng/Home/Record?app=fonandcol&IdNumber=103020&ecopy=.

Films and Programs

Jay Hunt, 'The Untold Story: Royal Canadian Air Force Leader Fowler Gobeil', *Canadian Aviation and Space Museum*, Ottawa, 2018.

Acknowledgements

As a lifelong reader, I finally know why the thank you notes in the acknowledgements of the books that I have read and loved over the years are a mile long. The work that goes into writing a book must be shared, or it will never happen. People came along who offered to help me research, who researched things for me, put up with being 'pestered' with questions, recommended sources and resources, lent me books, and came alongside with pep talks to boost my spirits. It turned into a nationwide Canadian project, with British assistance.

Christine Hayes and Carolyn Ryder, my friends from the Calgary Public Library who kept in touch, and listened to me talk about Bill … a lot. I had two of the best researchers in the world on staff to investigate Bill McKnight's Calgary years … not that I paid you.

Emma-lee Campbell for literally being the best thing that ever happened to me, my own wingman.

Barry Halliwell for (free) tours at the Hangar Flight Museum and for letting me climb in and out of vintage aircraft.

My wonderful and VERY patient editors and publishers at Pen & Sword. Your favourite Canadian author was an absolute beginner with this whole process, but it meant such a lot to me that you were understanding as I made a lot of blunders.

Karl Kjarsgaard for offering to help me with technical questions and then helping me explore Ray McKnight's story as well.

Darcy, for being so patient with me when I reached out and 'pestered' you a million times. I knew it was okay, because my Bill wouldn't have loved you if you weren't a such a good person.

Bert for the use of your fine library, so that I didn't have to make choices between buying groceries that week and purchasing books. I'm kidding, of course. Or am I?

Justin Campbell for buying me books and driving me places when I was broken in half, and for not letting me listen to my imposter syndrome (too much). Also, for many cups of tea. Having a professional driver on staff has been most appreciated.

Dilip Sarkar for the sundog omen, for agreeing to an interview with me about Douglas Bader, for writing books that helped me, and then for checking in with me again … and again. And recommending my wonderful publisher to me. It was the easiest thing ever. Time for us young pester-ers to get in on this.

Hugh Halliday, for being the single biggest and most influential and important source for this book. And for perhaps being the biggest pester-er in this country at one time. Without all your hard work, anything I tried to do would have been impossible. Also, thank you for emailing me Gobeil's file! I asked you about it and you understood immediately what I wanted to know, and why I wanted to know it. It turned out to be an interesting chapter in this book.

Kayla McAlister, my researcher at the Calgary Public Library, who researched Bill's years at Crescent Heights for me and tracked down the *Crescent Bugle* and found stories about 'little' Marian.

Rachet Bedet, for helping a person with a brain injury with the notes and the index. The book almost didn't happen but she saved the day.

Dave Hatfield for a fun morning ranting about Trump and teaching me about flying a Hurricane. Rob Erdos for filling in the Bf 109 angle, and for helping me think like a pilot just a little bit.

Jessica Zutz, Erin Hoar, Elizabeth Holt, Sandra Pallister, Deb Keller, Rob McIntyre. Essential buddies.

Kim and Tina Turner for sharing your amazing father's photographs, documents and artifacts. For your stories and ideas and encouragement.

To Richard, who spent hours driving me to physiotherapy appointments when I was in so much pain that I could hardly get in or out of a car and tottered around with a cane. During it all, you had the idea to transcribe the McKnight letters. Sometimes I had no idea what I was reading thanks to the concussion. But at least we were hanging out and having fun. The next thing I knew, I was writing an article. Then I was writing a book for some reason. And luckily for me, you are a top aviation historian and had a built-in network of people who I could reach out to. This book would never, ever, ever have happened without you.

And thank you especially to 'my' Bill, because without you this would never have happened to begin with. Thanks for picking me and for encouraging me so much that even I couldn't be confused. I am not sure what happens when we die, but I hope you're flying Hurricanes.

Notes

Bill Was from Edmonton

1. 'Wed 50 Years, Two Grandsons in Air Force', *Edmonton Journal*, 24 December 1940.

Calgary in the 1930s

1. Kate Reeves, *Rosedale Stories: A Community Remembers* (Calgary: Two Printers Inc., 2000), 10.
2. Ibid., 14.
3. Harry Reid, 'Ace Paid Ultimate Price,' *Calgary Herald*, 1997, 11.
4. Shirlee Smith Matheson, *A Western Welcome to the World* (Encino: Cherbo Publishing Group, Inc., 1997), 11.
5. Reeves, *Rosedale Stories*, 19.
6. Ibid., 21.
7. 'Fighter Pilot Lost in France', *Calgary Herald*, 1941, 1.
8. Guy Rhodes, 'Calgary Boy Gets His Commission', *Calgary Albertan*, September 30, 1939, 17.
9. 'Fighter Pilot Lost in France', *Calgary Herald*, 1941, 1.
10. Jeff Bartikiewicz, 'McKnight Boulevard Named after War Hero', *Calgary Herald*, August 29, 2004, B1–B2.
11. 'Wins Distinction', *Calgary Daily Herald*, 1931, 8.
12. 'Letters from Members', *Calgary Daily Herald*, 1931.
13. *The Crescent Bugle* (Calgary: Crescent Heights High School, 1937), 49, 70.
14. Ibid.
15. Ibid.
16. Ibid., 49.
17. Ibid., 70.

Bill's Moms

1. Jeff Bartikiewicz, 'McKnight Boulevard Named after War Hero', *Calgary Herald*, August 29, 2004, B1–B2.
2. Marian Osterweis, ed., *Bereavement: Reactions, Consequences, and Care* (Washington, DC: National Academy Press, 1984), 99–144.
3. Bartikiewicz, 'McKnight Boulevard Named after War Hero'.
4. Dougy Center, *Developmental Responses to Grief* (Portland, OR: Dougy Center, 2021), www.dougy.org/grief-resources/developmental-responses-to-grief.
5. Ibid.
6. Ibid.
7. Bartikiewicz, 'McKnight Boulevard Named after War Hero'.

Rebel

1. William McKnight, interview by Shelly McElroy, November 17, 2020.
2. Thane Burnett, 'The Amazing Willie McKnight', *The Calgary Sunday Sun*, March 3, 1991, S3.
3. Jeff Bartikiewicz, 'McKnight Boulevard Named after War Hero', *Calgary Herald*, August 29, 2004, B1–B2.
4. Harry Reid, 'Ace Paid Ultimate Price', *Calgary Herald*, 1997, 11.
5. Burnett, 'The Amazing Willie McKnight'.
6. Bartikiewicz, 'McKnight Boulevard Named after War Hero'.
7. Ibid.
8. Jeff Bartikiewicz, interview by Shelly McElroy, June 2, 2025.
9. Ibid.
10. McKnight, interview by McElroy, November 17, 2020.
11. Bartikiewicz, 'McKnight Boulevard Named after War Hero'.
12. Klaus W. Lange, Susanne Reichl, Katharina M. Lange, Lara Tucha, and Oliver Tucha, 'The History of Attention Deficit Hyperactivity Disorder', *Attention Deficit and Hyperactivity Disorders* 2, no. 4 (2010): 241–55, https://doi.org/10.1007/s12402-010-0045-8.
13. Paloma Scott, interview by Shelly McElroy, June 2024.
14. Bartikiewicz, 'McKnight Boulevard Named after War Hero'.
15. *The Toronto Star*, 'Planning to Build Bombers Here for Ocean Spanning', July 28, 1938, 3.
16. *Edmonton Journal*, 'Air Development Recruits', November 30, 1938, 2.

17. Clarence Simonsen, 'Notes from Noel Holland Barlow on No. 242 [Canadian] Squadron Nose Art,' Lest We Forget, November 20, 2014, https://athabaskang07.wordpress.com/wp-content/uploads/2014/11/a-street-in-calgary-named-after-him-but-nobody-knows1.pdf.
18. *Edmonton Journal*, 'Air Development Recruits,' November 30, 1938, 2.

The Fledgling

1. *Calgary Herald*, January 21, 1939, 14.
2. Jeff Bartikiewicz, 'McKnight Boulevard Named after War Hero', *Calgary Herald*, August 29, 2004, B1–B2.
3. William McKnight, postcard, January 25, 1939, McKnight Family Archive.
4. 'Willie McKnight Canada's First Ace', *WW2 Eagles* (blog), October 2011, https://ww2eagles.blogspot.com/2011/10/willie-mcknight-canadas-first-ace.html (accessed September 12, 2024).
5. ' – ', *Flight Global Magazine*, July 8, 1937, www.flightglobal.com/pdfarchive/view/1937/1937-1934 (accessed September 12, 2024).
6. William McKnight, Item ID Number 103020, May 3, 1939, Library and Archives Canada, https://recherche-collection-search.bac-lac.gc.ca/eng/home/record?IdNumber=103020.
7. Ibid.
8. William McKnight, 1939–1941. *Logbook*. AIR/77, The National Archives (TNA), Kew, United Kingdom.

'Tell Ted I'm Sorry About the Train'

1. William McKnight, letter, April 18, 1939, McKnight Family Archive.
2. Ibid.
3. William McKnight, Item ID Number 103020, May 3, 1939, Library and Archives Canada, https://recherche-collection-search.bac-lac.gc.ca/eng/home/record?IdNumber=103020.
4. Ibid.
5. William McKnight. 1939–1941. *Logbook*. AIR/77, The National Archives (TNA), Kew, United Kingdom.
6. McKnight, Item ID Number 103020, May 3, 1939, Library and Archives Canada.
7. Guy Rhodes, 'Calgary Boy Gets His Commission', *Calgary Albertan*, September 30, 1939, 17.

8. McKnight, Item ID Number 103020, May 3, 1939, Library and Archives Canada.
9. Ibid.
10. Paul Brickhill, *Reach for the Sky* (London: Collins, 1960), 28.

Summer of '39

1. William McKnight, Library and Archives Canada, Item ID 103020, July 23, 1939, https://recherche-collection-search.bac-lac.gc.ca/eng/Home/Record?app=fonandcol&IdNumber=103020&ecopy=.
2. William McKnight, Library and Archives Canada, Item ID 103020, June 25, 1939, https://recherche-collection-search.bac-lac.gc.ca/eng/Home/Record?app=fonandcol&IdNumber=103020&ecopy=.
3. Ibid.
4. Ibid.
5. Ibid.
6. Ibid.
7. Ibid.

'You can spot a Canadian right off'

1. Hugh Halliday, *242 Squadron: The Canadian Years* (Stittsville, ON: Canada's Wings, 1981), 20.
2. William McKnight, Library and Archives Canada, Item ID 103020, July 10, 1939, https://recherche-collection-search.bac-lac.gc.ca/eng/Home/Record?app=fonandcol&IdNumber=103020&ecopy=.
3. Ibid.
4. Ibid.
5. Ibid.
6. Ibid.
7. McKnight, Library and Archives Canada, Item ID 103020, July 23, 1939, https://recherche-collection-search.bac-lac.gc.ca/eng/Home/Record?app=fonandcol&IdNumber=103020&ecopy=.
8. Ibid.
9. Ibid.
10. Ibid.
11. Ibid.
12. Ibid.

Prime Minister Mackenzie King and Canada's Political Situation

1. Max Hastings, *Bomber Command* (London: Michael Joseph Limited, 1979).

Sick as Hell

1. William McKnight, Library and Archives Canada, Item ID 103020, September 16 and 24, 1939, https://recherche-collection-search.bac-lac.gc.ca/eng/Home/Record?app=fonandcol&IdNumber=103020&ecopy=.
2. William McKnight. 1939–1941. *Logbook.* AIR/77. The National Archives (TNA), Kew, United Kingdom.
3. Ibid.
4. Ibid.
5. Guy Mayfield, *Life & Death in the Battle of Britain* (London: Imperial War Museums, 2018), 41.
6. McKnight, Library and Archives Canada, Item ID 103020.
7. Ibid.
8. Ibid.
9. Ibid.
10. Ibid.
11. Ibid.

Meet No. 242 Squadron: The Official Troublemaker Squadron

1. Sir Gerald Campbell, 'Public Record Office, Group Air 2, Docket 3157, Air Ministry Files'.
2. Hugh Halliday, *242 Squadron: The Canadian Years* (Stittsville, ON: Canada's Wings, 1981), 8.
3. Ibid., 9.
4. Campbell, 'Public Record Office, Group Air 2, Docket 3157, Air Ministry Files'.
5. F.J. Hatch and Norman Hillmer, 'British Commonwealth Air Training Plan', *The Canadian Encyclopedia* (Toronto: McClelland & Stewart, 2000), 306.
6. Terry Reardon, *Winston Churchill and Mackenzie King: So Similar, So Different* (Toronto: Dundurn, 2014), 96.
7. Ibid., 97.
8. Halliday, *242 Squadron*, 11.
9. Ibid., 13.

Assembled

1. Fowler Gobeil, 'Reply to Letter D.A.P.C. 1580', August 22, 1940, 1.
2. Clarence Simonsen, 'Notes from Noel Holland Barlow on No. 242 [Canadian] Squadron Nose Art,' *Lest We Forget*, November 20, 2014, https://athabaskang07.wordpress.com/wp-content/uploads/2014/11/a-street-in-calgary-named-after-him-but-nobody-knows1.pdf.
3. Hugh Halliday, 'Rambling Through the Records: CAN/RAF Cards', *Observair* 62, no. 3 (2016).
4. Ibid., Simonsen.
5. Ibid.
6. Ibid., Gobeil.
7. Hugh Halliday, *242 Squadron: The Canadian Years* (Stittsville, ON: Canada's Wings, 1981), 17.
8. Ibid., 15.
9. Ibid., 16.
10. Ibid.
11. Hugh Halliday, *The Tumbling Sky* (Stittsville, ON: Canada's Wings, 1978), 258.
12. Halliday, *242 Squadron*, 16.
13. Ibid., 22.
14. Ibid., 21.
15. Ibid., 23.
16. Ibid.

Fighters and Fatalities

1. Hugh Halliday, *242 Squadron: The Canadian Years* (Stittsville, ON: Canada's Wings, 1981), 25.
2. Ibid., 26.
3. Ibid.
4. Ibid., 23.
5. Ibid., 27.
6. William McKnight, Library and Archives Canada, Item ID 103020, February 25, 1940, https://recherche-collection-search.bac-lac.gc.ca/eng/Home/Record?app=fonandcol&IdNumber=103020&ecopy=.
7. Ibid.
8. Ibid.
9. McKnight, Library and Archives Canada, Item ID 103020, April 24, 1940, https://recherche-collection-search.bac-lac.gc.ca/eng/Home/Record?app=fonandcol&IdNumber=103020&ecopy=.

10. Ibid.
11. McKnight, Library and Archives Canada, Item ID 103020, February 25, 1940.
12. Halliday, *242 Squadron*, 15.
13. McKnight, Library and Archives Canada, Item ID 103020, February 25, 1940.
14. Ibid.
15. Ibid.
16. McKnight, Library and Archives Canada, Item ID 103020, April 24, 1940.
17. McKnight, Library and Archives Canada, Item ID 103020, February 25, 1940.

Family and Friends

1. 'Parents Hear Son on British Radio', *Calgary Herald*, February 20, 1940, 9.
2. William McKnight, Library and Archives Canada, Item ID 103020, April 24, 1940, https://recherche-collection-search.bac-lac.gc.ca/eng/Home/Record?app=fonandcol&IdNumber=103020&ecopy=.
3. Ibid.
4. 'Ski-Ski-siana, From the Powder Snow Country', *Calgary Albertan*, March 22, 1940, 12.
5. Jeff Bartikiewicz, 'McKnight Boulevard Named after War Hero', *Calgary Herald*, August 29, 2004, B1–B2.

Where to?

1. Hugh Halliday, *242 Squadron: The Canadian Years* (Stittsville, ON: Canada's Wings, 1981), 26.
2. Hugh Halliday, *The Tumbling Sky* (Stittsville, ON: Canada's Wings, 1978), 210.

Meet the Hurricane

1. Dave Hadfield, interview by Shelly McElroy, May 6, 2025.
2. Douglas Bader, *Fight for the Sky* (Barnsley: Pen & Sword Aviation, 1973; repr. 2005, 2008), 38.
3. Rob Erdos, interview by Shelly McElroy, June 5, 2025.
4. Ibid., Hadfield.
5. Ibid.
6. Richard de Boer, interview by Shelly McElroy, March 5, 2025.

7. Ibid., Hadfield.
8. Ibid.
9. Ibid., de Boer.
10. William McKnight, Library and Archives Canada, Item ID 103020, April 24, 1940, https://recherche-collection-search.bac-lac.gc.ca/eng/Home/Record?app=fonandcol&IdNumber=103020&ecopy=.
11. Hugh Halliday, *242 Squadron: The Canadian Years* (Stittsville, ON: Canada's Wings, 1981), 25.
12. Dave Hadfield, interview by Shelly McElroy, May 6, 2025.

The Competition

1. Rob Erdos, interview by Shelly McElroy, June 5, 2025.

Willie McKnight: The Action Starts

1. Hugh Halliday, *The Tumbling Sky* (Stittsville, ON: Canada's Wings, 1978), 258.
2. Hugh Halliday, *242 Squadron: The Canadian Years* (Stittsville, ON: Canada's Wings, 1981), 44.
3. McKnight, William. 1939–1941. *Logbook.* AIR/77. The National Archives (TNA), Kew, United Kingdom.

19 May 1940: First Kill

1. Combat Report, AIR 50/175/22, The National Archives (TNA), Kew.
2. 'Fighter Pilot Lost in France', *Calgary Herald*, 1941, p. 1.
3. William McKnight, Library and Archives Canada, Item ID 103020, July 19, 1940, https://recherche-collection-search.bac-lac.gc.ca/eng/Home/Record?app=fonandcol&IdNumber=103020&ecopy=

The Rest of the Battle

1. 'Another City Pilot Missing', *Calgary Herald*, June 12, 1940.
2. Ibid.
3. Fowler Gobeil, 'Reply to Letter D.A.P.C. 1580', August 22, 1940.
4. Jay Hunt, 'The Untold Story: Royal Canadian Air Force Leader Fowler Gobeil', Canadian Aviation and Space Museum, Ottawa, 2018.
5. Hugh Halliday, *242 Squadron: The Canadian Years* (Stittsville, ON: Canada's Wings, 1981), 43.

Dunkirk: Operation Dynamo

1. Hugh Halliday, *242 Squadron: The Canadian Years* (Stittsville, ON: Canada's Wings, 1981), 46.

27 and 28 May 1940

1. Ronald Atkin, *Pillar of Fire: Dunkirk 1940* (London: Sidgwick & Jackson).
2. Combat Report, AIR 50/92/98, The National Archives (TNA), Kew.
3. Ibid.
4. Hugh Halliday, *242 Squadron: The Canadian Years* (Stittsville, ON: Canada's Wings, 1981), 55.

29 May 1940

1. Ronald Atkin, *Pillar of Fire: Dunkirk 1940* (London: Sidgwick & Jackson).
2. Hugh Sebag-Montefiore, *Dunkirk: Fight to the Last Man* (London: Penguin, 2006), 387.
3. Tom Lynch, *Dunkirk: The Real Story in Photographs* (Stroud: History Press Limited, 2017), 65.
4. Ibid., 388.
5. Combat Report, AIR 50/92/98, The National Archives (TNA), Kew.
6. Ibid.
7. Hugh Halliday, *242 Squadron: The Canadian Years* (Stittsville, ON: Canada's Wings, 1981), 56.

30 May 1940

1. Hugh Sebag-Montefiore, *Dunkirk: Fight to the Last Man* (London: Penguin, 2006), 416.
2. Ibid.
3. Hugh Halliday, *242 Squadron: The Canadian Years* (Stittsville, ON: Canada's Wings, 1981), 58.
4. Ibid., 61.

31 May 1940

1. Tony Holmes, *Hurricane Aces 1939–1941* (Oxford: Osprey, 1998), 51.
2. Hugh Halliday, *242 Squadron: The Canadian Years*, 59.
3. Combat Report, AIR 50/92/98, The National Archives (TNA), Kew.
4. Ibid.

5. Halliday, *242 Squadron*, 60.
6. Combat Report, AIR 50/92/98, The National Archives (TNA), Kew.
7. Halliday, *242 Squadron*, 60.

1 June 1940

1. William McKnight, Library and Archives Canada, Item ID 103020, July 19, 1940, https://recherche-collection-search.bac-lac.gc.ca/eng/Home/Record?app=fonandcol&IdNumber=103020&ecopy=.
2. Combat Report, AIR 50/92/98, The National Archives (TNA), Kew.
3. 'City Pilot with 14 Planes Leads Flying "Musketeers"', *Calgary Herald*, August 26, 1940, 26.
4. Ibid., October 2, 1940, 3.
5. Hugh Sebag-Montefiore, *Dunkirk: Fight to the Last Man* (London: Penguin, 2006), 440.
6. Tony Holmes, *Hurricane Aces 1939–1941* (Oxford: Osprey, 1998), 50.
7. Ibid., 51.
8. Ibid.
9. Hugh Halliday, *242 Squadron: The Canadian Years* (Stittsville, ON: Canada's Wings, 1981), 62.
10. *London Gazette*, June 14, 1940.

Meet the King, Pay the Price

1. Terry Reardon, *Winston Churchill and Mackenzie King: So Similar, So Different* (Toronto: Dundurn, 2014), 117–118.
2. Ibid., 113.
3. 'Canadian Aircraft Corporation Head Denies War Charge', *The Leader-Post*, June 7, 1940, 2.
4. 'André Verdier Sent to Prison', *The Windsor Star*, June 10, 1940, 21.
5. Hugh Halliday, *242 Squadron: The Canadian Years* (Stittsville, ON: Canada's Wings, 1981), 63.
6. Ibid.

Enemies in France

1. Hugh Sebag-Montefiore, *Dunkirk: Fight to the Last Man* (London: Penguin, 2006), 440.
2. Fowler Gobeil, 'Report by Gobeil', July 2, 1940, 1.
3. Ibid.

4. Hugh Halliday, *The Tumbling Sky* (Stittsville, ON: Canada's Wings, 1978), 259.
5. Hugh Halliday, *242 Squadron: The Canadian Years* (Stittsville, ON: Canada's Wings, 1981), 70.
6. Fowler Gobeil, 'Report by Gobeil', September 4, 1940, 5.
7. Air Marshal, Air Officer Commander-in-Chief, British Forces in France, 'Confidential Report', June 1940.
8. Ibid.
9. Fowler Gobeil, 'Report by Gobeil', July 2, 1940, 1.
10. Hugh Halliday, interview by Shelly McElroy, August 29, 2024.
11. Richard de Boer, interview by Shelly McElroy, March 2025.

Enjoying Himself Thoroughly

1. Fowler Gobeil, *Report on Operations in France: No. 242 Squadron*, 1940, 8.
2. William McKnight. 1939–1941. *Logbook.* AIR/77, The National Archives (TNA), Kew, United Kingdom.
3. William McKnight, Library and Archives Canada, Item ID 103020, July 19, 1940, https://recherche-collection-search.bac-lac.gc.ca/eng/Home/Record?app=fonandcol&IdNumber=103020&ecopy=.
4. Ibid.
5. Ibid.
6. Hugh Halliday, *242 Squadron: The Canadian Years* (Stittsville, ON: Canada's Wings, 1981), 69.

Margeaux

1. William McKnight, Library and Archives Canada, Item ID 103020, July 19, 1940, https://recherche-collection-search.bac-lac.gc.ca/eng/Home/Record?app=fonandcol&IdNumber=103020&ecopy=
2. Ibid.

Gobeil

1. McKnight, William. 1939–1941. *Logbook.* AIR/77. The National Archives (TNA), Kew, United Kingdom.
2. Gobeil, 'Report by Gobeil', September 4, 1940, 5.
3. Wing Commander Cyril Walter, Officer Commanding, No. 67 Wing, *Report on Squadron Leader Gobeil*, June 24, 1940.

4. Hugh Halliday, interview by Shelly McElroy, August 29, 2024.
5. Fowler Gobeil, 'Report to Chief of the Air Staff, R.C.A.F. Headquarters Ottawa', September 14, 1940.

Relieved of Command

1. Hugh Halliday, *242 Squadron: The Canadian Years* (Stittsville, ON: Canada's Wings, 1981), 80.
2. Hugh Halliday, interview by Shelly McElroy, August 29, 2024.
3. Clarence Simonsen, 'Notes from Noel Holland Barlow on No. 242 [Canadian] Squadron Nose Art', *Lest We Forget*, November 20, 2014, https://athabaskang07.wordpress.com/wp-content/uploads/2014/11/a-street-in-calgary-named-after-him-but-nobody-knows1.pdf.
4. Ibid.
5. Douglas Bader, *Fight for the Sky* (Barnsley: Pen & Sword Aviation, 1973; repr. 2005, 2008).

Leader of the Squadron: Stan Turner

1. William McKnight, Library and Archives Canada, Item ID 103020, February 25, 1940, https://recherche-collection-search.bac-lac.gc.ca/eng/Home/Record?app=fonandcol&IdNumber=103020&ecopy=
2. William McKnight, Library and Archives Canada, Item ID 103020, July 19, 1940, https://recherche-collection-search.bac-lac.gc.ca/eng/Home/Record?app=fonandcol&IdNumber=103020&ecopy=.
3. Hugh Halliday, *The Tumbling Sky* (Stittsville, ON: Canada's Wings, 1978), 209.
4. Hugh Halliday, interview by Shelly McElroy, August 29, 2024.

Meet Bader

1. Clarence Simonsen, 'Notes from Noel Holland Barlow on No. 242 [Canadian] Squadron Nose Art', *Lest We Forget*, November 20, 2014, https://athabaskang07.wordpress.com/wp-content/uploads/2014/11/a-street-in-calgary-named-after-him-but-nobody-knows1.pdf.
2. Guy Mayfield, *Life & Death in the Battle of Britain* (London: Imperial War Museums, 2018), 56.
3. Paul Brickhill, *Reach for the Sky* (London: Collins, 1960), 121.
4. Ibid., 123.
5. Ibid.

6. Douglas Bader, *Fight for the Sky* (Barnsley: Pen & Sword Aviation, 1973; repr. 2005, 2008), 367.
7. Ibid.
8. Ibid.
9. Ibid.
10. Stan Turner Documents, Turner Family Archive.
11. S.P. Mackenzie, *Bader's War*, 34.

Sick and Tired

1. William McKnight, Library and Archives Canada, Item ID 103020, July 19, 1940, https://recherche-collection-search.bac-lac.gc.ca/eng/Home/Record?app=fonandcol&IdNumber=103020&ecopy=.
2. Ibid.
3. Hugh Halliday, *242 Squadron: The Canadian Years* (Stittsville, ON: Canada's Wings, 1981), 71.
4. William McKnight, Library and Archives Canada, Item ID 103020, July 19, 1940, https://recherche-collection-search.bac-lac.gc.ca/eng/Home/Record?app=fonandcol&IdNumber=103020&ecopy=.
5. Ibid.
6. Ibid.

To So Few: the Battle of Britain

1. Douglas Bader, *Fight for the Sky* (Barnsley: Pen & Sword Aviation, 1973; repr. 2005, 2008), 15.
2. Ibid., 16.
3. William McKnight, Library and Archives Canada, Item ID 103020, July 19, 1940, https://recherche-collection-search.bac-lac.gc.ca/eng/Home/Record?app=fonandcol&IdNumber=103020&ecopy=.
4. Dilip Sarkar, *Fighter Ace* (Stroud: Amberley, 2014), 130.
5. Ibid.
6. Ibid.
7. Richard de Boer, interview by Shelly McElroy, March 2025.
8. Sarkar, *Fighter Ace*, 104.
9. Ibid., 94.
10. Douglas R.S. Bader, 'Dogfights', Ministry of Information Broadcast, n.d., 48.
11. William McKnight, 1939–1941, *Logbook*, AIR/77, The National Archives (TNA), Kew, United Kingdom.

12. Bader, *Fight for the Sky*, 30.
13. Ibid., 31.
14. Ibid., 125.
15. Sarkar, *Fighter Ace*, 120.
16. Hugh Halliday, *242 Squadron: The Canadian Years* (Stittsville, ON: Canada's Wings, 1981), 84.
17. The National Archives (TNA), AIR 127/1471/912.
18. Sarkar, *Fighter Ace*, 120.
19. Clarence Simonsen, 'Notes from Noel Holland Barlow on No. 242 [Canadian] Squadron Nose Art,' *Lest We Forget*, November 20, 2014, https://athabaskang07.wordpress.com/wp-content/uploads/2014/11/a-street-in-calgary-named-after-him-but-nobody-knows1.pdf.

Waiting for the Big Wing

1. Dilip Sarkar, *Fighter Ace* (Stroud: Amberley, 2014), 149.
2. Paul Brickhill, *Reach for the Sky* (London: Collins, 1960), 160.
3. William McKnight, Library and Archives Canada, Item ID 103020, July 19, 1940, https://recherche-collection-search.bac-lac.gc.ca/eng/Home/Record?app=fonandcol&IdNumber=103020&ecopy=.
4. Ibid.
5. Sarkar, *Fighter Ace*, 150.
6. Hugh Halliday, *The Tumbling Sky* (Stittsville, ON: Canada's Wings, 1978), 193.
7. Sarkar, *Fighter Ace*, 151.
8. William McKnight, Library and Archives Canada, Item ID 103020, September 22, 1940.
9. Halliday, *The Tumbling Sky*, 193.

30 August 1940 – Hat-Trick

1. Dilip Sarkar, *Fighter Ace* (Stroud: Amberley, 2014), 158.
2. Undated and unidentified clipping in Bob Grassick's scrapbook, n.d.
3. Hugh Halliday, *242 Squadron: The Canadian Years* (Stittsville, ON: Canada's Wings, Inc., 1981), 93.
4. Ibid.
5. Ibid.
6. Ibid.
7. Paul Brickhill, *Reach for the Sky* (London: Collins, 1960), 138.

8. Douglas Bader, *Fight for the Sky* (Barnsley: Pen & Sword Aviation, 1973; repr. 2005, 2008), 135.
9. 'Bill McKnight ... A Real Calgary Hero', *North Hill News*, 9 August 1957, 16.
10. Sarkar, *Fighter Ace*, 166.
11. Halliday, *242 Squadron: The Canadian Years*, 96.

Overclaims

1. Dilip Sarkar, *Fighter Ace* (Stroud: Amberley, 2014), 167.

Big Wings

1. Combat Report, AIR 50/92/98, The National Archives (Kew).
2. Ibid., 50/92/108 n.d.

9 September 1940 – Two More for the Reaper

1. Combat Report, AIR 50/92/98, The National Archives (Kew).
2. Ibid.
3. William McKnight, Library and Archives Canada, September 22, 1940, Item ID 103020.
4. Combat Report, AIR 50/92/98, The National Archives (Kew).
5. McKnight, Library and Archives Canada, September 22, 1940, Item ID 103020.

15 September 1940

1. Hugh Halliday, *The Tumbling Sky* (Stittsville, ON: Canada's Wings, 1978), 193.
2. William McKnight, 1939–1941, *Logbook*, AIR/77, The National Archives (TNA), Kew, United Kingdom.
3. Guy Mayfield, *Life & Death in the Battle of Britain* (London: Imperial War Museums, 2018), 97.
4. Ibid.
5. William McKnight, Library and Archives Canada, September 22, 1940, Item ID 103020.
6. Ibid.
7. Ibid.

Photogenic

1. William McKnight, Library and Archives Canada, September 22, 1940, Item ID 103020.
2. Dave O'Malley, 'The Return of the Reaper', *Vintage Wings of Canada*, April 25, 2022, www.vintagewings.ca/stories/first-flight-of-the-reaper.
3. Clarence Simonsen, 'Notes from Noel Holland Barlow on No. 242 [Canadian] Squadron Nose Art', *Lest We Forget*, November 20, 2014, https://athabaskang07.wordpress.com/wp-content/uploads/2014/11/a-street-in-calgary-named-after-him-but-nobody-knows1.pdf.
4. Paul Brickhill, *Reach for the Sky* (London: Collins, 1960), 138.

The Portrait

1. J.L. Granatstein, 2008, 'Vincent Massey', *Canadian Encyclopedia*, www.thecanadianencyclopedia.ca/en/article/massey-charles-vincent.
2. Eric Kennington, *Drawing the Royal Air Force* (Oxford: Oxford University Press, 1942), 12.
3. Ibid., 22.
4. Ibid., 33.
5. Ibid., 31.

18 September 1940 – 1 kill, 1 shared

1. Combat Report, AIR 50/90, The National Archives (TNA), Kew.
2. Ibid.
3. Douglas R.S. Bader, 'Dogfights', Ministry of Information broadcast, n.d., 48.
4. Hugh Halliday, *The Tumbling Sky* (Stittsville, ON: Canada's Wings, 1978), 215.
5. Dilip Sarkar, *Fighter Ace* (Stroud: Amberley, 2014), 200.
6. Ibid.
7. Paul Brickhill, *Reach for the Sky* (London: Collins, 1960), 161.

'Until the end … Or the other end'

1. William McKnight, Library and Archives Canada, September 22, 1940, Item ID 103020.
2. Dilip Sarkar, *Fighter Ace* (Stroud: Amberley, 2014), 120.
3. Ibid.
4. Ibid.

5. Shirlee Smith Matheson, *A Western Welcome to the World* (Encino: Cherbo Publishing Group, Inc., 1997), 17.
6. 'Four More Airfields to Be Built Near City', *Calgary Albertan*, July 31, 1940.
7. William McKnight, Library and Archives Canada, February 25, 1940, Item ID 103020.
8. William McKnight, Library and Archives Canada, September 22, 1940, Item ID 103020.
9. Ibid.

8 October 1940 – Bar to the DFC

1. Dilip Sarkar, *Fighter Ace* (Stroud: Amberley, 2014), 203.
2. McKnight, William. 1939–1941. *Logbook.* AIR/77. The National Archives (TNA), Kew, United Kingdom.
3. William McKnight, Library and Archives Canada, September 22, 1940, Item ID 103020.
4. Ibid.
5. 'Fighter Hit by Shell Bagged 2', *The Daily Mirror*, October 5, 1940.
6. Dilip Sarkar, *Fighter Ace* (Stroud: Amberley, 2014), 210.

5 November 1940 – Final Victory

1. *Calgary Albertan*, November 21, 1940, 5.
2. *Calgary Herald*, December 9, 1940, 11.
3. William McKnight, Library and Archives Canada, September 22, 1940, Item ID 103020.
4. Hugh Halliday, *The Tumbling Sky* (Stittsville, ON: Canada's Wings, 1978), 215.
5. Combat Report, AIR 50/92/98, The National Archives (TNA), Kew.
6. Ibid.
7. Ibid.
8. Ibid.
9. Dilip Sarkar, *Fighter Ace* (Stroud: Amberley, 2014), 220.

19 November – Emergency Jump By Parachute

1. Guy Mayfield, *Life & Death in the Battle of Britain* (London: Imperial War Museums, 2018), 102.
2. '20 Facts You Might Not Know About the Coventry Blitz', Coventry City Council, accessed September 2025, www.coventry.gov.uk/coventry-

blitz/20-facts-might-not-know-coventry-blitz#:~:text=The%20aim%20was%20to%20knock,on%20the%20road%20without%20light.

3. Ibid.
4. Dilip Sarkar, *Fighter Ace* (Stroud: Amberley, 2014), 223.
5. William McKnight, Library and Archives Canada, February 25, 1940, Item ID 103020.
6. McKnight, William. 1939–1941. *Logbook.* AIR/77. The National Archives (TNA), Kew, United Kingdom.
7. *Calgary Herald*, December 9, 1940, 11.

Winter

1. Guy Mayfield, *Life & Death in the Battle of Britain* (London: Imperial War Museums, 2018), 106.
2. Dilip Sarkar, *Fighter Ace* (Stroud: Amberley, 2014), 223.
3. Ibid.
4. Guy Mayfield, *Life & Death in the Battle of Britain* (London: Imperial War Museums, 2018), 122.
5. William McKnight, Library and Archives Canada, July 19, 1940, Item ID 103020.
6. Ibid.

12 January 1941

1. *Willie McKnight, Calgary's Battle of Britain Ace*, The Calgary Mosquito Society, accessed 15 January 2025, https://calgarymosquitosociety.com/feature16/feature16.htm.
2. McKnight, William. 1939–1941. *Logbook.* AIR/77. The National Archives (TNA), Kew, United Kingdom.
3. Combat Report, AIR 50/92/7, The National Archives (TNA), Kew.

Mosquito

1. Combat Report, AIR 50/92/7, The National Archives (TNA), Kew.
2. Ibid.
3. Willie McKnight, *Calgary's Battle of Britain Ace*, The Calgary Mosquito Society, accessed January 15, 2025, https://calgarymosquitosociety.com/feature16/feature16.htm.
4. Ibid. (Combat Report)

5. Stan Turner Documents, Turner Family Archive.
6. Guy Mayfield, *Life & Death in the Battle of Britain* (London: Imperial War Museums, 2018), 120.

The Telegram

1. 'Fighter Pilot Lost in France', *Calgary Herald*, 1941, 1.
2. 'Men Overseas to Hear Voices of City Friends', *Calgary Herald*, January 16, 1941, 11.
3. Ibid.
4. William McKnight, interview by Shelly McElroy, *Uncle Bill*, November 17, 2020.

Bill is a Prisoner

1. 'Hopes Are Raised for Safety of Ace', *Calgary Herald*, January 15, 1941.
2. 'Herald Correspondent to Go "Over There"', *Calgary Herald*, February 8, 1940, 1.
3. Ibid. (Hopes Are Raised for Safety of Ace)
4. 'Fighter Pilot Lost in France', *Calgary Herald*, 1941, 1.
5. Ibid.
6. *Calgary Albertan*, April 30, 1941, 'Follows Flying Trail of his Famous Brother'.
7. Letter to W.C. McKnight, July 15, 1941, AIR 81/4852, The National Archives (TNA), Kew.
8. Guy Mayfield, *Life & Death in the Battle of Britain* (London: Imperial War Museums, 2018), 79.

Missing

1. Combat Report, AIR 50/92/7, The National Archives (TNA), Kew.
2. Ibid.

Loose Ends

1. Hugh Halliday, *242 Squadron: The Canadian Years* (Stittsville, ON: Canada's Wings, Inc., 1981), 121.

Canada's Contribution to the Second World War

1. Paul Brickhill, *Reach for the Sky* (London: Collins, 1960), 251.
2. Ibid.

3. Stan Turner Documents, Turner Family Archive.
4. Terry Reardon, *Winston Churchill and Mackenzie King: So Similar, So Different* (Toronto: Dundurn, 2014), 97.
5. David J. Bercuson, *Canada's Air Force at 100* (Toronto: University of Toronto Press, 2024), 72–73.
6. Canada Remembers Program of Veterans Affairs, *The British Commonwealth Air Training Plan*, accessed June 2025, https://veterans.gc.ca/en/remembrance/classroom/fact-sheets/britcom.
7. Ibid. (Reardon, 97).
8. Terry Reardon, *Winston Churchill and Mackenzie King: So Similar, So Different*, 324.

McKnight Boulevard

1. Clarence Simonsen, 'Notes from Noel Holland Barlow on No. 242 [Canadian] Squadron Nose Art', Lest We Forget, November 20, 2014, https://athabaskang07.wordpress.com/wp-content/uploads/2014/11/a-street-in-calgary-named-after-him-but-nobody-knows1.pdf.
2. Vern Simaluk, 'Aviation Report', *Calgary Herald*, July 19, 1979, 52.
3. 'Heros Shrine Urged', *Calgary Herald*, July 27, 1957.
4. Ibid.
5. 'Bill McKnight … A Real Calgary Hero', *North Hill News*, 9 August 1957, 16.
6. Ibid.
7. 'Wartime Air Ace Proposes Honor for Calgary Hero', *Calgary Albertan*, July 27, 1957, 3.
8. 'Province Approves Naming Highway 2 "Barlow Trail"', *Calgary Herald*, December 22, 1966, 32.
9. 'Remembering the Heroes', *Calgary Herald*, November 6, 1991, 104.
10. Ibid.
11. Johnny Hopkins, *Calgary Herald*, February 14, 1967, 23.
12. Letter to C.D. Howarth, City Engineer, April 11, 1968, City of Calgary Archives.
13. 'Decision on City CD Fate Delayed', *Calgary Herald*, May 22, 1968, 24.
14. 'Richthofen Bombs As Street Name', *Calgary Herald*, January 22, 1970, 31.
15. Bartikiewicz, Jeff. 'McKnight Boulevard Named after War Hero', *Calgary Herald*, August 29, 2004, B1–B2.
16. 'Remembering the Heroes', *Calgary Herald*, November 6, 1991, 104.

17. 'Plaque Prepared at Airport for War Hero Bill McKnight', *Calgary Herald*, October 20, 1971, 49.
18. Ibid.

The Reaper in Canada

1. Dave Hadfield, interview by Shelly McElroy, May 6, 2025.
2. Dave O'Malley, 'The Return of the Reaper', *Vintage Wings of Canada*, April 25, 2022, www.vintagewings.ca/stories/first-flight-of-the-reaper.
3. Ibid.
4. Ibid.
5. Ibid.
6. Ibid.
7. Ibid.

On the Cover

1. Eric Kennington, *Drawing the Royal Air Force* (Oxford: Oxford University Press, 1942), 15.
2. Ibid., 30.
3. *Calgary Herald*, October 17, 1941.
4. 'Second McKnight Lad Starts His Air Training', *Calgary Herald*, April 30, 1941.

Mike, Marian, Ray

1. Bartikiewicz, Jeff. 'McKnight Boulevard Named after War Hero', *Calgary Herald*, August 29, 2004, B1–B2.
2. 'Carl Jones Was Oil, Gas Pioneer', *Calgary Herald*, August 1, 1999, B5.
3. Ibid., B1–B2.
4. William McKnight, Library and Archives Canada, 10 July 1939, Item ID 103020.
5. Ibid., B1–B2.
6. Ibid.
7. William McKnight, Library and Archives Canada, September 22, 1940, Item ID 103020.
8. Ibid., B1–B2.
9. Ibid.
10. Ibid.
11. Ibid., Item ID 103020.

12. 'Ray Joins the Royal Canadian Air Force', *Calgary Albertan*, April 30, 1941.
13. 'Carried on Brother's Job', *Calgary Albertan*, 6 March 1945, 12.
14. 'Bails Out of Plane 20,000 Ft. Over Desert', *Calgary Herald*, March 5, 1945, 16.
15. 'McKnight, Raymond – Obituary', *Times Colonist*, May 23, 2002.

And Ted

1. William McKnight, interview by Shelly McElroy, *Uncle Bill*, November 17, 2020.

Good at His Job

1. Hugh Halliday, *242 Squadron: The Canadian Years* (Stittsville, ON: Canada's Wings, Inc., 1981), 100–101.
2. Rob Erdos, interview by Shelly McElroy, June 5, 2025.
3. Ibid.
4. Ibid.
5. William McKnight, Library and Archives Canada, September 22, 1940, Item ID 103020.
6. William McKnight, Library and Archives Canada, July 19, 1940, Item ID 103020.
7. Edward M. Hallowell and John J. Ratey, *ADHD 2.0: New Science and Essential Strategies for Thriving with Distraction – from Childhood through Adulthood* (New York: Ballantine Books, 2021), 64–65.

Bill's Legacy in Canada

1. Hugh Halliday, interview by Shelly McElroy, August 29, 2024.

Author's Note

1. Bartikiewicz, Jeff. 'McKnight Boulevard Named after War Hero', *Calgary Herald*, August 29, 2004, B1–B2.

Index